SALMON FISHING

❖

on River and Stream

Alexander Baird Keachie

The Crowood Press

First published in 1995 by
The Crowood Press Ltd
Ramsbury, Marlborough
Wiltshire SN8 2HR

British Library Cataloguing-in-Publiaction Data
A catalogue record for this book is available from the British Library.

ISBN 1 85223 906 9

Picture Credits
All illustrations supplied by the author

Printed and bound in Great Britain at The Bath Press

CONTENTS

ACKNOWLEDGEMENTS

I would like to thank the following: Anthony Bridges, author of *Modern Salmon Fishing* (published by A. & C. Black), Arthur Oglesby, author of *Fly Fishing for Salmon and Sea Trout* (published by The Crowood Press) and Hugh Falkus, author of *Salmon Fishing – a Practical Guide* (published by Witherby) for granting me copyright permission to reproduce text from their books. Also, sincere thanks go to both Hugh and Arthur for allowing me to publish private correspondence between them and myself. I am also grateful to Michael Evans who very kindly allowed me to publish part of a letter which was first published in the letters to the editor section of the *Salmon & Trout* magazine, Geoffrey Bucknall who granted me permission to use text from an article he had published in the 1985 Spring edition of *Gamefishing & Fly Tying Quarterly*, and Peter Smith for allowing me to write about his microflies, the subject matter first appearing in an article written by himself and published in *Trout & Salmon*.

My appreciation goes to Gordon Dawson, the factor of the Smithston Fishings on the River Doon, for providing me with, and allowing me to use, catch records for the creation of graphs which I used to complement the text. Many thanks also to Dr Christina Sommerville, Head of the Parasitology Institute of Aquaculture, University of Stirling, for supplying information and diagrams on the life cycle of the sea louse. My appreciation to George Findlay for tying and supplying all the flies shown.

I would also like to thank John Wilshaw, editor of *Practical Gamefishing*, Sandy Leventon of *Trout and Salmon*, and Andrew Graham Stewart, publisher of *Salmon, Trout and Sea-trout* for allowing me to reproduce material from some of my articles which first appeared in their magazines.

INTRODUCTION

The British Isles are blessed with having a number of very good salmon rivers, from the world-famous east coast classics to the uncelebrated diminutive but abundant rain-dependent spate streams. However not all spate rivers are small in stature, many of them are the main or secondary tributaries of some of the major salmon rivers and highly productive in their own right.

For the majority of salmon anglers in the British Isles it is the medium-sized rivers or the smaller spate streams that provide them with their sport. This is not because they would not like to fish the dream beats of the Dee, Spey, Tay or Tweed. It is because access to the world-famous beats on these rivers is virtually impossible, regardless of how well heeled you are, the best fishing becoming available only through dead men's shoes or by invitation. Nonetheless there is still some easily accessible and excellent classic river fishing available to anglers. The Strathspey Angling Association water at Grantown on Spey is probably the best known and without any doubt the best value for money in the UK.

Although I am fortunate enough to be able to fish some of the rivers named above from time to time, my preference is for the smaller more intimate rain-fed rivers that fragment and break up the west coast of Scotland. Living in Ayrshire I am probably more fortunate than many by having some good rivers on my door step. These rivers are the Annan, Ayr, Bladnoch, Border Esk, Cree, Doon, Garnock, Girvan, Irvine, Nith, Stinchar and Tarf, all within an hour and a half's drive. As well as this I am only two hours away from the Tweed, Teviot, Ettrick and Tay, with the Spey only another hour.

By staying so close to these rivers I am able to be on the water at very short notice, which is of prime importance if the jungle drums start sending messages telling the arrival of fish. I am then capable of being on the right river at the right time, and if luck is with me catching fish. Although I have spent over thirty years fishing the rivers mentioned I have never become complacent.

I have heard it said that it is better to be a lucky angler than a good one. I do not agree. A lucky angler during the course of a week's fishing may catch an odd fish at times when others with more experience do not. A good angler on the other hand will probably take more fish home at the end of the week. This is because he will have gained experience from previous failures, thought about them, modified his approach and taken note of his successes. By constantly analysing, modifying and testing your techniques you will eventually enjoy sport when others are fishless.

Some angling authors try to explain in countless words and paragraphs the 'feeling' or 'sense' that they experience from time to time prior to catching a fish. For instance some may say that they 'felt' that they should be fishing a certain stretch of water, or that they should reassemble their rods after fruitless hours of effort and have another go, only to be rewarded for their efforts. What they are trying to explain is very difficult, because I am certain that they are trying to expound the 'Jungle Jim' aspect, a dormant sense that every angler has, but only some seem capable of using. I have had days when I *knew* I was going to catch fish; not only that, I have been aware of *where* I was going to catch them. This is not to mention the days when I knew I was wasting my time. When heading back to the car I have on a couple of occasions about-turned and fished one specific spot in a pool, and taken a fish, after perhaps fishing the entire pool thoroughly all day.

Like other authors I cannot explain it, however the following may help. A few years back I watched a series of documentaries about the life and beliefs of a tribe of Amazonian Indians. During one of the programmes one of the elders of the tribe was asked what was the greatest skill required to be a good hunter. After a short pause he replied 'It is not a man's skills, but his *spirit* that makes him a good hunter. If the hunted and hunter's spirit are one they will meet'. This profound statement, more than anything else that I have heard or read on the subject of 'feeling' or 'senses', seems to say what I and others cannot.

Nobody I know hooks or takes salmon every time they wet a line, I certainly don't and hope I never do. I have heard it said that anything which is not easy must be difficult, but this is not true. Salmon fishing is neither recondite nor easy, it is a delight. Most newcomers to the sport make the first mistake of assuming that it is only the gifted few who can catch salmon, but this is not the case. Right from the very first cast they lack confidence in what they are doing and start to question everything they do. This is all right if it is positive questioning, but more often than not it isn't. Salmon fishing is not a science – we cannot analyse the problems by using equative logic – but by keeping an open mind and adopting and adapting techniques which are either self-motivated or from the writings of others, we will catch fish. Most rivers are fairly secretive by nature, only giving up their secrets to those who are willing to court them over a long period of time. If you address rivers with respect, they will eventually give up their secrets, but only to those who are patient.

There have been many books written about salmon fishing, with the authors concentrating their writing around their own experiences on rivers such as the Dee, Tay, Tweed or Spey. This is fair enough, but the majority of anglers do not want to read solely about fishing these rivers, which is why I wrote this book. Initially I intended only to write about the methods and tactics I use while fishing medium-sized rivers and spate streams, but after further thought I changed my mind. This is quite simply because I have yet to know or hear of any salmon angler being monogamous to one type of river. Sooner or later all salmon anglers want to try something different. If an angler frequents a spate river the time will eventually come when he will want to fish a famous classic', it is all part of the natural progression of things. There will also be times when those who fish a major salmon river will fancy a change, or through no fault of their own – due to a change in employment circumstances, for example – have to move location.

The main problems faced by a spate river angler (SRA) arriving for the first time on the banks of a large wide river are many, including where to fish in the great watery expanse, what to fish, and how to fish it. On the other hand the classic river angler (CRA) faced with a smaller river may fail to recognize that the fish now have to be treated with more consideration. He is now no longer thirty yards or more away at the end of a fly line, but in some cases only a few feet. I have taken these points and many others into account in writing my book and hopefully the tackle and tactics herein will make it easier for the SRAs and CRAs to make the transition from one type of river to the other. The book only covers fly fishing and spinning, while the tackle and techniques outlined are the ones that I have adapted and developed through years of fishing busy association waters or modestly (and occasionally expensively) priced private beats.

Most anglers trying to venture forth for the first time to a classic river would find access to private beats difficult to obtain due to the infrequency of them becoming available. On the other hand many SRAs looking for classic river fishing may be unwilling to pay the high prices asked on a private beat for a day's, or week's fishing. Taking this into account I have decided when making reference to pools or stretches of 'classic river' fishing to write mainly about the inexpensive, excellent and easily accessible stretch of the river Spey leased by the Strathspey Angling Association at Grantown. This is because I feel it pointless writing about rivers and pools that many anglers are never likely to see or fish. If the methods that I describe in this book had only caught me one or two fish then I would not be writing it (unlike some who have caught a few fish, the majority of which were 'at the end of a pen', and as a result become overnight experts). I am not claiming to be an expert, nor am I ever likely to be one.

I am a full-time college lecturer in electronic engineering, with a passion for salmon fishing. Having some twelve weeks holidays during the year I am probably more fortunate than most to be able to indulge myself on my local rivers and, at times when vacancies arise and when finances allow, on other rivers a little further afield. This is particularly handy during July and August, especially if it is a wet summer. It is amazing how fast a rain-starved trickle can become a salmon highway, with silver sea-liced nomads rocketing through water which only a few hours previously could be walked across with shoes on.

All the rivers that I fish have very different characters: some are very fast flowing, with crystal clear water rolling over marble-sized gravel, while others run over stoney slabs through formidable rocky gorges. Some have a gentle slow flow meandering through rich agricultural land, washing out soil and turning the colour of potters' clay at the slightest hint of a rise in water height. A number of them drain moors and fells, flowing through peat that makes them run the colour of a well-settled stout, while others have pools holding more secrets than a Prime Minister 'covering up' a political scandal at question time. All rivers send their own unique message far out to sea, inviting their returning fish to come home.

While writing this book I have looked through many other books, some new, some old, trying to find the definitive explanation of 'spate stream', but with no success. Some anglers might be thinking they are called so because fish will only run upstream during times of high water. I am afraid that the answer is not quite as simple as this, as I know of small rivers that fish will happily run with no increase in water height. One or two ghillies that I know, when asked this question said that they are classified as such because this is when they fish best and are likely to be the most productive. For the want of a better explanation I am inclined to agree with them. I have also tried to find the meaning of 'classic'. Again there does not seem to be a universal meaning. The nearest that I can come to

finding a meaning for this description is that the word 'classic' is used as an expression to depict most people's idea of what a salmon river should look like, e.g. a classic example.

My first encounter with a salmon was at the age of eight, but to be honest it was my grandfather who hooked it, and then handed me his rod. The pantomime that followed I will never forget, with me backing further and further up the field behind with the rod bent almost to breaking point, or so I thought at the time. At the same time I was also receiving quiet instruction; this however was apparently falling on deaf ears, because I can remember that when the salmon started ripping yards of line off the reel the quiet words of instruction were quickly replaced by derogatory remarks about my level of intelligence. Eventually, however, after much ado and commotion an 11lb fish was safely landed. My next encounter occurred almost a year later to the day, but this time it was all my own work. I did not land the fish, but to this day I can remember the bright silver torpedo rising through the water, grabbing my Devon Minnow just below where I was standing and heading back to the depths. The fight that followed was short and explosive with the fish dancing wildly on the surface, before throwing the hook. My first salmon on fly, a fish of 7lb, was taken when fishing a small Black Pennell while fishing for trout. Since then I have taken many others under similar circumstances.

For me salmon fishing is a passion, not a pastime and I am glad to say that I am fortunate enough to have a wife who shares this passion with me. It is not a case of getting Mary to go fishing, rather one of getting her to leave the river. She simply will not give up. It is probably this persistence that makes her a much better angler than I am. Salmon fishing is the only thing I know of where a human being can experience the entire gamut of emotions in a single intake of breath, disbelief as a fish takes, the excitement as a fish runs, followed by disappointment as it comes off and the line goes dead. I once heard an old ghillie say that if you don't, or can't get excited with a fish on the end of your line, you shouldn't be fishing. I still get excited, even today after all these years my heart still races.

1 *SALMO SALAR*, THE FISH

Before looking at the different methods of catching this amazing fish it is best to look at the fish itself. By doing this we can get a greater understanding of our quarry, which as far as I am concerned is utterly essential if we are to become successful in our pursuit of it.

EARLY RIVER LIFE

It is the middle of March and from a gravel bed in a quiet stream a small fish wriggles and twists itself out from between the stones. As it breaks free it is grabbed and pushed downstream by an unseen force, but this is no ordinary fish but *Salmo salar*, the Atlantic salmon, King of fish. Very soon it is joined by other small fish each about half an inch long and carrying an umbilical yolk-sac, which will be their chief source of nourishment for anything up to six weeks. At this stage they are called alevins and a great number of them fall prey to trout and eels, while fish-eating birds like kingfishers, mergansers and goosanders also take their share. After the yolk-sac has been completely absorbed they are called fry and will be about one and a half inches in length. The fry's main source of food is very small insects such as midge larvae. After approximately two years the fish will be about three inches long. At this stage they are called parr and usually develop the characteristic six to eight fingerprint markings along their flanks. A great number of them are killed by mink and heron. Salmon parr, however, are expert hunters themselves having ravenous appetites and will attack and eat almost anything that they think they can eat. When spinning I have had salmon parr take a two-inch Devon Minnow intended for their larger kin. How they

ever hoped to swallow something that size has always amazed me. Usually when the parr get to about eight inches in length the urge to migrate to sea becomes great and they start to develop a silvery coat; they are now called smolts. The time of year when this occurs varies from river to river, but as a general rule:

> The first flood in May
> Takes the smolts away

At this stage the fish undergoes a drastic change in physiology – if it did not it would dry out in the salt water – and this is achieved by developing a skin which is impermeable. This is the silvery coat that the fish now sports in place of the characteristic fingerprint marks. Not all smolts, however, will migrate at the same time as some will spend a further year or two in the river. Why this is so I am not certain, but perhaps it is nature's way of providing a safety net in the event of a disaster. In addition, some cock parr become sexually mature and these fish are often seen nipping in under the milting adult cock fish at spawning time and fertilizing some of the hen's eggs. It would seem from scientific study that the longer a parr remains in freshwater the shorter the time it will remain feeding at sea. The inverse of this also seems to be true. Having made it to the sea many smolts will fall prey to a large number of predatory fish, such as pollock and cod, not to mention fish eating birds such as gannets and cormorants.

SEA LIFE

At sea, smolts put on size and weight very quickly, feasting on a wide variety of organisms that are found in the upper layers. This food supply consists of vertebrates such as capelin, herring, sprats and sand eels, not to mention a wide variety of invertebrates such as shrimps. These are described briefly below.

Capelin

These fish, which form an important part of the salmon's diet, have an olive green back with silvery sides and underbelly. During the day they are found at depths of around 500ft, but migrate to the surface at night where they feed on plankton. Adults range from about four to eight inches in length.

Herring

The herring has a high fat content and is an important food source for many fish. The herring spawns along the coast of Norway and, on becoming sexually mature at around five years old, migrates to the north of Iceland in search of food. These fish hunt mainly during the hours of daylight, close to the surface.

Sprats

The sprat is a silvery-green fish, which becomes sexually mature at around two years. At this stage they are about five inches in length. Like capelin and herring they are a shoaling fish. At night the shoals come to the surface, but during the day they are found at depths of thirty to 150 feet.

Sand Eels

These fish form a substantial part of the food chain for many marine animals and fish. The adults are between six and eight inches in length, and move around at night in small shoals. They are seldom found at depths greater than ninety feet. They are silver, long and slender.

Shrimps

There are two main species: *Parathemisto* and *Eusirus*. *Parathemisto* is present in vast numbers. It is a sandy orange colour, with large dark eyes. During the day it stays deep, only coming to the surface at night. It is about ⅜in in length. *Eusirus* is

The sand eel is one of the main food items of the salmon at sea. Commercial fishing of these small fish by the Danes and Norwegians could well prove to be disastrous to future salmon stocks.

very similar in appearance to *Parathemisto*, but have a reddish tinge down the back and is about one inch in length.

Prawns

The deep sea prawn is about 2¾ inches long and looks like the boiled prawn favoured by anglers. It is red in colour when viewed under light, but will almost certainly appear black in deep water beyond the reach of light. A smaller species is found at depths of 100–200 fathoms. It is similar in appearance to the deep sea prawn, but smaller.

All of these food forms are very high in fat and in the space of approximately nine to twelve months the smolts can increase their weight by thirty to sixty times. (This is assuming a smolt migrates one May at a weight of 3oz and returns as a grilse of between 6lb and 12lb, the following summer.) For many years it remained a mystery where these fish went; however it is now widely known that the majority of fish favour the rich feeding grounds of the North Atlantic around Greenland. When these feeding grounds were first discovered it was disastrous for world salmon stocks, because the drift netters quickly moved in and devastated whole shoals of fish. Today sanity prevails with many of the netting quotas being bought out.

SALMON SENSES

The salmon's sensory perception of its environment is highly detailed through the use of sight, smell and feel, the lateral line. Each sense has been evolved through thousands of years to ensure the salmon's prime objective, survival. Since the dangers of an adult salmon at sea are many, the detection of impending trouble has to be swift as its very life depends on early detection and reaction to continuously changing events around it. Why anglers ignore these highly developed senses has always been a mystery to me; they do not seem to realize that these senses, which are capable of acute detection in the vastness of the sea, now make the salmon highly attuned to the confined space of the river.

The fish are therefore conscious of everything going on around them. The salmon has three main senses that the angler must concern themself with: vision, taste/smell and feel.

Vision

The salmon is primarily attracted to its food by sight. The reason I say this is because the largest part of the salmon's brain is the *optic tectum*. This takes up approximately two thirds of the brain and is concerned specifically with visual information from the optic nerves. The construction of the salmon's eyes gives it diurnal variation, which means that through the use of cones and rods it can detect colour during the day, and see things in silhouette, i.e. black and white, during the night by the retraction of the cones. The construction of the eye also enables the salmon to detect very small objects in the roughest of water, which from my own fishing experiences certainly seems to be the case.

Have no doubt that a salmon has excellent eyesight and can see the smallest of flies in the roughest and dirtiest of water. I can recall an incident told to me by Bill Kerr of Kelso. Bill and his brother-in-law had access to fishing on the Sunlaws Beat of the River Teviot, which is situated about four miles above the junction of the Tweed. There had been no rain in Kelso so they saw no reason to check the water height before setting out. When they reached the river they discovered that it was in full flood and running red. However, since they had made the effort to get there they decided to put their rods up and have a go, even though conditions were completely unsuitable, or so they thought. Since they were not expecting the river to be in this terrible state they had left home with flies more suitable for the conditions which they had been expecting, low clear water. Bill tackled up with his 18ft greenheart, 13lb leader and a small ¾in tube. He had been fishing no more than about ten minutes when a fish took. It soon became clear that it was a large fish, and eventually, a quarter of a mile downstream from where it was hooked, the fish was landed, weighing in at 29lb. This is only one incident, but there are many stories of similar occurrences regarding salmon taking small flies in dirty water, just

Fishing the worm. Probably more salmon are taken on this bait than any other.

look through the river reports in the monthly periodicals. By the way Bill was photographed with his fish and appeared in a 1963 edition of *Rod and Line*.

Feel

The salmon feels through a sensor called the lateral line which is situated along both flanks of the fish. It is usually identified as a thin black line. These lateral senses are highly sensitive to vibration, and can pick up the slightest disturbance. This means that any vibrations caused in the water, such as an angler splashing about or a stone being knocked accidentally off a banking, will be felt by the fish. In addition, the lateral line helps the salmon to ascertain water strength, pressure and depth. It is a fact that noise carries much further and much more easily through water than air, something many anglers seem to forget.

Smell and Taste

These two senses are very important as far as bait anglers are concerned, but they are of little or no significance to the angler who uses flies or spinning lures. When it comes to taste, many authorities suggest that this is how the salmon accomplishes its fantastic feat of navigation, while others will argue that it is its sense of smell that guides it to the right river. Since the salmon is constantly opening and closing its mouth in order to pass water through its gills, it stands to reason that any information gained from this tasting could be used as a navigational aid.

When it comes to smell the salmon can only consciously detect smell if the olfactory is stimulated by the presence of a change in odour. As in humans, this is because if a particular odour is permanently present it very soon becomes ignored and fails to register on the conscious mind. If smell or taste does play a part in the salmon's fantastic feat of

One on the shrimp from the River Tay at Ballathie.

navigation back to the river of its birth then I am certain that the salmon is not consciously aware of it. It has been claimed by some authorities that the salmon can detect smells in concentrations as small as one part in 800 million. This may or may not be an exaggeration, but the fact remains that these fish have a sense of smell that is beyond doubt one of the best in the animal kingdom. Many anglers think that a salmon reacts to a lure by visual stimuli only and in the case of an artificial lure or fly this does seem to be the case, but when it comes to a natural bait, smell plays a major part in whether the salmon will accept or reject it.

Experiments have been carried out presenting fish with both a natural and an imitation shrimp. The results of these experiments showed that the salmon appeared to have a distinct preference for the natural bait. Although this is interesting it does not however provide conclusive proof that salmon will always prefer a natural bait to an imitation one. I remember reading a book where the author stated that a natural shrimp would nearly always guarantee a fish. Against such remarks I suspect that he is an angler of little experience. This is because any experienced salmon angler knows that *nothing* will guarantee a fish. In his book he said that he had come to this conclusion after many experiments with both the natural and imitation. Regardless of where or how the experiments were carried out, the salmon is such an unpredictable creature in its taking habits that there can be no controlled pattern of behaviour against which to make such statements. He also did not specify which fish showed a preference for the natural shrimp, stale or fresh. I have witnessed occasions when there has been an abundance of fresh salmon in a pool and the only fish taken that day on shrimp were red and stale. I have also seen the reverse situation when the majority of fish present were stale and the only ones that took any notice of the natural shrimp were the one or two fresh fish that happened to be about. Furthermore, I have seen a pool crammed with both fresh and stale fish that have refused everything offered to them, including the natural shrimp. Anyone who has ever fished for salmon with a shrimp or prawn knows that on some occasions the fish will go daft for them, while on others they will be completely ig-

nored. This is not to mention the times when the prawn or shrimp for some unknown reason causes them to panic and leave the pool in which the bait is being presented.

Taste without doubt plays a significant part when it comes to salmon taking prey into their mouths, because if the taste is unacceptable or unrecognizable, the salmon will be inclined to eject it rather quickly. When mouthing a natural bait such as a worm, shrimp or prawn it is a different matter. Now before we go any further I should make it quite clear that I am not talking about dyed shrimps or prawns, because anglers who practise this style of fishing will tell you that any fish mouthing these dyed naturals should be tightened into at once, failure to do so resulting in a missed fish. This is due to the fish tasting the dye and sensing that something is not quite right and spitting the shrimp or prawn back out. When natural undyed shrimp, prawn or worms are mouthed and squeezed they release enzymes that stimulate the brain through specialized receptors on the roof of the salmon's mouth and tongue. This stimulation, when related to a worm, seems to initiate a swallowing action resulting in the fish being hooked in the stomach.

Some might argue that this lack of additional stimulation (taste and smell) is why salmon that take an artificial lure are never hooked in the stomach. To me this reasoning, when related to an artificial fly or spinning lure does not stand up. This is because these baits are fished at the end of a relatively taut line, unlike a trotted worm which is presented on a 'free line' with additional line being fed to the fish when it is felt mouthing the worms. If a salmon takes an artificial lure fished at the end of a 'tight line' then any attempt to take and turn with the lure will be met with some resistance, resulting in the hooks being pulled into any skin that they happen to come into contact with. Sometimes, however, a fish that takes an artificial lure will be hooked right back in the throat, particularly if they move forward with it in the same instant. This, as far as I am concerned, indicates that the fish had every intention of swallowing it before the hooks were pulled into the flesh either by the angler or by the fish pulling against the line.

THE RETURN TO FRESHWATER

As mentioned earlier, on returning to freshwater the salmon has shown an extraordinary feat of navigation by returning to the river of its birth. Not only this, but some fish will even return to the gravel bed in which they were spawned. How this marvel occurs no one is really sure, but it is believed that smell and taste both play an important part. Not all salmon will return to freshwater at the same time, some will return to run the river in the spring while others will wait until the autumn. It used to be thought that 'like' breed 'like', i.e. grilse breed grilse, but this does not seem to be the case.

Regardless of how good the sea feeding is, all salmon must at some time return to freshwater in order to spawn. Salmon cannot spawn in salt water, because their eggs would float due to the buoyancy caused by the increased salinity. Small salmon returning to the river after only one winter at sea are called grilse and may weigh anything from 3 to 12lb. On returning to freshwater the salmon now faces the reverse change that it did so as a smolt. It is now in danger of becoming waterlogged and so must now be able to get rid of excess body water. The salmon's body cells are now more saline than the freshwater into which it has entered. Perhaps this physiological change keeps them unsettled for a period of time and is one reason why fresh-run fish are more easily caught!

PARASITES

Sea Lice *(Fig 1)*
One thing that anglers love to see on a fresh-run fish is the sea louse (*Lepeophtheirus salmonis*). This is because they believe that lice can only survive for a few days in freshwater and therefore any fish with lice attached must have been in the river for a very short time. Information kindly given to me by Dr Christina Sommerville of the Parasitology Laboratory of the Institute of Aquaculture at the University of Stirling seems to confirm this belief. These parasites go through ten stages of development, doing this by moulting. The ten stages are divided into five morphological phases, which are Nauplius, Copepodid, Chalimus, Pre-adult and Adult.

The first and second Nauplius stages are weak swimmers and generally disperse themselves by tide and current action. After the second Nauplius stage the parasite moults into the Copepodid. It is at this stage of its life that it infects fish. At this stage it has excellent optical senses which allow it to seek out and frequent areas where contact with a host is likely. It is now a strong swimmer and investigation has shown that the Copepodid may detect the presence of a host and manoeuvre itself to intercept it. It is approximately 1mm long and equipped with two large hooks at the front end which enables it to attach itself to fish, to various places, but mostly along the salmon's back or around the anal fins. Once they have attached themselves to the skin of the fish they begin to feed by means of toothed appendages, situated within a ventral mouth-like tube which they use to rasp the skin. The serrated skin tissue is then ingested.

After a feeding period the Copepodid moults into a Chalimus phase. There are four Chalimus stages, each of which remain permanently attached to their host by means of a frontal filament which is glued to the fish. Each stage of Chalimus development is larger than the previous, the final stage being about 2.5mm. The first of two moults then takes place into the Pre-adult stage. These Pre-adult stages are similar in appearance to the adult and are capable of becoming mobile over the body of the fish. From this stage onwards they are more easily identified as male or female, the females tending to be larger than the males. Although they look like the Adult stage, they are generally smaller and sexually immature. They attach themselves by the use of their shield-like bodies as a suction cup. Males mature faster and generally moult to the Adult stage prior to the females. Once mating takes place the genital segment of the female is enlarged for the production of eggs. The eggs are extruded in paired egg-strings, commonly called tails. As the eggs mature they darken in colour and eventually hatch, then to be discarded and replaced by further egg sacs. These egg strings have been reported to have been shed on entering freshwater in forty-eight hours. The minimum level of salinity to allow

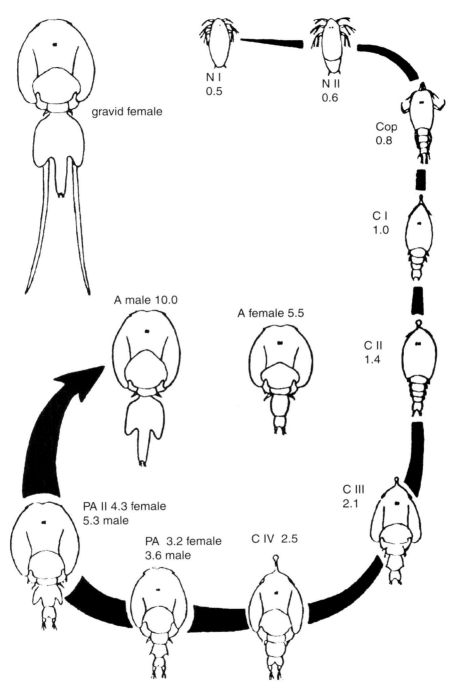

The life cycle stages of the salmon louse Lepeophtheirus salmonis *(Kroyer, 1883).*
N = Nauplius; Cop = Copepodite; C = Chalimus; PA = Pre Adult; A = Adult.
Figures indicate approximate size in millimetres. Modified from T. Turnbull 1991
Parisitology Laboratory, Institute of Aquaculture, University of Stirling, 1994.

survival of Adult stages has been suggested to lie between 12 and 16 per cent. It has also been suggested that their survival is greatly improved if they are attached to a salmon, rather than free swimming. Free-swimming lice have been reported to be capable of osmoregulation between 13 and 42 per cent. In freshwater they cannot carry out this process and may die within a period of eight hours.

The longest recorded survival of lice on salmon in freshwater is twenty-five days, although five to six days is more common.

The smaller species of sea louse, *Caligus elongatus* is suspected of swarming, which can cause mass infestation to sea trout and migrating smolts. There have been reports of these lice covering a host from nose to tail. One sea louse on its own will pose no great threat to a smolt, but in a swarm they are extremely pernicious.

Sea Lampreys

One parasite that is not so welcome is the sea lamprey *(Petromyzon marinus)*. In its juvenile form in freshwater it is a harmless larva feeding on organic matter, but as an adult it is a different story. As an adult it looks like a jawless eel and when about six to eight years it migrates to sea where it preys on a wide variety of fish, which includes returning salmon. They attach themselves to their hosts by use of a suctorial mouth, which creates a vacuum. Next the teeth, which are placed all around the mouth, are brought into play. The lamprey now cuts its way through its victim's skin with circular motions of its jaws. The cut flesh, now in a soft pulp like consistency, is swallowed. The hole at times can extend right through organs to the bone. On detaching themselves from their hosts the victim's wound soon becomes infected, which can lead to premature death. The adult lamprey can be as long as three feet in length and weigh as much as six pounds.

Gill Maggots

Another parasite is the gill maggot *(Lepeophtheirus salmonis)*, which breeds in freshwater. They are free swimming and attach themselves to the gill rakers of salmon. These maggots are usually about half an inch long and grey in colour. The gills of infected fish are usually eaten away in places. One old ghillie once told me that the presence of these gill maggots is the sign of a good spawning, but I will reserve judgement on this.

GRILSE

Grilse are slender, graceful fish, with a small head and forked tail. It is these fish which produce the majority of sport for the summer and early autumn spate stream angler. On initially entering the river, grilse have very soft mouths and because of this they are the very devil to keep on a hook, with their splashy acrobatic displays. These grilse have very little in the way of a wrist at the tail which can make them difficult to tail out by hand. It is difficult to tail a grilse by hand, but not impossible as some authorities would have us believe. With larger grilse of around 10lb or so, or with two-sea-winter salmon there is no difficulty as the wrist is quite pronounced.

On their return to freshwater, scientific research has shown that grilse and salmon stop actively feeding. This is because they have accumulated large reserves of fat due to the rich feeding while at sea. Some salmon will occasionally take items of food, however the majority very seldom if ever take anything. This is why only a very small percentage of salmon that run a river ever get caught. This self-imposed fast, as far as I am concerned, is nature's way of protecting the species. If salmon were to continue with their voracious feeding habit on return to the river, they would very quickly become extinct.

RUNNING FISH

On their return to freshwater, salmon that ascend the larger 'classic' rivers generally have a running speed of approximately 2mph. The fish that run these rivers are more leisurely in their upstream migration. However, spate stream salmon are a different kettle of fish (sorry about the pun) the whole

A typical summer grilse, taken on small fly and floating line.

affair being much more hectic. Their prime object when running is to travel maximum distance upstream at that particular time. The salmon that run the smaller rain-dependent rivers will usually travel as fast and as far as the spate allows. This means that their running speed can be anything from 3 to 6mph, but this depends primarily on the river's location, which governs the rise and fall rate. Salmon for some reason do not like to ascend high dams or weirs at night, but they will run from pool to pool at this time.

SEXING SALMON

In order to distinguish the difference between a cock fish and a hen we must look at two things.

The Shape of the Gill Covers
The gill covers on a cock fish are pointed on the rearward edge, while the gill covers on the hen are more rounded.

The Length of the Head
The length of the cock's head when measured from the tip of the snout to the centre of the eye is longer than that of the hen. Usually for the same size of fish, the distance between snout and the centre of the eye will be about one inch. As the season advances towards spawning time, the distance increases with the development of the gonads. At this time the kype will start to develop on the lower jaw. It is not known fully what function this kype performs, but perhaps it helps the fish to fight and drive off other males that are seeking the attention of the hen.

SPAWNING

As September arrives most fish will be starting to develop their spawning livery and at this time the cock fish turns red and becomes thin and very ugly to look at. (They are commonly referred to in Scotland when they turn red as having their 'tartan breeks' on.) The skin at this time also becomes very slimy. The hen fish on the other hand becomes very black with an extended belly due to the ripening roe within her ovaries. On sexual maturity a female fish will have approximately 500 eggs for every pound of body weight.

As her eggs ripen and the time draws near, the female will make a 'redd' or hollow in medium-sized gravel, usually about an inch in size. This usually takes place some time in late November or early December. When cutting the redd she will turn on her side and start fanning the desired area with powerful motions of her tail, periodically stopping and lying along the redd with her body while fitting her anal fin into the hollow to gauge its depth. When finished the redd can be up to two yards long and three inches deep, but this depends on the hen. Only when it is to her satisfaction can spawning begin. At this stage the male will position himself just a little upstream of her. Soon he will start to encourage her to shed her eggs by pressing and rubbing his flank against hers. At the instant when the eggs are released the cock will release his milt, which will be washed down over the eggs by the current. As the eggs (small orange-like 'rubber balls') and milt are released both fish will have their mouths open at the moment of orgasm, fertilization

taking place immediately. During the shedding of her eggs, one or perhaps two male salmon parr may have nipped in under the cock and fertilized some of the eggs with their own milt. Male salmon parr have also been known to fertilize the eggs of adult salmon when there is a scarcity of adult cock fish about. After all her eggs have been fertilized she will cover them with gravel by once again turning on her side and fanning the gravel upstream of the 'redd' with her tail.

After spawning the male will die. Very few males survive to spawn a second time because of the effort they exert in seeing off other male salmon which hang around the redd trying to steal their ladies away. In this weakened state they are thrown against rocks and boulders which open wounds which then become diseased. However, scientific research has shown that some hens will spawn twice, but it is only a very small per centage about (10 per cent), with about 1 or 2 per cent managing to spawn a third time. The period of incubation of the eggs depends on the water temperature; the colder the temperature the longer the time it takes. Generally, however, they will hatch between sixty

An autumn cock fish showing large kype on lower jaw.

and 120 days after fertilization. Out of all the eggs that are laid, only a small number (about five) will become adult salmon from one spawning pair.

After spawning, fish are called kelts and are now emaciated in appearance with ragged fins and extended vents. These fish are protected by law and must be returned. Most kelts will have gill maggots (*Leroepoda salmonea*). Although gill maggots are mostly found on kelts they can also be found in gravid stale fish close to spawning. Some kelts have been known to start feeding again when descending the river, taking the odd small fish or two. This is why during the early spring they become a nuisance to the angler in pursuit of a fresh-run spring fish. Salmon which for some reason do not spawn are called 'baggots' or 'rawners'. These fish are also protected by law and must be returned to the water. Since these fish are usually caught by anglers after spring fish they are easily identified by having a large, soft 'baggy belly', compared to a fresh-run springer, which is very streamlined and solid to the touch. These fish generally return to the sea and absorb any unshed milt or roe.

SALMON DISEASES

The salmon is subject to a variety of diseases, some of which are the cause of high mortality rates. One disease, *Furniculosis*, is caused by a bacteria *Aeromonas salmonicida*. Salmon that catch this disease are recognizable due to congestion of fins and haemorrhage of the vent. Fish which are heavily infected and dying will swim close to the surface, going round and round in circles. This disease is more likely to occur when the water is low and the temperature rises above 55°. Another disease is *Vibrio anguillarum*. The external symptoms of the disease are haemorrhagic blotches on the body and belly. These should not be confused with the red marks on the belly of a fish which has been running hard and pushing up through rough water. An internal sign of the disease is the degeneration of internal organs.

The most widely known disease is *ulcerative dermal necrosis* (UDN). This was first noticed in the rivers of south-west Ireland during 1964. However within four years it had spread to most of the mainland rivers with very few exceptions. Initially the disease is recognized by the appearance of small, white, bleached patches on the back of the head. These patches usually make the fish very conspicuous in the water and in the advanced stages of infection the majority of the body can be covered in this white growth. Fish which contract this disease are prone to aquaplaning and flapping with an agitated movement when they jump. These fish, although ugly and horrible to look at, should not be removed from the water as some might think, but should be left to spawn.

2   WHY DO SALMON TAKE?

Of all the questions asked by novices and experts alike, this perhaps is the most difficult to answer. There are many uncertainties in the sport of salmon angling, but the one thing that I am certain of is that the majority of salmon that run up a river do not, if ever, eat anything while in freshwater. Through the years there have been many theories put forward as to why salmon will take a lure when they don't actively feed on their return from the sea. Taking this into account it is surprising that any ever get caught at all. The six most common reasons put forward as to why some salmon will take a lure or bait are (in alphabetical order): aggression, curiosity, feeding response, inducement, irritation and playfulness.

AGGRESSION

Aggression is very often put forward as a reason why a salmon will take a lure, but the salmon is a gregarious creature by nature and as such cannot, on the whole, afford to be aggressive towards its fellow travellers. Nevertheless, like with most other male creatures, when it comes to the time for procreating the species, there is a certain degree of competitiveness involved when it comes to

Two new-run summer grilse from the River Doon, one on fly the other on a Devon Minnow. Both had nothing in their stomachs when cleaned so why did they take?

attracting and keeping a mate in order to pass on their genes. Any aggression consequently displayed at spawning time is almost without doubt stimulated by the sexual desire to mate. Therefore male fish with well-developed gonads and approaching sexual maturity do become sexually aggressive. This will possibly be their only chance, because very few cock fish survive to return to the river to spawn a second time. Just prior to and during the spawning season I have observed cock salmon driving off other cock salmon and smaller fish, such as parr or trout, that happen to get too close to their hen. If this is not aggression then what is? Having observed male fish during the autumn I am certain that the majority of them that do get caught at this time of the year are done so because of their sexually generated aggression. The take of these autumn fish is generally very fierce, a take that indicates the fish means business.

Curiosity

Some anglers will tell you that a fish has taken their lure because they were curious or inquisitive. This to me is not a valid reason for a fish taking a lure. A creature that is preyed upon during all stages of life by many predators cannot afford to be curious in the fashion we know. The salmon's self preservation depends on its reaction to potentially dangerous and continually changing events around it. If fish are uncertain of something that could be potentially lethal, they will be more inclined to shy away from it, rather than head towards it. 'Curiosity' as defined in the dictionary is not feasible when related to a salmon taking a lure. The salmon is of a low order as far as neurological capability is concerned and therefore does not possess the ability to learn from investigation. Some anglers, when explaining curiosity as a reason for a salmon taking a lure, will relate its reaction to that of a cat pawing a leaf that has been blown past. A cat, however, is much further up the scale when it comes to neurological activity and therefore cannot be compared with the salmon. In saying this, though, not all salmon will react or respond similarly to the same external stimuli and I am certain that they have different 'psychological profiles'.

Some anglers will argue that some fish are being curious and merely mouthing the lure or bait to see if it is edible. This is possible, but I would not describe it as being an act of curiosity, but merely an investigative response associated with the feeding habit, that is, touch and taste. I believe this is what happens when we get a tentative pluck at the lure and all goes dead. Some anglers will simply put this down to parr or small trout and perhaps at times it is, but having experienced this peculiar type of taking behaviour myself I believe differently. The first time it happened to me I was fishing the Stinchar in Ayrshire. On that particular day I had no fewer than eighteen fish come to the fly. The first few fish merely plucked at the fly very gently and initially I suspected parr, but later in the day some of the plucks resulted in a yard or two of line being pulled off the reel. Now in all my years of fishing I have never known, or heard of parr taking line. Salmon that take in this fashion are seldom well hooked and from my experience do not stay on for very long. I

One on a Toby spoon from the Spey.

did, however, on this occasion finish the day with a fish of 16lb and lost two others while being played.

FEEDING RESPONSE

It has long been conjectured by some anglers that the salmon's stomach shrinks and atrophies on return to freshwater, but this does not seem to be the case. By carrying out a table-top autopsy on three fish of the same weight, a fresh-run wild fish, a stale fish and a farmed salmon, the following came to light. On dissection I found that the external stomach dimensions of all three fish were very similar. Further dissection of the inner stomach revealed that the inner walls of the wild fresh fish were sticky and dry to the touch, while the stomach walls of the farmed fish were lined with what appeared to be a secretion of digestive fluid. Surprisingly the stale fish's stomach was similar to the fresh-run fish's. Now I am no expert on the digestive system of the salmon, but it would appear that the secretion of digestive fluid in the wild fish had become arrested. This is perhaps why nothing is found in the stomach of most salmon – they are incapable of digesting anything. However, the fact that a lot of salmon swallow a worm makes one think! (The reason for including a farmed salmon is that they are fed almost right up to the time of slaughter, that is feeding usually stops about two weeks prior to slaughter.)

Although there have been many studies made regarding the cessation of the salmon's feeding instinct, none have ever answered the question fully. The fact remains nonetheless that on returning to freshwater the salmon's feeding instincts are indeed suppressed. It is widely believed by some authorities that the feeding suppression is brought about by a physiological change prior to the fish running upstream, similar to that of the anorexia that affects humans. They will take food into their mouths, but seem incapable of swallowing it. Now I am not saying that salmon cannot swallow anything, because they obviously can, for example a bunch of worms. Could it be that these worm-chewing salmon still have their feeding instincts fully or partially intact!

The physiological change that influences the feeding habit of the fish does not seem to affect all salmon at the same time, which thankfully means they do not all run in from the sea with the same level of appetite suppression.

If salmon arrive off a river mouth to find the river in spate and do not have to hang around for a period of time awaiting a rise in water they seem more inclined to take. This is why I think that some salmon seem to be very good takers, while the majority seldom if ever take anything. I am certain that this is the main reason why some fresh-run fish will take a lure more freely than a long-time resident that has been in pool for some time. Although the majority do have their feeding instincts totally suppressed, some do not, and therefore it is wrong to say that salmon never feed in freshwater. Most salmon do not take anything while in the river, but I feel that a small number of fish may, on occasions, mouth something with the intention of deriving nourishment from it, particularly fresh-run fish when presented with the necessary stimuli. Taking what I have just said into account I am therefore inclined to suspect that it is these fresh-running fish we catch during a spate.

INDUCEMENT

I have two modes of thought relating to why a salmon will take a lure. The first is as follows. If we look at inducement when related to the salmon's feeding habit it may be possible on occasions to induce or coax a fish into taking a lure. This is perhaps what happens when a fish is covered time and time again, ignoring all offerings and then quietly with no fuss or commotion moves forward and quietly takes hold of the lure. It is quite unlike the take of an aggressive autumn fish. I bring to mind an incident that I witnessed on the Border Esk at Burnfoot, a few miles upstream of Langholm. I watched an angler fish a worm over the same salmon from early morning to late evening. The river was crystal clear and every move of the fish could be seen. I do not know how many times the worms had been trundled past its nose, but after many hours of ignoring them it moved slowly forward and gently sucked them in. There was no increased commotion from the fish. I am pretty certain that the salmon in this instance was taken by the persistence of the angler, inducing or reawakening the feeding memory.

The other form of induced take that occurs is when the salmon's predatory instincts are triggered by something suddenly appearing in its field of vision and then disappearing. This type of take is an instinctive and purely automatic response. It is usually a violent take, as the fish takes and turns with the lure, causing a great vortex on the surface. These fish I find are usually very well hooked and according to my diaries seem to be made up largely of fresh-run fish. I suspect that the two forms of induced take just described are directly related to the feeding suppression factor, that is both are induced responses from fish that have their feeding responses suppressed to differing degrees.

IRRITATION

This at first sight might seem a perfectly logical reason for a salmon taking a lure. However, I am not so sure that a salmon can be irritated by a lure alone. On many occasions I have fished a pool all day that has been absolutely stuffed with fish, only to have them ignore everything. Over the past few years I have come to believe that the lies that a salmon occupies may contribute towards its catchability. If fish take up uncomfortable lies they will become restless and more snappish towards anything passing overhead. Generally the fish that occupy these comfortless lies will periodically leave them and circle around a few times, like a dog prior to settling in front of the fire. I can think of no other reason for a salmon doing this. I do not want to dwell on this theory too much at the moment, because I explain it at greater length in a later chapter.

I believe that sexually frustrated males or fish

Fishing for summer salmon on the Stinchar.

Two anglers fishing the Weir Pool on the Skeldon Estate House Beat of the River Doon. It was in the calm water just above the small weir behind them that I first witnessed tail-slapping salmon.

physically damaged by nets or seals will often be more easily irritated and consequently react to a lure, when other fish in the same pool have ignored all similar offerings. Usually the fish that do react will not do so until the lure has passed over their heads a number of times, the take generally occurring after the lure has passed the fish. Frequently, prior to the fish turning on the lure, there is an increase in pelvic and pectoral fin activity, indicating that it is becoming more and more agitated with this annoying 'entity' continually passing overhead. The take is usually very positive and results in a well-hooked fish. In my opinion this type of take is 'aggressive' in nature. After all, is swiping a fly or wasp that continually buzzes around your head not an act of aggression on your part towards the annoying insect? According to my diary, salmon most likely to take in this fashion are cock fish at the back end, and fresh-run fish (both sexes) suffering net damage, seal wounds or heavily bruised bellies. These wounded and damaged salmon, due to the

discomfort of their open wounds, cannot get their heads down, that is they cannot switch off. They are thus wide awake, fully alert and much more likely to take notice of our lure. The lure passing overhead seems in many cases to be the final straw.

PLAYFULNESS

It is very difficult to imagine a salmon playing in the sense we know it, but if the salmon can enjoy sexual pleasure from the orgasm of shedding milt or roe, suggested by the open gape of its mouth, then perhaps it can also enjoy pleasure by 'playing' with something. I have on a few occasions seen salmon gently knocking large olives off the surface with their tails. As well as this I remember watching a salmon sucking thistledown off the surface, blowing it out and swinging around in the current and catching it again. I have watched a particular fish repeat the process on more than one occasion.

Some salmon, on entering a pool that has been difficult to enter, will slap the surface of the water with their tails. Why they do this I am not particularly sure, but perhaps the salmon in question are feeling elated, like athletes punching the air with their fists after having won a race or achieving a personal best. Salmon that slap the surface of the water with their tails are fresh-run fish. I have never seen a stale or gravid fish perform in this way. These tail-slapping salmon are usually very good takers. On this subject I wrote to two of the best-known names in the sport, Hugh Falkus and Arthur Oglesby. Their replies were as follows:

> Many thanks for your interesting letter. Although I have seen salmon occasionally slap the surface with their tails, I have never seen it happen as you describe. Apart from the possibility that it may have been a kind of signal to other fish in the party running upstream … that the fish in question has surmounted the falls … I can think of no explanation for it'.

> *Hugh Falkus*

I find it most difficult to comment on your dilemma. I have studied salmon behaviour for countless hours without a rod in my hand and have only come up with one or two ideas on the subject. For instance I have always assumed that fish which throw themselves up and alight backwards on their flanks are fish which are settled in a lie or kelts on their slow downstream migration. Fish which head and tail in a porpoise-like manner may be potential takers, but they may also have been disturbed by deep wading or simply running fish. Generally I have assumed that fish which splash the surface with their tails are new, running fish … I am sorry not to be more helpful; but the more I study these creatures the less I seem to know about them.

Arthur Oglesby

The salmon is totally unpredictable and can take a lure at any time. I have hooked salmon that have taken my Devon Minnow as it was lifted out of the water in preparation for my next cast. As well as this I have had fish that took my lure the instant that it landed on the water. Having given these takes considerable thought through the years, I must confess I am still at a loss to explain them. If they had only occurred with red cock fish I might have opted towards aggression, i.e. an invasion of territory response, but I have had a number of silver sea-liced fish that have taken my lures in the same way.

All the reasons given above for salmon taking lures are based on my own personal observations and should not be taken as definitive explanations. Although I have categorized them I feel that they can and do overlap into each other. Perhaps none of the reasons given are correct, but they are based on observation and common sense and until someone finds a way to communicate on a piscatorial plane and can tell me otherwise I shall continue with my beliefs. The crux of the matter is that no one actually knows why a salmon takes a lure, but the sheer magic of those rare occasions when the line does go tight is sufficient to keep me going.

3   WHEN DO SALMON TAKE?

WATER LEVEL AND APPEARANCE
(Figs 2–3)

Salmon can be caught at any time and because of this there is no 'right' time. They can also be caught in all heights and colours of water, but the two most likely times of taking a fish are just when the water starts to rise after rain, and when the water level has fallen to about two-thirds of the height of the full spate height and started to clear. To determine if the water is rising look at the side of a rock; the water around it will appear convex. This is called the meniscus effect. Another indication of rising water is the sudden appearance of flotsam, such as dead leaves or grass that was once high and dry being lifted by the rising water and carried out into the flow. To check if the water is falling, look around to see if any overhanging tree branches or rocks show

a wet belt. The width of this line will indicate how much it has fallen. The water surrounding a rock at this time will be concave.

The rise and fall characteristics of one river I fish is shown in Fig 3. It must be noted however that all rivers are different and this is only given as a guide.

When the river initially starts to rise after rain, the fish during the first inch or two of the increase seem willing to take a lure, sometimes after many days or weeks of disinterest. Why this is so I am not exactly sure, but I feel that it is perhaps because the fish come alive again and become more restless, knowing that they will soon once again be on their journey. From my own experience any fish which are caught at this time appear to be ones that have been in the river for some time and are starting to get a bit stale. Any chance of sport at this stage of

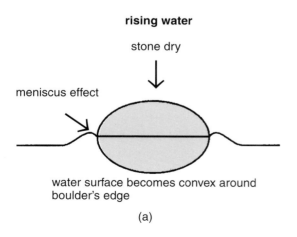

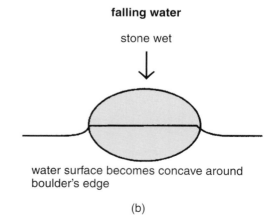

Fig 2 Determining whether the water level is rising or falling.

The River Stinchar in Ayrshire, a river that needs rain in good amounts before it fishes at its best.

the flood will not last long, so one has to be quick before the river starts to rise further and colours.

I have fished rivers at full flood height and still caught fish, but I have only done so if the beat is booked and paid for, a local one and not too far away. As the full flood height is reached, no fish migration will be taking place. The resident fish which came on the take during the early stages of the flood will now have moved on or taken to the quieter water along the edges, while any fresh fish waiting to enter the river will bide their time in the estuary until the volume of water has dropped back a little. If the river runs dirty and muddy, fresh fish will generally wait until the water has cleared a

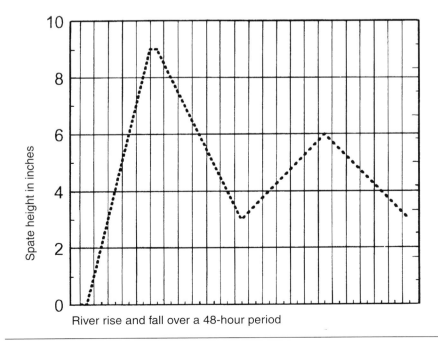

River rise and fall over a 48-hour period

Fig 3 Rise and fall characteristics of a typical river.

little. This is because they do not seem to like the mud 'soup' passing through their gills. If the river, on the other hand, has been low for a long period of time some fish will not wait for the suspended matter to clear.

I have caught fresh-run fish while the river has been running high and dirty, but this has been the exception rather than the rule. I can recall an incident some years back, when after many weeks of dry weather, a localized summer thunderstorm put the river up about a foot. The next day the river was running very dirty with mud, weed, and all sorts of flotsam being washed down. I was spinning at the time and it was impossible to keep the hooks on my Devon Minnow clean, as they were continually picking up things among the assortment of rubbish.

To be honest I did not expect to catch anything with the water running in this state. As it happened, however. totally to my surprise I hooked and landed a small, bright silver grilse of 5lb. This sort of thing has happened to me a few times since, but not often, and has generally been after a prolonged drought when fish have taken the first opportunity coming their way to ascend the river. Generally it is not until the river has risen and fallen back to about two-thirds of the maximum flood height. At this stage it usually starts to clear a little and provides the best chance of sport with fresh fish. In saying this though there must be a sufficient rise in water height to enable the fish to run and a nine-inch rise on some rivers may well not be enough. When the river falls to the magic two-thirds height, fish will

When the river is in spate it is best to concentrate ones efforts in the slower calmer water along the edge. This area is shown by the hatched section.

be migrating in numbers. At this stage they will be moving up through the quieter, slower water along the edges of the pools. Fish activity is summarized in the table below.

Water height	Fish activity	Fish response
Water starting to rise 1–2in in height	Some migration	Good
Water 3–9in	Very little migration	Poor
River starting to fall back to about 7 or 8in	Limited migration	Fair
River falls to about 6in	Maximum fish migration	Very good
River falls to about 4in	Limited migration	Good
River starts to rise after further rainfall	Fish become unsettled	Poor

If further rain makes the river rise once again, within a short period of time the fish will become unsettled. Generally if the river rises and falls and then rises again within a short period of time, (approximately 48 hours) the fish will go 'off' the take and your chances of tempting a fish will be very poor. Yet as is always the case with salmon, just when I think I am starting to understand them something happens to shows me just how little I do know.

I can remember a day's fishing on the River Stinchar when the river had been up and down like a yo-yo all week. On arrival at the hut all the tell-tale signs were that the river was falling, but due to heavy overnight rain I was certain that it would not be long before it would rise again. The Stinchar is a very productive river, but it does tend to rise and fall very quickly. I had just fished down the first pool when I remember glancing across to have a

look at the gauge. This showed that the water had started to rise. To cut a long story short, by the time that I had fished down the pool for the third time, the river had risen a good foot and was running the colour of milky tea. I had started off fishing with a small fly and floating line and within the space of an hour I was fishing a fast sinking and a 2in Waddington.

Although spinning is allowed in high water, it had not quite reached the mark and I therefore continued using the fly. Within a short period of time fresh fish arrived in the beat and started to show everywhere. In fact, at one stage when my wife was fishing down the pool, fish were felt brushing past and running through her legs. By the end of the day I had taken two fish. Although it is generally best to wait and fish after the river has fallen back to about two thirds of the maximum flood height, you can never tell when it comes to salmon. If I had arrived at the river to find it in the high and coloured state that it had quickly turned into, I would probably not have bothered fishing.

Arthur Oglesby in his book *Fly Fishing for Salmon and Sea Trout* (Crowood) wrote about fishing in a rising water: 'Too often I have experienced total frustration in trying to catch fish at this time. As soon as the river starts to fall, however, it is a different story.' The decision to fish in rising water is really a personal choice. The majority of times it will be a waste of time, but if you do not go fishing you cannot catch fish. Salmon, because of their unpredictable taking behaviour, can come on the take at any time, even with no discernible rise in water height or noticeable change in conditions.

AIR TEMPERATURE

Sometimes a change in air temperature will bring about a change in behaviour. On more than one occasion I have been fishing away the best part of the day and seen nothing. Then all of a sudden the feel of the occasion changes, like the hush that befalls a theatre audience just prior to the curtain going up. This change usually occurs with any wind dying away and the air taking on a warmer feel. At this point I have stepped back into the pool and caught a fish. If you notice an increase in the air temperature then make use of it, because from experience it does not seem to last very long, sometimes only a few minutes. Some might argue that taking fish at this time is just coincidence, but I don't think so, because I have taken too many fish too often during these periods of 'hush'.

I can recall an incident that took place during one cold wintry day on the River Bladnoch. I had fished away the best part of the morning and seen nothing. Around midday I decided to move further down river to escape the cutting wind. On arriving at the pool that I intended to fish, I discovered two anglers sitting having lunch. I gestured my intention to fish down through. Both anglers kindly indicated for me to go ahead. As I started to pull line off the reel to make my first cast the bitterly cold wind that had been blowing all morning died away and the air took on a much more pleasant feel. Having made no more than about three or four casts I had a take, a 9lb cock, which was duly landed. Some might argue that it was my choice of fly or line that was the crucial factor in bringing about its downfall, but in this case I am sure that they were not, because as it transpired all three of us, myself and the two other anglers were all using the same line and fly combination, a Wet Cel ll and an Ally's Shrimp tied, believe it or not, on a size 8 low-water double. The other two anglers had fished the pool all morning and had moved nothing. It may be that the fish had just moved into the pool as I started to fish, possibly, but knowing the river reasonably well I think not, as the river was too low at the time for any fish to run.

Why then did this particular fish respond to my fly, when it had refused similar offerings fished in the same fashion all morning? It could be that my fly was presented a little slower or a little faster than the flies fished by the other two anglers, but I don't think so because a little later I watched them fish down another pool and I could see no difference. I am pretty sure that it was the increase in the air temperature that brought about my success and not any great angling skill on my part. A cool breeze on a hot day can bring about a similar response from fish.

During the summer when rivers are running low,

it is best to leave the water alone during the day and fish only at dusk and dawn, with one's efforts being concentrated in the streamy water at the neck of the pool. It is soul destroying and self-defeating to flog the river all day, because any fish present will be in the deeper middle sections of the pool with their heads well down. Come the hours of darkness and the fish will start to move and cruise about the pool. It is the change in light conditions that seems to trigger the salmon into moving. Why, I have no real idea, but I feel that if the water has been running low the salmon will seek out the shallower, more oxygenated part of the pool under the cover of darkness. Perhaps this helps to invigorate the fish, just like taking a shower makes one feel a lot fresher at the end of a hot, sticky day. Salmon have excellent eyesight and it is always worth fishing well into the dark, as many salmon are taken by sea-trout anglers. Why anglers stop fishing for salmon when the light goes I don't know, but in doing so they are missing many opportunities of a fish or two.

TIME OF DAY (Fig 4)

The time of day is also very important. From catch returns very kindly given to me by Gordon Dawson, the factor of the Smithston Fishings on the River Doon, I have made up a graph showing the number of fish caught during late summer and early autumn for the time of day over three seasons, 1991, 1992, and 1993. We can see that between 11.00 a.m. and 12.00 noon the catch returns are consistently very good. This is because fresh fish running into the river on the early morning tide will be arriving in the beat around this time. The fish which ascend the river during the hours of darkness take longer to arrive in the beat than fish running on the afternoon tide. Why this is so I am not completely sure, but I suspect it is because salmon do not like ascending weirs or high obstacles during the hours of darkness.

If we look at the catch returns you will see that between 1.00 and 2.00 p.m. the number of salmon caught took a drop. This is easy to explain because the beats are rotated at 1.00 p.m., with most anglers taking lunch between 1.00 and 2.00 p.m. By looking again at the chart we can see that the catch

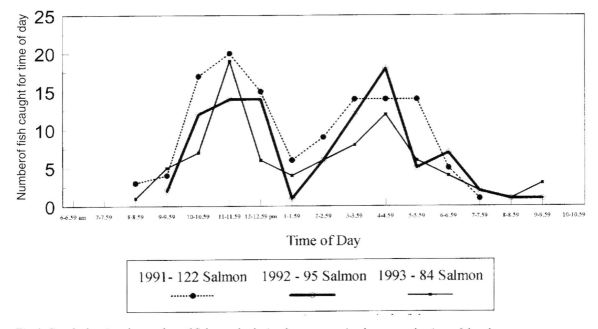

Fig 4 Graph showing the number of fish caught during late summer/early autumn by time of day three seasons.

returns peak once more between 4.00 p.m. and 5.00 p.m. This is because the fish that ran on the high tide that occurs around midday at this time of year are starting to arrive in the beat. Such consistent sport over a period of three years cannot be ignored. (It must be noted that the catch returns are not the total for the season. They are only the fish that had their time of catch recorded.)

WIND

Wind can also bring salmon on the take, particularly if the river is low, a steady moderate wind being the best. An upstream wind seems to be more productive that a downstream one, but this depends on the location of the river. A northerly or easterly wind is generally cold and not desirable, whereas a westerly or southerly is warmer and seems to bring the fish alive, at times after many days of bright sunny weather. Additionally, salmon will sometimes, prior to and just preceding a thunderstorm,

become active and start showing themselves. Some authorities say that if fish start splashing and rolling about on the surface they will seldom take an angler's lure. This to me does not seem to be a logical assumption to make. Anytime that fish become active they become alert, which means that they will be more likely to take notice of any lure passing over them. To waste opportunities during the brief times that fish do become active is wrong. One can never say never when it comes to salmon.

SHADE

Salmon can also come on the take due to the presence of shade. If the day is bright a single cloud can turn the angler's fortune. I have had occasions when the blotting out of the sun by a cloud for a few minutes has brought me the only take of the day. From time to time I get allocated a beat that has the sun shining right down the pools. Some years ago I would have persevered with this most unfavourable

On a bright day make use of any available shade. Here I am fishing a known lie under the tree.

situation, but now I either enjoy the scenery or take photographs of others fishing until the Earth spins on its axis and puts the sun behind a hill or some trees. I bring to mind the occasion when I suddenly became aware of the effect that shade can have on fish. I had been fishing most of the day and had been unlucky enough to have two fish come to my fly and then have them come off during play. I was starting to get a little hungry and returned to the hut for something to eat. The other rods were also back at the hut for the same purpose. As it transpired one of the other rods had recently hooked and lost a fish. On asking where, I was told that it was from a good holding pool that was difficult to fish because of the canopy of leaves on the other bank. A bulb lit, all the fish that had been hooked and lost were done so in pools blessed with shade. There was only one unfished shaded pool on the beat. Needless to say it

was here that I took my fish, a slightly stale one of 7lb.

RIVER LOCATION *(Fig 5)*

From my own experiences the easiest time to catch salmon, without any doubt, is when they are fresh run. If the water is of the correct height to allow fish direct from their feeding grounds access into the river when they arrive off its mouth, they will be more likely to take a lure. Catch percentages made at this time are usually greater than if the river had been low for some time. The fish are not having to hang around the estuary, getting staler by the day as they nose in and out of the river mouth on every high tide. There may be a very fine difference in the feeding suppression between a taking and a non-

Faskally Dam at Pitlochry.

taking salmon, possibly only a day or two, and this is the reason why some will take a lure relatively freely, while others – probably the majority – with a higher feeding suppression factor take nothing. Fresh-running fish are alert and are full of 'energy'. This energetic state wears away the longer they are in freshwater and there is no salmon more difficult to catch than one that has been in a pool for a while, has its feeding response totally suppressed and is lying in a self-induced semi-comatose state. Regardless of how many fish run a river very few of them get caught. From various sources of data that I have from different salmon fishery boards and associations it would appear that the total amount caught on rod and line is about 8 to 10 per cent of the total river stock.

In order to give ourselves the best chance of a fish we must therefore fish the water at just the right time, as indicated by Fig 3. Some rivers run through peat, which means that they seldom if ever run dirty, but even though they can be fished at the height of the flood, it is best to wait until the river has dropped. This is because the fish will be put off the take due to the increased acidity from the peat. Many rivers, however, run through low lying agricultural land, meaning that they run dirty for a large part of the time due to the suspended mud and matter. With these types of river it is best to wait until the water takes on the colour of brandy. When this colour transformation has taken place the magic time has arrived. It is not so much the water height with these rivers, but the water colour that is important. It is not always easy to coincide our arrival with this colour change, because it depends on the amount of suspended matter at any one time. These rivers, however, should be fished as soon as they start to clear. When the fish are running we must try to time our arrival on the stretch of water we will be

An angler fishes down the Swallow Braes on the River Doon. This pool is less than half a mile from the sea. As a result the majority of fish caught are very fresh.

Obstacles such as the one shown, although relatively easy to surmount, will slow down the upstream migration of running fish.

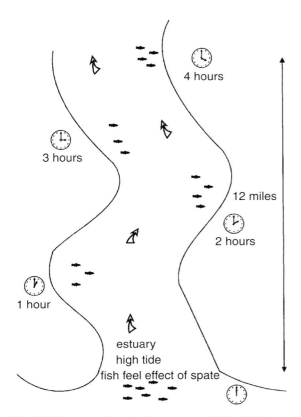

Fig 5 Salmon running time from estuary. If the fish have a running speed of 3mph it will take them approximately 4 hours to run 12 miles; however if there are many weirs or obstacles it will take them a little longer.

Most anglers do not have access on a river from sea to source, therefore it is imperative to know when the fish are likely to arrive in a particular beat. It is then a simple question of starting at the bottom of the beat and if possible following the fish as they move upstream through the pools. Knowing a river helps enormously, but if the river is new to you then watch the locals, because everything stops for fish. If this is not possible then consult a local tide chart, because most fish will run on a high tide and will have an average upstream running speed of 2–3mph (3–5km/h). It is now a simple matter of working out when the fish are likely to arrive in our stretch of water, which can be done by dividing the beat distance from the sea by the running speed of the fish. This time can then be added on to the high tide time. For example, if the high tide time is 12 noon and we are fishing some 12 miles (19km) from the sea we can expect the fish to arrive around 4 p.m., assuming of course that the fish average 3mph (5km/h).

If there are a number of weirs then the time taken by the fish will be longer. If all this sounds too much, then contact the ghillie or keeper for the stretch that you are due to fish, as these people have a good knowledge of when the fish are likely to be in their particular beat. The secret of success when fishing any river is without question to be in the right place at the right time. What I have written in this chapter is only a guide and should not be regarded as a definitive approach to guaranteeing sport. When it comes to salmon there is no fool-proof method of predicting when they will come on the take. The greatest success comes to those who observe, take note and persevere through thick and thin.

fishing with that of the fish. If we arrive too late the fish will have moved through, too early and they will not have arrived yet.

4   SALMON LIES, THE COMFORT FACTOR

Two questions that are often asked by salmon anglers are, what is a salmon lie and how can I identify one? A salmon lie is quite simply a stretch of water where a salmon has decided to rest during its upstream migration. They are usually places that allow the fish to keep stationary in the current with the minimum effort. As to what makes a good lie, it is very difficult to know. No one really knows, or is ever likely to know, but if any of the readers in a previous life was of the genus *Salar* and can remember the experience I for one would be only too willing to listen.

Anthony Bridges in his book *Modern Salmon Fishing* wrote 'it is often impossible to deduce, from appearance of the surface currents, the features at the bottom which are likely to appeal to a salmon'. Many lies are indeed impossible to detect, especially in slow, featureless, canal-like pools, like the one shown of the Ash Tree Pool on the River Bladnoch or the Long Pool on the association water below Grantown. Fortunately, however, not all salmon pools are this featureless, and with a little experience it is sometimes possible to identify areas or pockets of water where fish are likely to be resting up.

The Ash Tree Pool on the River Bladnoch. Featureless, but nevertheless a pool where a great many salmon decide to rest up. Identifying any lies on water like this is difficult if not downright impossible.

The lies tenanted by fish will depend on the time of year, the temperature and the height of the water. Generally, though, for a given set of conditions they will be in the same spot year after year, provided nothing disastrous occurs, like a winter flood altering the geography of the river bed. Surface indications can sometimes show if a section of water will hold fish, but there are many lies where there will be nothing visible to make us think that a salmon would find it a desirable place to be. Generally, where a stone creates a 'V' in the current is a good place to find fish so give it a try. Where this occurs there is generally a calmer spot, a slowing of the current, either in front or behind such an obstruction. Wherever there is a change in direction or a slowing down of the current the chances are that a salmon will take advantage of it. At the edge of a stream is another likely spot, particularly if the stream happens to be a fast one. Where the current boils and bubbles on the surface of a glassy glide is again a very good spot, because the breaking of the surface generally indicates some subsurface obstruction to the flow. Salmon will also choose to lie on flat rocky slabs, especially if the largest proportion of the river bed is made up of mud or sand. Very seldom can these slabs be identified by a surface disturbance. In order to locate them a low water survey is necessary. Never be put off by the surface pace of the current, because very often the pace of the current along the river bed is very much slower.

In low water salmon frequent the slower, deeper water during the day, but with the coming of darkness they will move up into the thinner, shallower water. The neck of the pool at such times is always worth a try. During the autumn salmon will often take up lies in these thinner runs, at times with their

This pool is a little easier to read. The salmon tend to lie on both sides of the central flow, the take usually coming in the slacker water closest to the bank being fished.

backs out of the water. As the water starts to rise after rain, fish will move, and at this stage it is well worth concentrating one's efforts in the very neck of the pool. But, as soon as the water starts to colour up the fish will have moved position to the slower water along the edges of the pool, and at this stage the fish will have usually gone off the take. In times of flood knowledge of the lies is of little consequence, because the fish seldom, if ever, take during this period.

Over the years I have come to the conclusion that there are three main types of lie frequented by salmon; short stay, medium stay and long stay. The short-stay lies are frequented only by running fish, while the medium-stay lie, the one of most interest to the angler, is tenanted by fish between rises in water height. In some cases this might be as short as a few minutes, or hours in a large river, or if in a small river suffering from a drought, several weeks. Long-stay lies, on the other hand, are occupied only by resident fish, which for some unknown reason have decided to stay put for a while. On some occasions fish occupy a lie for many months and only move on later in the season when their sexual urge becomes too great to stay.

Running fish will generally tuck themselves in behind stones and boulders in fast, rough water, or just above the lip of a weir, at times with no more than a few inches of water over their backs. These short-stay lies are of great importance to spate stream anglers. Fish that are steadily moving upstream and spending a longer time in a lie are of most interest to the classic salmon angler, because these fish will take up medium-stay lies for a reasonable time, before continuing their journey. They will generally choose water about 4–6ft (1.2–1.8m) deep, but this depends on the river, the river height and the time of year. At times the lies tenanted will be no more than a flat, rocky surface out of the main flow. I am certain that the majority of fish that get caught on rod and line come from a medium-stay lie.

Although there are productive lies (PLs) and non-productive lies (NPLs), both must be identified. Some anglers might think that only the PLs are worth knowing, which is all right provided that we know for sure. If, however, we spend time covering fish in an NPL then all we will be doing is wasting valuable fishing time, sacrilege on a spate river.

Some anglers will call a productive lie a taking area, but there is a great difference between the

Running fish in this pool tend to frequent the central run. The fast water in the left of the photograph is also worth a cast.

This is Tarric Mor on the Spey. During the summer this pool holds an uncountable number of salmon and sea trout.

two. A taking place and a productive lie can often be in two very different sections of the river. It must be understood that some PLs produce taking fish locally, but very often the fish will leave its lie to intercept a lure. It is this section of the water where the fish actually takes the lure that is called the taking area. Often a fish will follow a lure and take it some distance from the spot where it was first presented. In order for a fish to take our offering we must first present the lure to the fish, this being why it is crucial to know where the salmon will be lying. If we present our lure in the taking area the likelihood is that 'the' fish will not respond, because very often this area happens to be in a different part of the pool from where the salmon has actually been resting. If the taking area is a little upstream of a lie, accurate knowledge of its exact location is not necessary because if the fish is in a taking mood it will either move forward upstream to intercept it or wait

until it passes overhead. If on the other hand the taking area is downstream or across the river from the lie it will be a waste of time presenting our lure into the taking section of water, because the chances are that the fish will be oblivious to its presence, that is, it may not see it. This is why local knowledge is absolutely essential. If one is fishing a stretch of river for the first time the service of a ghillie is indispensable. If a ghillie is not available consult the locals, who if approached in the right fashion over a pint or a half are usually only too keen to help.

On the subject of unproductive lies, these are of unequalled interest so that we do not waste our time fishing over unproductive water. Why a particular lie produces taking fish while another does not, often under similar conditions, is not fully known, but I am certain that it is the lie itself and not the salmon that is responsible. How often have you heard of an angler taking salmon, one after the other from the same spot, while other anglers fishing at the same time over different lies catch nothing? The reason for this must be something to do with the lie under certain conditions.

From our point of view, a good lie will keep the salmon restless and on the fin, that is, it will not allow the salmon to get their heads down and go to sleep. I consider these lies to be the equivalent of sitting on a hard wooden bench. If the lie is a comfortable one it stands to reason that the fish will have their heads down and be switched off. It is by this reasoning that I have no doubt that the majority of salmon that get caught come from an uncomfortable medium-stay lie, while the lies that produce the fewest fish are tenanted by very comfortable resident fish. The short-stay lies are occupied by fish actually engaged in running upstream at the time, and therefore unlikely to be looking for a place to get their heads down. Anyway these short-stay lies used by running fish are not always ideally situated for a long-term stay, perhaps being in fast, rough water with little depth at the head or tail of a pool, an unlikely place for a fish to have a nap. This is why a running fish in a short-stay lie can be caught – the fish is permanently restless and wants to be pushing on upstream, and for this very reason alone is likely to be fully alert and conscious of what is going on around it. The fish will therefore be more likely to take a lure.

A short-stay lie must therefore have a very low comfort factor as far as the fish is concerned. I suppose some anglers might argue that the fish might take my lure out of irritation. They could be right, but what about the fish that took the first time it was covered? If it was irritation that caused the fish to take the lure, then surely it must have been irritation brought about by the lie itself, and not by the angler presenting the fish with a lure, bait or fly of their choice. The lure might have been the final straw, but as far as I am concerned the fish was already irritated by the lack of comfort in its chosen lie. This is also why I think that some lies are well known for producing large fish. It would seem that when small fish occupy one resting place very few get caught, but when a large fish takes up temporary residence in the same place it becomes uncomfortable due to its size.

5 CLOTHING AND ACCESSORIES

When it comes to specifying or recommending clothing and tackle it is very difficult not to mention brand names. It is not my intention in this chapter to advertise products, but I do make reference to the ones that make my fishing safer and more enjoyable.

CLOTHING

The first item of tackle that should be considered is clothing. In order to get the maximum enjoyment from the sport we must dress appropriately – with field sports we must therefore 'dress to kill'. This used to be an expression given to young ladies who had made themselves up for going out on the town, but when related to field sports, of which fishing is one, it quite simply means dressing in a manner that is befitting the event. It is amazing how many anglers disregard the issue of fitting dress. Visit any stillwater rainbow fishery and you will see what I mean. Some anglers will be clad sensibly, but the majority seem to think nothing of dressing themselves in glow-bright yellow or orange tops, along with denim jeans and trainers. When it comes to playing bowls or golf, however, the selfsame people would never think of not wearing the correct regalia.

Not everyone likes to wear a hat. If you happen to do a lot of spring or late autumn fishing then I would thoroughly recommend one. Since there is more heat lost through the head than any other part of the body, it stands to reason that if the head becomes cold the rest of the body will very quickly follow suit, regardless of how well insulated it is. Purchase two, one that is waterproof for fishing in the rain and another made of cloth for use during dry weather.

Another useful item that should be considered is a rain choker. There are two types available, the towelling and the moleskin. The moleskin is a little more expensive, but much smarter in appearance. Wearing a choker will help to stop any rain dripping down the back of your neck and stop your shirt collar from getting wet.

When it comes to shirts the 100 per cent cotton types are without doubt the best. Do not go fishing in a shirt made from synthetic man-made materials, as these cause you to perspire terribly. Cotton shirts can be purchased in heavy, medium or lightweight styles for fishing at different times of the year. As for pullovers, I have tried many types through the years, but have now settled for the green military or blue naval types. These pullovers can usually be purchased from army and navy stores for a very reasonable amount. They are extremely hard wearing and will last for many seasons.

Which type of trousers to wear for fishing is something that most anglers do not pay very much attention to and this is a great mistake. Many anglers will opt to wear denims, but this type of legging material is a nightmare if it gets wet. The first choice when purchasing trousers for myself has to be a pair of plus-twos made from tweed, corduroy or moleskin. They do not necessarily have to be plus-two style, but trousers made in this style are much more comfortable inside a pair of waders or wellingtons as they do not gather up around your knees when sliding your legs inside.

For stockings, I prefer a thick pair of woollen ones such as the types worn by hill walkers, mountaineers or trekkers. I used to wear two pairs, but now I settle for one pair with a pair of Bama Sokkets worn over the top. These Sokkets will stop your socks from riding down your leg and becoming uncomfortable around the heels.

The most important item of clothing is without any doubt the jacket. There are many different types and styles on the market, but the two most favoured by me are the traditional waxed cotton types as manufactured by Barbour or the Gore-Tex types, manufactured by Musto and Partridge. The Barbour waxed jackets are extremely hard wearing and will gave many years of service. I have only just recently retired a Solway Zipper which gave me over twenty years of service and replaced it with a new Spey wading jacket. The one disadvantage with the waxed cotton jackets is that they are inclined to make you perspire, whereas the ones made from breathable material do not. Although the latter do not cause you to sweat nearly as much as a waxed jacket they are not so hard wearing. The great advantage they have over a waxed jacket is that you can wash them when they need it. When a waxed jacket looks dirty and shabby the only real way of

restoring it is to return it to the manufacturer for an overhaul and rewaxing.

The style and length that you choose will depend on whether or not you intend to wear wellingtons, thigh waders or chest waders: a long jacket for wellingtons, three-quarter length for thigh waders and the short Spey style for chest waders. When it comes to choosing a jacket you will only get what you pay for, so invest in a good one. Cheap ones from a market stall will not stand up to the wear and tear that one from a reputable manufacturer will.

Another aspect worth considering is a floatation aid of some description. These aids come either as a separate round-the-neck, strap-on appliance, or incorporated into a waistcoat garment or jacket. These are further divided into two main types, the standard buoyancy kind, and the manual and automatic inflatable types that are inflated with a small replaceable carbon dioxide cartridge when they become submerged. The buoyancy aid will keep

Choosing the correct clothing is essential.

you afloat, but it will not right you in the water if you happen to knock your head on a rock or something and become unconscious. The automatic inflatable ones will inflate whether you remain conscious or not, turning you over and keeping your head above the water. These auto-inflating types are expensive at the present time, but there again what price do you put on your life?

As regards waders I have tried most makes on the market at one time or another and have only just recently found a pair that I really like. Barbour, a long- established name for quality waxed clothing, have only recently started to manufacture waders. They do, however, appear to have got it right. Quality waders do not come cheap and, like jackets, I would recommend paying for a good-quality pair from a reputable manufacturer.

Regardless of which make you finally decide to purchase they will be made from one of the following materials: rubber, PVC/nylon/PVC sandwich, PVC/cotton/PVC sandwich, or neoprene. The two most popular construction materials are the PVC/cotton/PVC and the neoprene. The rubber types have a bad reputation for perishing after only a season or two, whereas the ones manufactured from the PVC sandwich type construction last longer. Of these two the PVC/cotton/PVC is the more comfortable, while the PVC/nylon/PVC is heavier. In saying this, though, the nylon sandwiched ones are inclined to be stronger and are less likely to be torn or holed if caught by a thorn or barbed wire spike. One word of warning: whatever type of sandwich construction you do decide to choose, avoid the ones with the weld seam on the inside of the legs. These seams catch and chafe on each other when walking, and after a very short period of time they will rub each other away, resulting in a leak which will lead to wet legs. Neoprene waders are very good, but they are again very expensive. If most of your fishing is done during the early spring or late autumn months then I would thoroughly recommend that you consider buying a pair, as they are very warm and comfortable. Although excellent for cold weather fishing, if worn during the warmer summer months you will not need to join 'Weight Watchers'!

One other interesting development on the wader front is that Barbour are now producing waders specifically shaped for lady anglers. These are long overdue considering the number of women who have taken up the sport in recent years.

When purchasing a pair of waders you must take into account where they are going to be used. Many anglers do not give this aspect any thought when buying them. The style of sole is very important and must be taken into consideration, for if you have the wrong type for the river bed on which you are intending to wade then they will not give adequate grip, and it will not be long before you get a soaking. There are three main types of sole to choose from – rubber-cleated, rubber-studded or felt. Felt soles, although excellent on wet rocks, are inclined to be a bit on the slippy side on wet grass. I know of one angler who lost his fish of a lifetime because he was wearing felt soles at the time. He slipped on wet grass while making his way up the banking, fell and slid down back towards the water. As he slid closer to the river he let go of the fish to try to stop himself from sliding further. The fish was carried away by the current, never to be seen again. The rubber cleated type soles, although better on wet grass than felt, are prone to be a bit lethal on wet rocks or weedy surfaces. If money is no problem then the ideal solution is to purchase two pairs, one with studs and another with felt. The waders that have micro studs on their soles offer the best compromise.

When it comes to buying waders it really is a case of you pay your money and you take your choice. There is no use spending a large sum on a pair of neoprenes if you fish on a stretch of river where access to the water is difficult due to barbed wire fences or nasty thorn bushes. They would not remain watertight for very long!

For fishing during the warmer months I would recommend a waistcoat, as these are very good when fishing at times when a jacket is not required. Again these come in many types, from waxed cotton to brushed corduroy, but whichever type you choose, pick one with a lining and a multitude of pockets.

One item of tackle which is often overlooked by anglers who frequent medium-sized rivers or spate streams, is a wading staff. It is true that on the majority of smaller rivers there is no need to wade in order to cover the water, but on many occasions it is necessary to cross to the opposite bank. A wading staff can on small rivers be a bonus, especially where the banking has become overgrown, since it gives you something to use as a prod to discover if there is solid ground beneath the vegetation. The feeling of walking into thin air is a most unpleasant experience. Wading staffs are also handy to give some inquisitive bullocks a prod on the rump with, or to give unrestrained dogs that come snapping around your heels a friendly warning. Perhaps, on the other hand, it would be better if the friendly warning was given to the irresponsible owners!

On a large, fast-flowing river a wading staff is absolutely essential. The first time I fished the Spey I inadvertently went 'staffless', and as a result did not have a happy week's fishing. This was not because I did not catch any fish; I did. It was because I knew that I was not fishing to my maximum potential. A wading staff gives you a third leg, enabling you to keep your footing better, and allowing you to get yourself into the optimum position to cover the maximum amount of water. It also makes it safer and easier to wade, especially where the current is fast, or where the river bed consists of boulders. One pool in particular that springs to mind is the Lurg Pool below the Old Spey Bridge, where it is like wading on wet bowling balls.

When purchasing a staff choose one with a good lump of lead in the end, because if you don't pick one with a bit of weight in it, it will lift in the current when being left to hang at the end of the lanyard when casting. Also, pick one that has a rubber cap on the end, so as not to create any unnecessary noise if it happens to strike against any rocks as you probe about. A wading staff without a rubber button on the end will almost certainly frighten fish. When it comes to makes and types I like the Spey ones manufactured by Sharpes of Aberdeen. As well as being well made they are also the heaviest currently available that I am aware of. Of course, if you do not want to buy a wading staff you could always make one, but with the Spey staff so modestly priced it is hardly worth the bother.

One word of warning: do not allow the staff to give you a false sense of security. Remember that very often the water in front of you will be deeper than the water behind. Further, beware of gravel shifting under you feet – if it starts to move, back up upstream immediately.

SUNDRIES

Other items of tackle that I would recommend are described below.

The *thermometer* is very important to monitor water and air temperatures. It has long been accepted that these are a significant factor in the taking behaviour of salmon and for this reason a thermometer is of vital importance.

Another useful item to have is a pair of *artery forceps*. These are essential so that we can quickly and easily unhook any fish that we are intending to return. As well as this it is far safer removing a hook, even from a dead fish, by mechanical means. I have witnessed some nasty injuries caused by hooks. The most likely time and cause of injury is when a fish has been landed and despatched and the successful angler is busy trying to remove his hooks. The injury is generally caused by some passer-by not looking where they are going and catching any loose line around their feet. When this happens the hook is usually pulled free of the fish and straight into its new catch, the angler.

Never go fishing without a *priest*, there is nothing worse than watching someone looking around for a stone or stick to administer the last rites while their prize flaps about on the banking. This is a disgraceful practice and I shudder when I see it.

During a day's fishing it is inevitable that at some time or another our lure will hook something other than a fish. If we manage to get it out it will almost certainly have lost its needle-like point. I would therefore recommend that you purchase a *hook sharpener*. So often I have seen anglers fish away with flies or spinners that have had the hook point blunted or removed, which as far as I am concerned is foolish. This practice is complete madness considering that Murphy's law generally dictates that salmon prefer a lure with a damaged hook!

Whether a fish is dead or alive it should be treated with respect. So often I have seen anglers flush with the joy of success reach for a black plastic bin liner to put their fish in. To me this shows the utmost contempt for the fish they have just killed. A black plastic bag will only cause the fish to rapidly decompose, especially if the day is hot and the bag is left in the sun. If the bag and fish are left out in the sun the fish will start to sweat and partially cook in its own juices. A salmon or any other fish which has been killed and kept for the pot should be put into a proper fish holder, such as a *straw bass* or a *cool bag*.

For cutting nylon I would recommend a pair of *nail cutters*. I do not like scissors because they are dangerous items. A river bank is an easy place to slip and fall, and scissors that are kept in a pocket or, worse still, hung around the neck can all too easily cause severe injury if fallen upon.

Insulating tape is also essential to tape up the joints of fly rods so that the female ferrules do not crack while Spey or switch casting.

One final thing that I would recommend is a *wader repair outfit*. Most manufacturers supply such a kit with every new pair of waders, but as a rule these only cater for very small tears. I therefore like to carry with me at all times a tube of *Aquasure* as well. This is a clear flexible sealant which can be used on rubber, PVC and neoprene. Carrying this enables me to repair any tears or holes quickly without having to return to the car.

When it comes to keeping your flies together there are a multitude of boxes on the market. As far as I am concerned the majority of them are a waste of money. For keeping singles, doubles or trebles the best fly container that I have ever used is an *empty video cartridge box,* which can be purchased very cheaply from most video hire outlets. Choose the ones which do not have two retaining capstans for securing the video tape. These can then be lined with self adhesive single-sided ethafoam, which can be purchased quite cheaply. The added advantage that these have over a metal box is that they float. If a metal box falls in the water it will sink and be bounced along the bottom by the current until it comes to rest in some deep hole. The plastic boxes, on the other hand, can usually be netted out a little further downstream. For tubes and Waddingtons I still prefer a custom-built aluminium one such as the *tube fly box* made by Wheatley.

6   FLY TACKLE: CHOICE AND PREPARATION

DOUBLE-HANDED SALMON FLY RODS

Before deciding on a rod you must decide where and when you are going to use it. This will determine its length and to a certain extent its action. I like to fish with rods which do not have too stiff an action. Also, when fishing small spate streams I like to use a rod which is a little on the long side. By choosing a long rod even on these small rivers I feel that it allows me to control the fly better through any likely holding water. The more we can control our fly the better. Using a longer rod than is necessary enables me to fish the maximum amount of water and hopefully cover a far greater number of fish. This aspect of fly control I will cover in later chapters.

For the smaller rivers like the Stinchar or the Doon I like a rod of not less than 13ft, while for the larger rivers such as the Nith, Annan or Spey I use one of 15ft, this being the most common and pleasant length for fishing such rivers. Anything smaller on a large river will not do. A longer rod of 16 or 17ft may allow us to cover more water, but they can become very tiring after a few hours, especially if there is a bit of a wind blowing. I have watched visiting anglers to the Spey using short 12 or 13ft rods. True, some of them still catch fish, but I feel that by using such rods they are failing to maximize their chances.

When it comes to purchasing a rod ignore the marketing hype so commonly found in the adverts of the monthly periodicals. The only sure way of

The Lurg Pool on the Spey. Running fish, particularly grilse, are frequently taken from this stretch of water on a floating line.

choosing a rod is to try as many as possible. This can sometimes be difficult, as many tackle dealers are reluctant to give equipment on approval, although some of the 'better' dealers will take a credit card number as security. My own view concerning tackle dealers who do no let you try out rods prior to purchasing is that they do not deserve the business and therefore should be avoided at all costs. Many of the larger mail order companies that advertise in the monthly magazines will send you a rod on approval on giving them your credit card number as security, but it could mean returning a few rods before you finally decide on the one that you like. By purchasing a rod in this fashion you are not stuck with one you may not like, which in all probability will end up locked away in the corner of a cupboard gathering dust. All you lose contracting rods on approval is the money spent on returned postage fees. The best way without any doubt is to go along to one of the many game fairs that frequently take place up and down the country during the summer months. This way you can try a wide variety of rods from many manufacturers. Most companies will have a wide selection set up and available with the correct line ratings for this very purpose. This means that you can try one, sit it down and pick up another to compare actions.

There are many manufacturers, some producing good rods and some not so good. Some rods are very expensive, but this does not necessarily mean that they will better suit your needs or casting style. One manufacturer who offers rods with a variety of different actions is Bruce & Walker. Their new Powerlites are excellent and should be considered by any discerning salmon fisher. I first tried the new Powerlite models at the 1993 Game Fair and was highly impressed. Like their predecessors they are available with two distinct actions.

The Walker range of rods comes in four lengths, 12, 13, 14 and 15ft, the 14 and 15ft versions being line rated AFTM 7–10, while the 12 and 13ft rods are rated AFTM 7–9. These rods are designed to have sufficient power to fish sinking lines and large flies, but they are first class Spey casting rods, which makes them ideal for fishing with a floating line. They are better suited to the caster who likes a rod with a fairly stiff action. The Bruce comes in the same lengths as the Walker range. The three shorter rods take lines AFTM 7–9 while the 15ft type is rated AFTM 7–10. These models are ideal for female anglers or for those who like or prefer a softer, more traditional through action in their rod. I have tried both models and prefer the Walker.

For those with limited storage or carrying space the 14ft and 15ft Walkers are also available in a six-section travelling range. Those who prefer an action about midway between the two or something less expensive would not go far wrong by considering the Expert range. These rods are described as being 'general purpose' budget rods, but do not let this put you off considering them. They are made from ungrounded blanks finished over with a clear varnish. They do not have the black or green enamelled finish as found on the more upmarket ranges.

For many years I fished with split-cane and fibreglass rods and liked both. When the time came to move over to carbon fibre I tested many different makes, including the ones made by Bruce & Walker. I eventually settled for the 13½ft Cordon Bleu, line rated AFTM 8–10, and the 15ft Expert, line rating 9–11. The Cordon Bleu rods are no longer produced as part of the standard production run, but Ken Walker tells me that they will still make them to order. If ordering a new one is not to your liking then some good second-hand models can still be purchased from reputable mail order companies that regularly advertise in *Trout & Salmon* magazine. Both the 13½ft Cordon Bleu and the 15ft Expert perform very well with a number 10. This means that if you are limited to a moderate budget you do not need to purchase two sets of line ratings. I have both of these rods and they have done everything which I have ever asked of them. We are old friends, and together we have caught many fish through the years.

I am not concerned about a rod's cosmetic appearance – it is its action which is of paramount importance. All of the models mentioned are excellent for overhead and Spey casting, and capable of putting the backing splice through the top ring with ease. If I was asked to limit my choice to only one rod I would have to choose my 15ft Expert.

There comes a time when some rivers during drought conditions will fall right back and run with

Two summer fish from the Stinchar. The rod is 13½ft, an ideal length for such a river.

a vastly reduced flow. During this time they are better fished with a single-handed rod. Some anglers prefer a single-handed salmon rod specifically designed and built for the job. These rods are generally line rated AFTM 7–9. In my experience they usually need the heavier line to work them properly and because of this I don't like them. I prefer a rod with a lighter line rating of AFTM 6–7, my own choice being the 10½ft Multi-trout as made by Bruce & Walker. This rod might lack the back bone of the 'specialized' salmon and sea trout rods, but I like using it, and there is a lot to be said for using what you are happy with. According to Bruce & Walker the 10ft Merlin Stream King, line rating 6–7, is their nearest current alternative.

FLY REELS

When buying a fly reel choose one that is in the middle to upper price range. A salmon fly reel is a very important part of equipment and should not be skimped on. There are some very cheap and nasty reels on the market and these should be avoided like the plague. My own preference is for one manufactured by Bruce & Walker (the Expert series), Young's or Hardy's. Those of Young's and Bruce & Walker have a 4¼in drum and are almost identical in appearance; however, the latter has one advantage in that it is lighter due to a drilled back plate, but because of this you have to be careful where you sit it down so as not to allow sand or grit ingression. All these reels have an excellent drag system and can be used either right- or left-handed. In saying this why some anglers choose to wind a fly reel with the right hand escapes me, considering that the same angler when using a fixed-spool spinning reel or multiplier will wind with the left.

When choosing any of these reels pick the wide drum version. This will allow you to put on at least 100yd of backing. The backing serves two functions; first it widens the reel arbour, meaning that the line can be retrieved much faster, and second it gives us extra line if a fish decides to leave a pool.

Some might think that 100yd plus of backing is excessive, but not at all. I can recall a fish on the River Doon, a small river, that took my fly in the thin, fast water at the tail of a pool. The fish turned in the same instant and was quickly into the heavy water below. In the space of a few seconds the fish was out of sight and two pools below me, a distance of some 150yd. The fish had taken out the remaining length of Wet Cel II from my reel and the best part of 100yd of Dacron backing. After a hectic 20 minutes of passing the rod around the half dozen or so trees between me and the fish I eventually caught up with it. When I saw the size of it I was shocked. Initially I thought that it was one of the greybacks – a fish in the 20lb bracket that run the river – but as it happened it weighed 8lb.

The Hardy reels are machined from a single block of aluminium, making them the lightest of those mentioned. They are also as far as I am concerned more aesthetically pleasing than the others. If you decide to purchase a Hardy reel I suggest the Marquis Salmon 2, because the Marquis Salmon 1 will not allow you to put on a good amount of backing with a number 10 line. Hardy reels are excellent, and though they are expensive, they will last a lifetime. In saying this I do have one small dislike, the drag adjustment control. While the other reels mentioned have a screw adjustment, which allows fine changes to be made, the Hardy Marquis reels have an adjustable cam regulator. Although it does not give the same fine adjustment possible with the screw mechanisms found in other reels, it is still excellent. All the reels cited have an exposed rim which allows fingertip- or palm-controlled braking of the drum if a fish decides to run. Although from time to time I do fish with the mechanical drag ad-

On narrow pools such as the one shown a single-handed rod could be used. A longer rod, however, allows you to keep well back from the water's edge and gives you better control of the fly, especially if the fish lie from midstream towards the other bank.

justed to provide braking my own preference is to leave the drag control set to a minimum and 'palm' the rim. By doing this I feel that I can apply just the right amount of pressure.

My first choice of fly reel for the single-handed rod would have to be one from the three makes mentioned previously. With the Bruce & Walker or Young's I would opt for the 3½ in wide drum versions, otherwise the Hardy Marquis 8.

FLY LINES, BACKING AND BRAIDED LEADERS *(Figs 6–12)*

When buying a fly line we must get one that suits the rod on which we are intending to use it. The fly line is a weight that when lifted from the water causes the rod to flex, and store energy. If the wrong line rating is used the rod will not 'work' properly. If too light a line is used, the rod will not flex correctly and it will be difficult to cast short distances, while a heavier line will overwork the rod, meaning that it will perform short casts well, but be incapable of long casts. The correct flexing of the rod is of paramount importance. In order to get the best from any rod we must use the correct line rating. All line weights are classified by the AFTM (Association of Fishing Tackle Manufacturers) system.

Like many other things in life you only get what you pay for when buying fly lines. So often I have seen anglers purchase the best rods and reels that money can buy and then load up their reels with a line that cannot do justice to the rest of their tackle.

Cheap lines are usually rough to the touch and have a high memory factor, meaning that they try to coil themselves into tight loops after being pulled

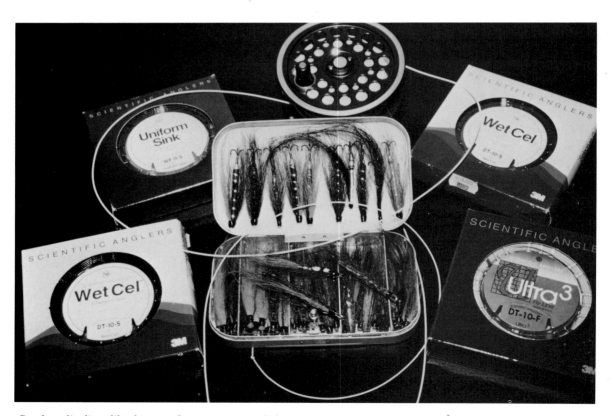

Good-quality lines like the ones shown are essential if you are to derive the maximum pleasure from the sport.

One on a small fly and floating line from the Little Stream on the Spey.

off the reel. Both these undesirable qualities result in a set-up which does not allow the angler to get the maximum from his tackle. This is because a line with a rough surface has a much greater air resistance, meaning that it will not cut through the air as well as a smoother one. At the same time the coiling of the line due to the memory will not allow extra line to be 'shot' easily. A set-up which does not allow us to fish at our best will needless to say result in reduced catches. Furthermore, a line with a rough surface will cause an annoying grating noise as it passes through the rod rings. Even worse is the fear that this noise is caused by the rough surface of the line filing away the rod rings.

Good-quality lines are smooth and supple and have the minimum of memory. Lines made by Cortland, 3M Scientific Anglers (imported by Leeda) and Hardy are all excellent, but they are expensive. Some anglers prefer the Cortland while others prefer the Hardy, while my own preference is

for the lines manufactured by 3M Scientific. I have used these lines for many years and they have never let me down.

For the double-handed rod the double-tapered (DT) profile is the first choice of most anglers because of its versatility. With this line type you will be able to perform the overhead, roll, switch and Spey casts with relative ease. It is also reversible, which means that when one end is starting to show signs of wear and tear it can be reversed. If most of your fishing is done on a large river then this is usually not possible, because very often the entire length of line is cast beyond the rear taper, resulting in both ends wearing. However, on smaller river systems we are generally casting a shorter line, 15 to 20yd (13–18m) being the norm. This means that for the majority of the time the rear taper of the line is seldom off the reel, apart from the odd times when a spirited fish will leave a pool while being played. Generally, though, on smaller rivers any fish hooked can usually be kept within the pool in which they are hooked.

Although some anglers prefer a weight forward (WF) profile for most of their fishing, I do not. This is because it does not give the flexibility of being able to perform the wide variety of casting styles that the DT gives. Also, if these lines are cast any distance then any length of the running line which is shot beyond the top ring must be pulled back through it prior to casting, and this is something that I don't particularly like to do when I am fishing with a long double-handed rod.

Nonetheless, in saying this I do use a Wet Cel II 'Universal' WF sinking line when I am backing up a pool. By analysing the principle of backing up I have modified my presentation to that commonly practised. When using this line it helps me present my flies 'properly' for a longer period of time than I could when I used a standard sinking DT Wet Cel II. My technique will be explained later in the book. When fishing with the single-handed rod where there is ample room for a back cast I will opt for the WF, because on a wide pool it will give you more distance for the same effort. One word of warning when using a WF, if you don't pull the running line back through the top ring it will start to split and crack. When fishing overgrown stretches where my

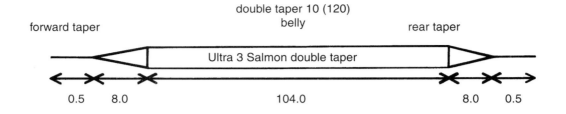

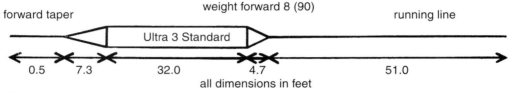

Fig 6 *Line profiles.*

back cast is restricted I will opt for the DT line, which will enable me to roll or Spey cast, depending on locus.

The length of time that a line will last depends on many things, but most of all it is the angler himself who will dictate its life expectancy. Let me explain. No two anglers cast in the same way, but a good caster (and by this I don't mean someone who can cast to the far horizon, but someone who casts with style, so that their actions look easy and effortless) will go through fewer lines than someone who has no timing and merely waves the rod back and forth. In addition, a line which is trodden on, or forcibly pulled free from riverside vegetation or from around a rock where it has become snagged, will

certainly not last very long. A line which is treated with respect will give many years of service.

There is no need to have a great assortment of line densities; I recommend three, an AirCel Ultra 3 or Supreme 2 (floaters), Wet Cel I (slow sinker) and a Wet Cel II (fast sinker). Using these lines, we can present our flies to the fish in most heights of water. All the lines mentioned are manufactured to a very high standard and represent the best that money can buy. In later chapters I will explain where and when to use each line to best effect.

Although I prefer to fish with one of the three line densities listed above, many anglers are now starting to use only a floating line in conjunction with braided monofilament leaders which come in a

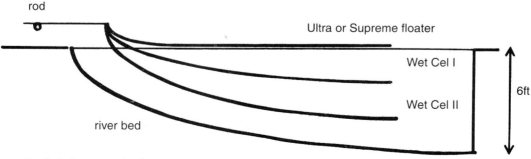

Fig 7 *Sinking rates for floating and sinking lines in a medium-paced flow.*

wide variety of densities, from floating to ultra-fast-sinking. These leaders were first introduced on to the market during the early 1980s and since then they have found favour with a great number of anglers. The one advantage of fishing with this type of set-up is that you only need to buy and carry one line, a floater. You can then simply purchase a selection of braided leaders in a variety of densities to cover most situations. By using these you can fish a small fly just under the surface during the summer months, or a large tube or Waddington during the spring and autumn using the same line. Another advantage is that these leaders can be fitted very quickly to the fly line by means of a small length of silicon rubber sleeving. The fly is attached to the other end of the leader by a short length of nylon, usually 3–6ft. I have watched Bill Pennington, a regular contributor to *Trout & Salmon* magazine, use these leaders to great effect on the Smithston Fishings on the River Doon.

The next thing we must do to our set-up is to connect the backing line to the drum of the reel. First tie an overhand knot near the end of the backing, then feed it around the arbour of the reel. Now form a small loop of line by taking the end with the knot over the backing and back towards the body of the reel. Next make three or four turns around the bottom section of the loop. At this stage moisten the loop and then gently pull the completed knot tight around the drum. This is a safe and secure method of attaching the backing to the reel, because the harder it is pulled the tighter it gets.

The next step is to attach the backing to the fly line. There have been many ingenious methods devised through the years, but the simplest and easiest is by means of a braided leader loop.

These can be bought ready-made, or can be created very cheaply and simply by purchasing a spool of 30lb braided shooting monofilament.

Once the braided loop is secured to the fly line the backing can be connected. This is done by means of passing the backing through the loop and securing by means of a half-blood knot.

There are many variations of this knot, some good, some bad, but they are all easy to tie. First pull about 6in (15cm) of backing through the braided loop. Now rest a finger on the main line backing and then bring the working length up and over your forefinger, so that a small loop or opening is created between your finger and the backing. Next secure this between forefinger and thumb. Now lay the working length of backing along the main line and make four or five complete turns. Bring the remaining length down and back through the loop between your finger and the braided loop. Before pulling tight wet all parts of the knot, and then gently but firmly, in one complete action, pull the coils tight. Some anglers will add a small overhand knot to the end of the backing line, while others will put the backing through the braided loop twice. I prefer to put the line back through the loop between my finger and braided loop twice, because I feel that this is a better and safer method. I also use this knot for attaching nylon to flies and spinners, although some

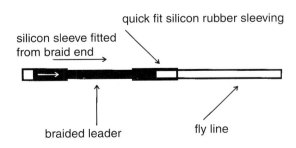

Fig 8 Attaching the braided leader to the fly line.

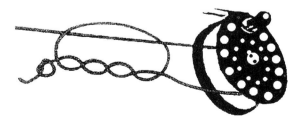

Fig 9 Connecting the backing line to the reel drum.

contemporary angling authorities do not like it for attaching flies because they claim that the fly has a tendency to hinge at the end of the nylon and there-

fore fish badly. Perhaps with the version they tie it does, but I have never experienced this problem.

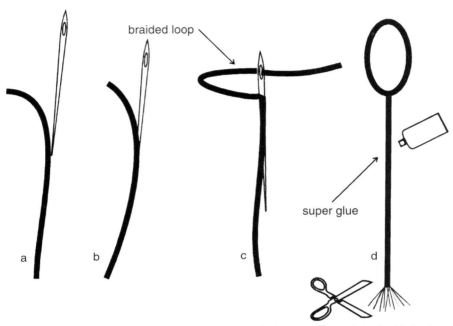

Fig 10 Making a braided leader loop. (a) Pass a needle down and through the braided nylon. (b) Push the needle down and through the centre of the braid and then bring the point back out at the side. (c) Now thread the top section of the braid through the eye of the needle. This will form a small loop. Before the needle can be pulled down and through the braid to form the loop it is best to put a pencil or knitting needle through the loop to stop it disappearing when the needle is pulled through. (d) After this has been done the pencil can be removed. Although the design of the braid will stop the loop coming undone, a drop of super glue will give added security. Next trim away any frayed ends and gently heat the end which is pushed onto the fly line with a candle. This will stop it closing up and make the job a lot easier.

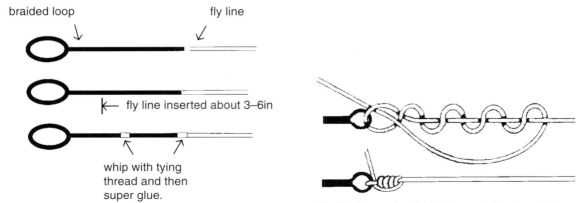

Fig 11 Securing the braided loop to the fly line.

Fig 12 Connecting the fly line to the backing with a half-blood knot.

MONOFILAMENT NYLON LEADERS

There are many makes on the market and through the years I have tried most of them, but the one that I prefer, and now use to the exclusion of all others, is Maxima Chameleon. The manufacturers claim that the fish cannot see it, though I am not certain of this. I like it because it is resilient to abrasion and has a very good knot strength; some anglers don't like it because of its dark colouration which they think might cause fish to refuse to come to their lure. Perhaps under some conditions this is true, but I cannot say that I have seen any evidence to confirm this. If, however, you feel that a dark nylon is not to your taste, Maxima now produce an Ultragreen version.

To cover most of your leader needs I would recommend that you buy 100m spools in the following breaking strains; 8, 12, 15 and 20lb. The reason for having a selection of breaking strains is so that we can match the nylon to the size of fly. It is no use connecting 20lb nylon to a size 8 or 10 fly, or 8lb nylon to a 2in brass tube. In the first instance it would be difficult to get it through the eye of the hook, but more importantly the fly would not fish properly tethered to such a heavy breaking strain. A small fly, if tethered to such a gauge, would not be able to rise and dance in the current, giving it a 'lifeless' presence through the water. On the other hand a 2in tube tied to light nylon would probably fish properly across the pool, but would be a nightmare to cast. Also, if used for a prolonged period of time it would soon weaken the nylon, a dangerous situation. I have seen heavy tubes snap light nylon like a thread and go rocketing across the river. Let me assure you that being hit by a 2in brass tube travelling at over 50mph is not a pleasant experience. We must not only take our own safety into consideration when fishing, but that of other anglers as well.

In order to keep your nylon in good condition keep it either in your pocket or in a dark corner of your tackle bag, anywhere out of direct sunlight, as the ultraviolet rays will weaken and destroy it. In saying this, though, it does take some time before the nylon is affected. When assembling your tackle

tie on your own flies, do not let some well-meaning friend or ghillie do the job for you. Trust only your own knots. One last piece of advice when it comes to nylon – if it becomes damaged replace it. There is no use fishing away to hook the only fish of the day, only to lose it because the nylon had suffered some previous damage.

Although many anglers use braided leaders with short monofilament extensions I still like to use a long conventional monofilament one. I join these leaders to the fly line by connecting another braided leader loop in the same fashion described earlier to the business end of the fly line. I then simply tie the nylon leader to this by means of my modified blood knot.

TACKLE CARE AND TIPS

If tackle is deprived of maintenance then it stands to reason that it will inevitably fail. Time spent giving tackle a once-over prior to an outing costs nothing, especially when weighed against the disappointment of an early return home, or lost fish, not to mention the price of a day's fishing. The two most common failures concerning fly rods I have witnessed are ring guide faults or loose or frayed whippings. The most disastrous of these is the damaged ring guide, especially if it happens to be the top ring on the rod, which if not replaced will almost certainly result in the fly line being ruined and a new one having to be purchased. The top ring on any rod always seems to be a magnet for disaster, simply because of its position. How many times has the top of one of your own rods been accidentally knocked off something while walking along the bank between pools? For this very reason alone I like to carry my rods with the handle out in front, and the rod tip behind, well out of harm's way. After such accidents, if damage is not checked for then sooner or later its results will be known, inevitably at the worse possible time, while playing the best fish of the season. If the rod does fail at this time the angler will no doubt curse the manufacturer for producing faulty goods, forgetting the knock off an overhead branch that it received a few days earlier, or the knock it received on a boulder when it was sitting-down on some rocky banking while the angler was changing a fly or unhooking a fish.

One part of my own fly rods that I like to check at least once a year are the whippings that strengthen both the male and female joints on the rod. This is because I like to Spey cast, and because of this I tape up the joints to stop them working loose while casting. It is surprising how much varnish the tape can remove throughout the course of a season, so I give these whippings two or three coats of clear polyurethane varnish at the end of each season. These whippings are not there for show, and therefore must be revarnished to stop them from coming undone. If they do come undone, do not be surprised if the female joint splits during casting. In addition, if a rod has to be repaired then just like a car that has been in an accident and repaired, it never quite feels the same, regardless of how well the repair has been carried out. After revarnishing the joint whippings you should also rewax the male spigots with some candle wax, but wait until the varnish has dried!

At the end of each season it is also a good idea to check your fly lines for damage. Not much can be done about cuts and cracks, but if part of the line has only been flattened or squashed by being accidentally trodden on then all is not lost. Some gentle heat applied from a hair dryer may be all that is needed to repair the damage. Hold the dryer approximately 9in (24cm) away from the line and with the dryer set to a low heat setting move it back and forth over the damaged area. At the same time roll the flattened section of the line back and forth over a flat surface until all the damaged section has returned to its original cylindrical shape. This technique works well with PVC-type lines, provided that not too much heat is applied. It does not, however, work with the new Teflon-coated lines.

It is surprising how many anglers will fish away with a floater that does not fully float due to the amount of dirt that it has accumulated over the seasons. A floater should be on the surface, nowhere else, and since if it gets dirty it may not float it, should be cleaned regularly.

You can purchase custom-made cleaning agents from most tackle shops, but my choice when it comes to cleaning lines is a mild hair shampoo. Put the same amount that you would use to wash your own hair into a basin of lukewarm water, and agitate into a good lather. Now submerge the entire length of line for a few minutes before cleaning the line with a soft cloth, while still in the basin. Next rinse the line with some clean water and wipe with a dry soft cloth. I have cared for my own fly lines in this fashion for a number of years and as a result have not had to purchase any new ones due to premature deterioration resulting from lack of care. Not only does the line last longer, it also makes it much easier to fish with, because a dirty line is a sticky line. Sinking lines should also be cleaned in a similar fashion. At the same time as cleaning the line check your backing splice to the line. If there is any doubt about its security then retie it. A good splice should, if done properly, last the lifetime of your line, or if a double taper until the line is reversed.

Most modern reels of reputable make will give many years of service provided that they are looked after properly. At the start of each season, and prior to use, I like to give my reels an overhaul. I give the spindle and the line roller (where fitted) a coat of new light machine oil, which if not done, particularly to the drum spindle, may cause jamming. Many of today's modern reels are designed for ambidextrous use which gives us an in-built source of spares since the ratchet and drag mechanism is duplicated on many reels. It is not a question of disengaging one pawl and engaging another to change from left- or right-hand wind – if we are only using one pawl and spring it means that the other set is redundant, and because both sets are identical they can be swapped over should failure of one occur.

7 SALMON FLIES: FACTS AND FANCIES

SINGLE HOOKS *(Fig 13)*

At the turn of the century most fly tiers tied their salmon flies to look like large trout flies because they believed that when salmon returned to freshwater they continued to feed. The flies they dressed were almost exclusively tied on single hooks and were large in comparison to the small doubles or trebles preferred today. Nearly all the dressings tied on large single hooks during the late nineteenth and early twentieth century were opaque. This meant that they could be seen quite easily, albeit in silhouette, if viewed from beneath against the light of the sky, which is the fish's point of view.

Almost all of these early dressings incorporated a tail, which more often than not was made up of a few fibres of golden pheasant topping. The reason for this was that anglers at the time thought that they were representing some form of insect, and by incorporating a tail in the dressing to simulate the tail filaments of such, they imagined that if it looked right, it would tempt more fish. If the flies were fished just under the surface to represent some form of ascending nymph then I can see some logic to this thinking, but the single hooks used at the time were not small, but large and heavy, which meant that they could not be fished high in the water. As well as this the lines and tackle used at the time did not facilitate the shallow fishing of a fly, therefore any flies fished were not just below the surface, but in mid-water. The fly was therefore being fished a good foot or more down. For this reason I think that these large single-hooked flies were taken by salmon because they closely resembled a small fish, and not some species of hatching ephemeral invertebrate.

By taking into account the bend of the hook and

Some will tell you that a change of fly will bring about a change in luck. Numerous fly changes, however. do nothing to promote confidence and as a result seldom bring fish to the bank.

the tail of the golden pheasant topping, so commonly used at the time, we can see by looking at the outline of the flies that they had a general fish-like shape. This theory also holds more water if we take the action of the throat hackle into account as well. If the throat hackle is fixed and has no action in the water then we can ignore it, but being mobile, and moving back and forth in relation to the force of the current acting upon it we cannot. Could this action from a salmon's viewpoint not be interpreted as the lateral movement of the pectoral fins of a small fish, trying to keep position in the flow? We shall never really know why salmon took them, but I like

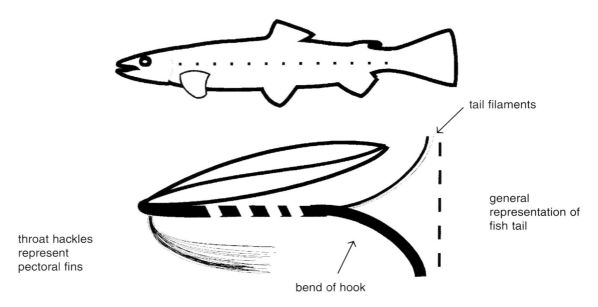

Fig 13 Tying a fly to resemble a fish.

to think that it was because their overall shape and outline represented a small fish. Therefore when tying flies on single hooks I like to take into account what I have said above and use a solid winging material like bronze mallard or teal, rather than hair.

DOUBLE HOOKS *(Fig 14)*

When it comes to double hooks you either love them or hate them. Regardless of one's likes or dislikes, though, flies tied on them do catch a lot of fish. A fly tied on a double hook in my opinion fishes better in the water than a single hook. This is because the two downward bends help to keep it on an even keel. Low-water double hooks are ideal for tying shrimp- or prawn-type patterns, such as the General Practitioner or Ally's Shrimp. This is firstly due to the overall shape of the hook, which I shall look at a little further on, and secondly the long shank of the low-water double hooks are perfect for representing the elongated body of these crustaceans. By selecting a hook that is in harmony with the general outline of the entity that we are trying to

represent we can tie patterns that are more representational of the 'prey' that we are trying to create. If the overall shape looks right, that is edible, then it probably is as far as the salmon is concerned. It must be understood that it is not an exact likeness that I am trying to create, but something which gives the illusion of a creature previously preyed upon by the salmon.

Geoffrey Bucknall in an article published in the 1985 spring edition of *Gamefishing & Fly-Tying Quarterly* wrote,

> The argument about imitative salmon flies hinges on that even older argument as to whether or not salmon feed in freshwater. Those who oppose the idea point out that the salmon's digestive organs have already atrophied before it begins that ascent to its spawning bed, but I'm reminded of the old soldier who could still feel a twinge of rheumatism in the toe of his amputated foot. And it is beyond dispute that one vital digestive organ remains intact: the salmon's mouth.

In order to help create the illusion the hook must become part of the dressing and not be something on which the dressing is merely tied. Low-water double hooks are ideal for tying shrimp or prawn patterns on, because the two bends of the hooks look just like a set of legs or feelers, especially if they are varnished red or orange to match the overall colour of the shrimp. If you are fishing these patterns deep, right in front of the salmon's nose, then the varnished bends of the hooks might make a difference on the day, but if the flies are to be fished high in the water and viewed against the light, then it probably does not make that much difference because under these conditions everything will appear dark and in silhouette.

Brief success. The fish came off seconds after this shot was taken.

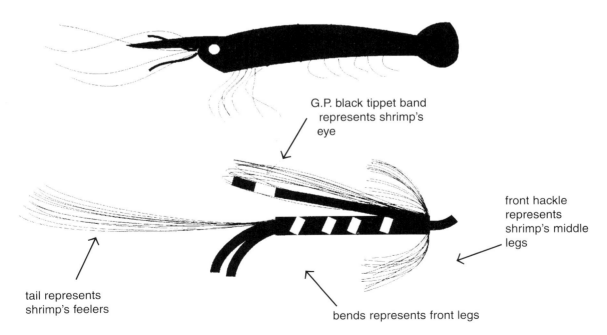

G.P. black tippet band represents shrimp's eye

front hackle represents shrimp's middle legs

tail represents shrimp's feelers

bends represents front legs

Fig 14 *The outline of a general shrimp pattern showing the bends of the hooks as viewed from the side.*

TREBLE HOOKS *(Fig 15)*

Treble hooks such as the Esmond Drury types, or the Partridge Long Shank Salmon Fly Trebles, code X2B, are excellent hookers of fish, the latter in my opinion being the better of the two. Both of these hooks, however, have a tendency to turn on their side when being fished, which is all very well if the dressing is a symmetrical hairwing pattern with the hair of the wing being tied in 360 degrees around the shank, but if the dressing is of a standard type with a wing, beard and tail, or a shrimp pattern they are the very devil to get to swim in an even keel. Some will be saying that this is not so if they are secured to the nylon by a Turle knot. I have tried this knot with these treble hooks, and in my experience it makes little difference, they still turn on their side. The reason for this, I believe, is that the eye on these hooks is positioned the wrong way, the hooks having the eye bent so that there are two hooks above the shank and only one below. This causes the hook to be top heavy and therefore unbalanced. If the eye of the

hook was bent so that there was only one bend above and two below, the fly would then have a double keel and keep in the 'correct' plane when being fished. Some might argue that if the hook was manufactured in this fashion it would be difficult to incorporate a tail, because the top hook would make it difficult to facilitate this. Why tie in a tail when there is one already there, the top hook? If golden pheasant topping is your first choice then why not just varnish the top bend of the hook yellow. Trying to bend the eye in the opposite direction without the hook breaking is very difficult, so perhaps the manufacturers of these hooks could start to produce them in both styles just to keep people like me happy. If the eye of the hook were bent in the desired direction they would then be ideal for shrimp and prawn patterns, but unfortunately they are not. Nevertheless they are ideal as mentioned previously for tying general hairwing-type patterns.

These hooks are excellent when tying representations of small squid, a known major food source of the salmon at sea – the three bends on these

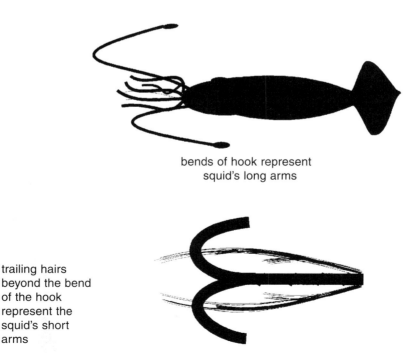

bends of hook represent
squid's long arms

trailing hairs
beyond the bend
of the hook
represent the
squid's short
arms

Fig 15 Tying a squid pattern.

hooks just shout 'squid', due to their tentacle-like appearance. The hook, therefore, when tying a squid pattern is the major ingredient, because all that is needed is a small collar hackle to represent the tail rays, a layer of body floss, and a bunch of hair tied in between the hooks to represent the smaller set of arms.

FLIES FOR AUTUMN FISHING
(Fig 16)

During the autumn when the majority of salmon have long left the feeding grounds, and their feeding instinct has long since been suppressed, a large deeply sunk fly generally proves to be much more successful than a small fly fished just subsurface. At this time of the year I believe that most fish are caught because of 'sexual induced aggression'. For this reason it is best to fish with something that will bring about a hostile reaction from the salmon. A fly that has a slim fish like-profile will often induce a salmon into taking at this time of the year, when a shrimp, or prawn pattern will not. Possibly this is because they see the fish-like object as a sexual rival. Large single hooks tied in the fashion described previously could be used, but these are

better suited to fresh fish with soft mouth tissue – they are not very good hookers of fish which have been in the river for some time and whose mouths have gone hard.

In order to increase our chances of success at this time of the year these flies should be tied either on brass tubes, Waddingtons or Brora-type shanks. This is because not only do they offer the correct profile, but they utilize the facility of a treble hook, and when armed with a small outpoint treble, they are deadly. When these tubes and Waddingtons are dry they look nothing like a fish, but when wet, with the hair flattened against the shank by the force of the stream they have a very fish-like appearance. The treble attached at the rear of the tube or shank adds further to the illusion by effectively representing the tail of a fish.

SHRIMP PATTERNS *(Figs 17–18)*

As mentioned at the start of this chapter, salmon flies from the 1850s through to the 1920s were tied mainly to represent large trout-type flies, because anglers at the time who saw salmon taking natural flies believed that if they used large trout patterns then they would invariably catch salmon. Perhaps

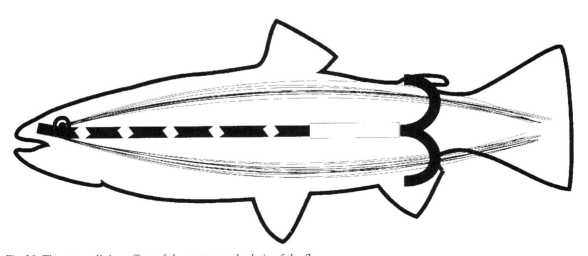

Fig 16 The streamlining effect of the water on the hair of the fly.

they had a point, but what they should have been doing was tying up patterns that represented prey on which the salmon had been feeding prior to ascending the river. It has always surprised me how few salmon fly patterns there are that represent a form of food on which the salmon feeds at sea, a major source being shrimps or prawns. I know there are a number of shrimp and prawn patterns about, but considering the many thousands of other salmon fly patterns in existence, very few of them resemble any food items that the salmon could recognize. The trout angler on the other hand has gone a long way in trying to imitate the insects on which his quarry feed, so why then not the salmon angler?

Some of the more enquiring contemporary salmon anglers have given this aspect some cognizance, by coming up with a pattern or two that extends a long way towards representing a shrimp or prawn. The better tried and tested patterns such as the General Practitioner as invented by Esmond Drury, or the more modern Ally's Shrimp, by Alastair Gowans, have both proved effective salmon-catching patterns. If each of these flies are looked at more closely the one thing that they have in common is the colour orange.

This I am sure is the secret when it comes to their success, because if we look at the natural colouration of two of the salmon's main food items, a shrimp-like amphipod of the *Parathemisto* genus, and a prawn-like crustacean called a Euphausiid of *Meganyctiphanes* genus, we see that they are a translucent 'orangey' colour. Although it is less opaque than the orange found in the Ally's Shrimp and the General Practitioner patterns, the orange floss in association with the orange of the golden pheasant tippet create the necessary visual stimuli, which at times seem to trigger off the salmon's predatory feeding instinct. This is especially so if

Two fresh summer fish taken on a large Ally's Shrimp.

the salmon has only just arrived back from its rich sea feeding and has not yet undergone the physiological change that suppresses its feeding habit. The Curry's Red Shrimp also has this translucent effect due to the badger hackles used, but in saying this if I was asked to choose only one shrimp fly, it would have to be without any doubt the Ally's Shrimp, its success probably due to the grey squirrel tail tied in under the golden pheasant tippet. This gives the fly a ghostly, almost translucent effect in the water, when viewed against the orange of the tippet.

By looking at a fly catch percentage bar chart for a beat on the River Doon, we can see that shrimp patterns accounted for a staggering 33 per cent of all the fish taken, with the Curry's Shrimp taking 13 per cent, Ally's Shrimp 12 per cent, and the General Practitioner 8 per cent. Also, we can see that 25 per cent of the total fish were taken on orange hairwing tubes or Waddingtons. The percentage of the total

number of fish taken with a predominantly orange fly is therefore 45 per cent; this is of course only if we ignore the Curry's Shrimp, because it is not a predominantly orange fly. Why then are the figures so high? One reason for this is that. I correlated all the catch returns made on fly over a period of three years and put a catch percentage chart up inside the hut. The majority of the anglers fishing the stretch were time share owners with limited experience of the river. When their week to fish arrived, in a bid to optimize their chances of catching a fish, most put on a shrimpy orange-coloured fly, something which was seen to be successful on the beat.

When going after fresh-run spring or summer fish my first choice of salmon fly has to be one that will trigger off the salmon's predatory feeding instinct. This can sometimes be done by using one of the shrimp-type flies mentioned previously, particularly if the feeding instinct of the fish has not

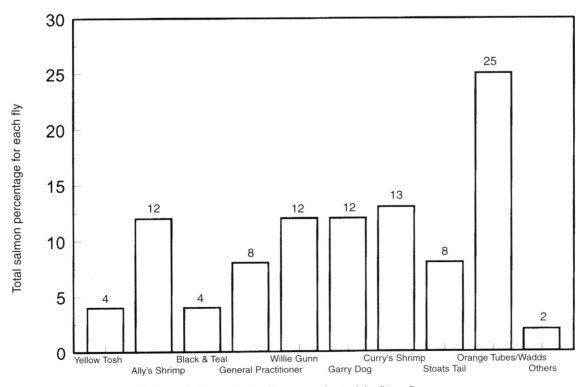

Fig 17 The percentage of fish caught by particular flies on one beat of the River Doon.

Fishing below a small weir during a spate. When fish are running, the water above the weir would probably give the best chance of a fish.

been totally suppressed. The reason why I think that these flies are so successful is that the fish have not been away long from their feeding grounds and the feeding instinct in many of them still burns bright. In times of drought, however, when the fish cannot run and have been hanging about in the tidal estuaral stretches for some time these flies are not so effective, possibly due to the feeding resopnse being by now almost totally suppressed. As is so often the case in salmon fishing, however, ideas and techniques that produce fish for one angler may not be so productive for someone else.

Ally's Shrimp (variant)

When fishing a river that is fining down after a spate, and when in with a chance of a fresh-run salmon straight in off the tide, my first choice will be an Ally's Shrimp. The dressing and tying for this are as follows:

Hook	Partridge low-water doubles 12 to 8, and 1–2in Waddington shanks.
Tail	Orange bucktail, length of hook.
Rib	Oval gold, or silver depending on taste.
Body	Rear half orange floss. Front half black floss.
Wing	Grey squirrel tail with golden pheasant tippet on top.
Throat	Bright orange cock hackle.
Head	Red varnish.

1   Lay down a bed of tying silk along the shank of the hook, starting and finishing just in front of the bends.
2   Now cut approximately thirty strands of orange bucktail, the length being about two to three times, the length of the shank being used. Tie in and secure.
3   Next tie in a suitable length of either gold or silver ribbing. At this stage leave hanging free.
4   Tie in and secure a length of orange floss.
5   Wind the orange floss half way along the shank of the hook. Secure and trim.
6   Secure and wind the black floss along the remaining length of the hook.
7   Wind the ribbing material towards the front of the hook, five to six turns being enough.
8   Cut some grey squirrel tail about the length of the hook and tie in at the head.
9   Select a golden pheasant tippet and tie in so

Spinning for summer salmon on MacKenzies Pool of the Smithston Fishing's on the River Doon. Note the low rod point. On such small rivers a high rod point is detrimental to good lure presentation.

Spinning a lure through a quiet glide during a dirty spate.

Holding the rod as shown, especially with a long one, is far more comfortable than holding it at arm's length when leading the line round.

Casting a fly on the Stinchar, a river that fishes very well during the summer given rain.

Tailing out tired fish. Note the index thumb and forefinger of the right hand is placed on the torso of the salmon's tail wrist.

Choosing the correct size of fly for the prevailing conditions is what generally separates the average fly fisher from the good fly fisher.

During bright overhead conditions salmon that frequent lies shaded by trees will sometimes be tempted to move to a fly, unlike salmon in open holding water.

Small obstacles like the one shown behind me often cause fish to halt before ascending further. Places like this are always worth a cast or two during a spate.

Fishing down a good holding pool. The fish during the height of water shown tend to lie just on the edge of the central flow.

A selection of flies for high and/or cold water. The four on the left are tied on Waddington shanks while the other two are on Brora type shanks of different gauge.

A selection of shrimp flies favoured for summer fishing.

A grilse from the Strathspey Angling Association water of the Spey at Grantown.

Two anglers fish the Manse Pool on the Castle Grant water of the Spey.

Fishing huts come in all shapes and sizes. They don't, however, come much better than this.

Fishing for a July salmon.

Mary Keachie fishing the type of fly water that the Spey is famous for.

that the black bars extend about two-thirds of the way along the shank of the hook.

10 Finally select a suitable orange cock hackle and wind it around the shank just behind the eye of the hook. Take care not to wind it too close, as room will be needed to make the head of the fly. Take it around the shank three or four times. Now with the aid of a hackle guard hold it back and secure, finishing off with a whip finish to keep it in place. When this is done give it a coat of clear varnish and allow to dry. When dry give it a coat of red varnish.

Note When tying this pattern on to a Waddington shank, only take the orange bucktail past the treble hook by about an inch. Also, before tying in the gold or silver ribbing, put a collar of orange hackle around the rear of shank and pull back as for the front collar.

I tie this shrimp mostly on low-water doubles in sizes ranging from 12 to 8, for the majority of my summer and early autumn fishing. These flies, with their tail extending beyond the bend of the hook, throw all hook size theory out the window. The tail of these flies effectively doubles, or in some cases trebles, the overall length of the fly, which means that a fly tied on a size 8 will be very close to 2in in length, a size 10 about 1¾in (45mm) and a size 12 somewhere between 1½ and 1¼in (30–36mm) in

length. When it comes to fly sizes you must consider their full size – do not go by hook size alone.

During late autumn if the river is running at normal height and is not too cold I will use a size 6 or 8 fished in conjunction with a Wet Cel II line. If on the other hand the water is cold or very coloured, then I will fish the same pattern tied on a brass tube, Waddington or Brora shank from 1 to 2½in (25–60mm) in length, depending on the river and prevailing conditions at the time. Shrimp flies tied on tubes or Waddington shanks do not look as 'good' as the same fly tied on a double hook, but they are very effective in high or cold water. One thing to look out for when connecting the treble hook to either the shank or the tube is to make sure that you position two hooks of the treble so that they run parallel to the underside. This is more easily achieved with the tubes since the hook can be manoeuvred once tied to the nylon. With the Waddington the hook must be positioned correctly prior to putting on the dressing. Practising this will help you to keep your flies swimming on the right keel.

If you do not position the treble as suggested the fly will turn on its side and will lose its effectiveness. I also position the treble in this fashion when fishing standard hairwing tubes or Waddingtons to help keep the fly swimming in the correct plane, that is, with the hair lying true in the current, and

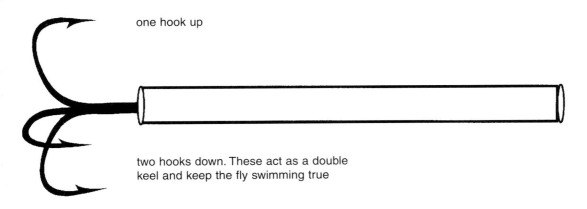

one hook up

two hooks down. These act as a double keel and keep the fly swimming true

Fig 18 Correct positioning of the hooks when tied to shank or tube.

An Ally's Shrimp, tied on a Waddington shank.

not turning and swimming with the hair down one side. On a medium-sized river or small spate stream there is no need to use a tube or shank longer than 1½ in (30mm). This is because the overall size of the fly will be in the region of 2½ in (60mm), this size being about the upper limit for such rivers. On a large river anything from 3 to 4in (75–100mm) might be needed. (Remember I am talking about the overall fly size and not the size of the tube or shank.) The size of fly used will generally be determined by the water and air temperature, but the physical size of the river will also in many cases dictate the maximum size of the fly. A large fly fished in a small spate stream will be totally out of place, unless fished when the river is very high or coloured. If the river is of such a colour or height we would need something larger than 2½in/60mm (total length including tail and hook), then a spinning rod is better suited. To be successful the fly size selected must be of such that it is in 'harmony' with the river and its mood at the time.

Other Shrimp Patterns

There are other prawn and shrimp patterns that are very successful, with some even going as far as having two black beads for eyes, along with a length of latex or plastic pulled down the length of the shank and segmented by monofilament to give the impression of the crustacean's shell. These seem to work well for some anglers who use them, but I have not found them very successful. One of the best examples of this type of imitation prawn is the one created and tied by James Waltham, 'The Red Devil' on Andy Nickolson's video *The Game Fly*. If exact imitation is your choice, then this is probably as close as you will get. In saying this I am not so sure that exact imitation is all that necessary. My own preference is for a fly that suggests a previous food form in shape, and colour. It is the triggering factor that I am interested in, and not the exact likeness. As I said earlier, if something looks edible, then it probably is as far as the salmon is concerned.

When choosing the type of shrimp fly to use, or any other kind of fly for that matter, it is quite simply a case of using the one you have the most confidence in. If you cannot decide on a fly then ask the ghillie or someone more experienced than you to pick one for you. Rely on their judgement. When faced with this situation I have on some occasions given someone a fly and told them that it has caught a number of fish. On other occasions I have cut off my fly and handed it to them after I have taken a fish on it. The fact that they are now fishing with a successful fly does wonders for their morale. If you have belief in a fly then you will fish it 'better' than one you are not sure about. It goes without saying that the 'better' you fish a fly the more fish you will catch.

A question that is often asked by anglers is, can a fish see colours? I think that they can for the reasons I gave in Chapter 2. Also if we look at the spawning livery of cock salmon in the autumn we see that they undergo major colouration changes. I do not know why this colour change takes place, but suspect that it is a visual deterrent to ward off other cock salmon that may try to indulge in 'piscatorial adultery'. The colour red in the animal world often signals danger, or stay away, and this is why I think that the cock fish go through this change in skin pigmentation. If we look at the male minnow its belly goes a bright red at spawning time. When setting the minnow jar at this time of the year, a piece of red wool or other similarly coloured material will bring a violent reaction from the males, as they try to rip it to pieces. Many anglers who fish the natural minnow for salmon get their supply at this time, because they believe that the red-bellied males are more productive than the more drably coloured males or females caught earlier in the year.

The Garry Dog

The spawning livery of a cock salmon contains red and to a lesser extent a mottling of yellow and orange in paler shades. This is why my favourite fly at this time of the year is a Garry Dog, because it contains two of the three colours mentioned above. I like to tie them on brass tubes or Waddington shanks 1–2½in (25–60mm) in length.

Tag   Wide oval gold tinsel, four or five turns.

Rib   Wide oval gold tinsel.

Body   Black floss.

Wing   Red bucktail under yellow bucktail, extended beyond the end of the shank by about an inch, so that the hair goes past the bend of the treble hook.

Head   Black varnish.

1   Lay down a bed of tying silk thinly along the tube or shank, finishing back at the hook end.
2   Tie in and secure the oval gold ribbing, leaving hanging.

3   Tie in the black floss and wind along the length of the shank or body and secure. Do not forget to leave room for the head.
4   Take the ribbing and wind in open turns over the black floss. Five or six complete turns should be enough. Secure and trim.
5   Cut approximately thirty strands of red bucktail long enough so that it will extend beyond the bends of the treble hooks by about one inch. Once you have done this level up the uncut ends with a stacker. Next split into two even bunches and tie one half on top and the other underneath at the head of the fly. Secure with two or three turns of thread and trim away protruding hair.
6   Prepare approximately forty strands of yellow bucktail in the same way and tie it in at the head of the fly over the top of the red bucktail. Secure and trim away any waste.
7   Finish by making a head. Seal with clear varnish, wait until dry and then give it a coat of black varnish.

Note By varying the amounts of yellow and red we then have a fly suitable for both clear and murky conditions.

I used to fish this fly throughout the season, but now only during the autumn, as this is when it has brought me the most success. For some reason it does not catch the same number of fish during the summer as the Ally's Shrimp. I have tried it at other times of the season, but have not found it very successful if used before late summer. This fly tied on 1 to 2½in (25–60mm) brass tubes with a ribbing of wide oval gold instead of the silver rib as the original was dressed, is the ideal autumn fly. This is particularly so when the river is running a bit on the high side and carrying a touch of colour. It is also very effective when tied on similar sized Waddington shanks when the river starts to fall away and slows through the streams.

The Orange Lodge

Sometimes one particular fly on a river will gain a legendary reputation for producing salmon, but this is almost certainly not because the fish in that river will only go for that dressing, rather it is because no one ever fishes with anything else. In many instances it is better to fish a fly that the fish have seldom or ever seen. I have no doubt that fish that have been in a pool for some time get fed up seeing the same fly day in day out and for this reason I like to pass something over their heads that they have not seen before. In saying this, if the ghillie or keeper for the stretch recommends a particular fly then give it a try, but do not stick to it if it does not produce a response relatively quickly. It maybe diplomatic to give it a couple of times down the pool, then if nothing is forthcoming change to one of your own choice, say change from a Stoats Tail to a bright, hot-orange hairwing. This technique is best tried with a fairly garish fly a size or two larger than would normally be used for the conditions. A favourite fly that I have used for this on some rivers with considerable success is a tying of my own called the Orange Lodge. The dressing and tying are as follows:

Hook	Partridge low-water doubles, sizes 12 to 2.
Tail	None.
Body	Black floss.
Rib	Flat wide silver.
Wing	Hot orange bucktail or squirrel tail.
Throat	Bright blue cock hackle.
Head	Black varnish.

1   Lay down a bed of tying silk the entire length of the body ending up at the hook end.
2   Tie in a suitable length of flat silver ribbing. Leave this hanging for now.
3   Tie in the black floss and secure.
4   Wind the floss to just behind the eye, secure and trim.
5   Take the silver ribbing along the shank in no more than four or five turns. Secure and trim.
6   Take one small- to medium-sized bright blue cock hackle and tie in behind the eye of the hook.

Do not forget to leave room for the head.
7   Wrap the hackle around the shank three or four times to make a collar. Now tie in, secure and trim away waste material. Wet your forefinger and thumb and pull the fibres down below the shank to form a beard. When this is done secure with a few turns to keep the fibres in place.
8   Cut a bunch of orange hair long enough to extend to the bend of the hook. Level the ends and tie in. Trim away any waste.
9   Finish the head and whip finish. Seal with clear varnish and when dry give a coat of black varnish.

There is no doubt that since the introduction of hair-wing patterns many of the legendary multi-layered fixed-winged types have fallen out of favour. Perhaps this is because in today's instant, hectic, throw-away world, no one wants to bother with tying and fishing patterns that take time and skill to create.

There has been much written about why these hair-and-feather creations are called flies since they do not look anything like an insect, other than perhaps some extinct Jurassic species! There has been many a reason put forward, but in my opinion it is because of the manner in which they are constructed. Some anglers will take great pain tying flies, insisting that it is crucial to stick to the exact tying of the original and wanting to know how many turns should be put around the head, while other saner individuals will merely lash a bunch of hairs onto a shank.

The Willie Gunn

It has always puzzled me why some anglers will choose one pattern at the exclusion of all others, (although in saying this I do it myself). It is very often because they have taken their first fish on that particular tying, or perhaps it was recommended by another angler. If the fish have been difficult to come by and all of a sudden fish are taken on a particular pattern the local tackle shops will quickly be sold out of the successful tying. This was what happened with the Willie Gunn. Here is the true story of how one of the most famous salmon flies in the world came to be invented, as told to me by Rob Wilson himself.

At the time Waddington shanks had just become patented and a lot of the Helmsdale anglers were forming paper clips into Waddington-type shanks. At the same time there was an explosion of hairwing patterns and colours on the new articulated bodies. Although the home-made shanks were very successful they were inclined to be unreliable due to the mildness of the metal. In an attempt to overcome this Rob Wilson engaged the services of a company dealing in the manufacture of stainless steel wire, different gauges being purchased so that light or heavy flies could be tied for a wide variety of water conditions. This shank style became very successful and was soon to become the 'Brora' style as known today.

Since there were so many different fly patterns Rob Wilson decided to rationalize his 'Brora' flies to only twenty. It was during this streamlining process that the Willie Gunn was conceived. The fly was originally tied in 1970 by an RAF navigator called Dusty Miller who worked for Rob Wilson of Brora. The fly came about when Dusty was instructed to come up with a hairwing pattern of the famous Thunder and Lightning. The 'new' fly consisted of a black body, gold rib and equal bunches of yellow, orange and black hair tied down on top and under the shank. The original fly did not have the hair mixed as so many fly tyers would have us believe. It is thought by many that the fly takes its name from the ghillie Willie Gunn, because he initially tied it, but this too is wrong. One day, Willie Gunn, a ghillie for the Countess of Sutherland, walked into Rob Wilson's tackle shop and out of a selection of the twenty patterns lying on the counter picked up one that he thought looked good. It was in fact one of the new hairwing versions of the Thunder and Lightning. After looking at it and playing with it for a while, Willie was told to take it and go!

What happened next made angling news around the globe. His first two outings with the fly gave him double-figure catches and needless to say there was great demand for the fly that Willie Gunn had done so well with. The fly from then on was renamed the Willie Gunn. As time went on the fly was developed by Rob Wilson and he eventually arrived at the fly dressing so widely used today, with the hair being well mixed in equal amounts of

yellow, orange and black. This dressing proved to be more successful for autumn fish than the original fly tied with separate bunches of hair, which was originally tied for spring fish.

Some might think that which of these two styles the hair is tied in makes little difference, but Rob Wilson assures me that in his experience it does, the autumn salmon for some reason preferring the equally mixed hairwing version. The fly has taken countless salmon through the years, and although initially only tied for spring fish it very soon become an accepted 'all rounder', being tied on hooks from size 10 long-shanked trebles for low-water summer fishing, right through to 3in (75mm) brass tubes for use during early spring or late autumn. Incidentally, Rob Wilson tells me one of the most popular dressings now is tied on long-shank trebles up to size 4, with the hair being at least twice the length of the hook. For larger sizes the Brora shank is better. The dressing and tying is as follows:

Thread	Black.
Tag	Four or five turns of wide oval gold tinsel.
Rib	Wide oval tinsel as used for tag.
Body	Black floss.
Wing (Spring)	Yellow under orange under black bucktail tied in bunches with hair extending about one inch beyond end of shank.
Wing (Autumn)	Equal mix of yellow, orange and black bucktail extending about one inch beyond end of shank.
Head	Clear or black varnish.

1 Start by tying in the silk near the front of the tube and wind openly towards the rear. This helps to keep the body floss in place around the tube and stops it from working loose.
2 Tie in the oval gold tinsel, taking care that it is secure.
3 Wind the gold tinsel around the shank four or five times to make the tag. Secure with a couple of

turns. Do not trim and cut off as the tinsel will later be wound along the tube to form the rib.

4   The black floss can now be wound along the tube. Do not wind it right up to the end, leave about 5mm. Tie in and trim off surplus floss. This is where the hair will be tied in.

5   Wind the oval gold tinsel around the tube to form a rib. For a 2in (50mm) tube five turns will be enough. I have found that too many turns for the rib spoils the overall effect of the fly. Tie in and secure, taking care not to cut the tying thread in the process.

6   Prior to tying in the hair, a bed of tying thread should be laid down along the remaining section of the tube. This will help to keep the hair in place while it is being tied down. When tying the mixed hairwing pattern, the hair should be mixed by rolling the different colours between your fingers. The hairs can now be brought to the same length by putting them into a stacker points down and gently tapping. It is best to mix enough hair at the time for the quantity of flies that your are going to tie.

7   Tie in the hair on top of the tube with a good dozen or so turns of the thread. Repeat the process when tying in the other wing. Before finally whipping the hair down on to the tube, it is best to check how the hair is lying along the length of the tube. At this stage final adjustments are possible. If no adjustments are necessary finish off the head of the fly and complete with a whip finish and varnish. (For durability I generally give my own flies two coats.)

Like every other fly in salmon fishing, however, there is no guarantee of it providing sport.

Deciding on a Fly

Some anglers will swear that it is the *style* of fly that is important, because they think that one style will have a better action in the water than another style under the same conditions; for example, choose between a long flowing hairwing like the Collie Dog or a short solid feather wing like the Blue Charm. If the fly is of the right style for the conditions it will create the illusion of life much more convincingly. When it comes to style the type and weight of hook both play an important part in how it will swim and must be taken into consideration when tying a specific style of fly. It is no use putting a long fixed wing on a long Waddington-type shank if it does not look good or fish well. Taking all this into account I cannot find fault with this theory.

Others will fervently argue that it is the *colour* which is the most important factor, which I am inclined to agree with to a certain extent, especially late in the season when salmon are starting to show their full spawning livery, reds and yellows. When the fish are fresh run and straight in from the rich sea feeding, I believe colour also plays a part in stimulating a response from a running fish and from my own experience orange appears to be the best. It is a belief and nothing more based only on personal preference and experience, while the current thinking by a number of respected authorities on the subject of fly selection is that colour plays no part in determining whether a fish will find a fly interesting or not.

It used to be thought by some (and probably still is by many) that on a bright day one should fish a bright fly and on a dull day a dull fly. Leading contemporary angling authorities, however, place greater emphasis on the overall swimming speed of the fly in relation to its size, and in this reasoning I can find no fault. The main object when presenting anything to a salmon, whether it is a fly or lure is to make the fish take hold of it, and for this reason it must have some semblance of life and 'swim' at the correct speed. Although salmon will occasionally take objects into their mouths other than for the purpose of eating, the main reason for anything being mouthed must as far as I am concerned be connected to the feeding habit. Some anglers prefer a fly tied to represent a shrimp or prawn and why not, since the salmon is known to include these in its diet. When fishing for fresh-run fish I am inclined to be fishing with this in mind and favouring an Ally's Shrimp for this very reason. Whether this is a valid explanation of why the salmon takes these flies we shall never know, but they do kill their fair share of fish.

Why any angler considers his chosen fly to be more successful than another is really irrelevant, since there is no positive evidence to prove or disprove his theory. It is probably a fly that has brought him success in the past and is therefore likely to be the only fly that gets a swim, even though the fly box is filled with a wide variety of patterns, styles and colours. Bear in mind that the only fly that can catch a fish is the one which is being fished. Certain flies from time to time seem to gain a legendary status, not because they are better slayers of fish than anything else, but because very often the fish in that particular beat or river see nothing else. This happened with the Willie Gunn, when everyone starting fishing with it. If a fly does not produce a fish relatively quickly and with some consistency for an angler, it generally falls out of favour very quickly. This is why some patterns fall by the wayside. Some anglers seem to think that salmon will not take their choice of fly, because the ghillie has told them that the only fly that kills fish on his beat has to be of a particular pattern, colour or type. This is nonsense: next time one comes away with this rubbish ask him when he last spoke to a fish. Some ghillies have the infuriating habit of cutting off a well-tied fly, saying 'Ah, that will never do', and while putting it into their own fly

boxes, replace it with one of their own shoddy creations. I don't grudge them a fly or two, but all they have to do is ask.

Although I have great faith in a certain colour of fly for a specific fish, for example, orange for fresh-run fish and yellow and red for autumn fish, I am certain that if a salmon is in a taking mood it will take virtually anything passing over it. I have been fishing away on more than one occasion with a small wisp of a fly and have taken a fish or two, only to have someone step in at the head of the pool with a spinning rod and take a fish on a 3in (75mm) Toby. These incidents above all others have proved to me that there are no hard and fast rules when it comes to taking salmon.

Some anglers, however, including some well-known angling authorities, have put much thought into the selection of the correct fly. The late Reg Righyni divided his floating line flies into four main groups: Flashing Illusion, Normal Image, Silhouette, and Translucent Illusion. The first of these, the Flashing Illusion, he used as a last resort when all other types had failed. As the name suggests they were bright patterns such as a Silver

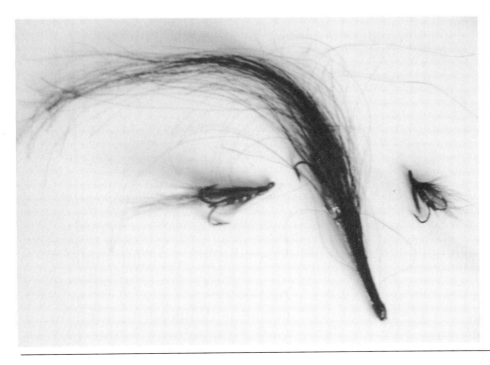

The photograph shows a 6in (150mm) Collie Dog, size 8 Munro Killer and a 14 Stoat's Tail. I have experienced days when all three flies killed fish.

Doctor, which was used to grab the fish's attention and was primarily used in difficult conditions. The Normal Image flies such as the Hairy Mary or Thunder and Lightning were used in dull weather and bad light conditions or when the river was carrying a touch of colour. Righyni argued that if fishing under a strong, bright light all colour in a fly would be lost and would therefore be a waste of time. This is why he preferred a fly with a solid wing such as the Blue Charm when fishing under these conditions, while the Translucent Illusion type flies such as Silver Grey were preferred when the sun was shining obliquely down the river.

Reg Righyni was without doubt one of the great anglers of the century; he was a 'thinking' angler and caught many a salmon on the fly, but I think that his secret of success was that he had the greatest confidence in his choice of fly for the prevailing conditions. The result of having confidence in the fly that we are fishing is that it is likely to be fished for a longer period of time and in a 'better' fashion than one in which we have little or no faith.

Therefore it would seem to make very little difference, as far as the fish is concerned, what fly we tie to the end of our leader. It has always amazed me that so many anglers seem to bestow on the salmon human powers of deduction. Neurologically, the salmon is of a low order and cannot make decisions based on information collected by its senses. The salmon merely reacts to continuing changing events around it in order to perform its prime function, that of spawning. There is no solid evidence relating to why a salmon takes anything into its mouth while in freshwater and for this very reason no scientific approach can be used in selecting the correct fly.

Although each individual has his own beliefs and methods when it comes to fly selection, it would appear from my own experience and that of other anglers that as good a way as any of choosing a fly is to sort your flies into three separate boxes: fill one with large, another with medium and the other with small flies, select the correct box for the water conditions, then simply close your eyes and take your pick.

8 DOUBLE-HANDED CASTING

As I mentioned in Chapter 6, it is absolutely essential when purchasing a fly rod to acquire one that suits your own particular style of casting. If you do not you will not derive the maximum pleasure from the sport.

ROD ASSEMBLY *(Fig 19)*

Having hopefully made the right choice the next thing we must do is assemble it properly so that it will perform the task for which it was designed. It is no use just pushing the sections together, attaching a reel and line and walking down to the water. To assemble a rod incorrectly will only result in its premature breakage. This is because during the casting process the flexing and twisting action that occurs when the rod is loaded and unloaded will cause the male and female joints to work free of each other. If this happens the female ferrule will crack and break. In order to stop them working loose we can do two things.

First push and twist the two sections firmly together (it is no use just pushing one section into the other). Make sure that the rod rings of all the sections align once you have finished. One thing that makes the aligning of the rings a little easier is to put small dabs of coloured varnish or paint opposite each other on all the sections. When these marks line up the rings will be running true down the length of the rod.

Second we must tape the sections together. One author of eminence has stated that this should not be done with electrical PVC-type tape, but with masking tape instead. Masking tape in my opinion should *not* be used, since if it happens to get wet it will lose its adhesive qualities and therefore will not

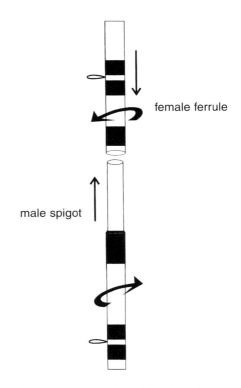

female ferrule

male spigot

Fig 19 *Lining up the male and female rod sections.*

prevent the sections from working loose. I prefer to use the PVC-type tape, which when stretched and wound over the two joints with overlapping turns and in the same direction that the female ferrule was twisted over the male spigot, will ensure that the sections never come loose during casting.

Now that we have secured the rod joints the next thing to do is attach the reel and feed the line through the rod rings. If we do not thread the line through every rod ring the line will not be cast easily. It is always advisable to double check that all the rings have been threaded before starting to fish.

PREPARING TO CAST

Before starting, adopt a comfortable casting position. This is done by resting the butt of the rod against your lower abdomen and moving your right hand (if right-handed) slowly along the length of the handle until your arm is taking the weight of the rod comfortably. Generally this occurs when the elbow is almost straight, but still partially bent. I have never favoured a totally straight arm for supporting a long rod, as it tends to become tiring after a while. Once we have our own position of comfort the left hand can take hold of the butt section below the reel to act as a support. Note it is the right arm that casts the rod, the left arm only supports and provides a fulcrum point. For left-handed casters this will be the other way round. Then position your feet so that you can rock back and forth, back with the back cast and forward with the forward power stroke. With right-handed casters the right foot should be placed slightly in front.

We are now ready to start casting. First pull a good two to three yards of line off the reel and pull it through the top ring of the rod. Flick this line out onto the water. Do this two or three more times and then let the current carry the line downstream. Once there is enough line beyond the top ring to load the rod we can begin casting.

CASTING STYLES

Before I start to describe how each type of cast is performed I would just like to say that a book is a limited medium for representing this topic, a video being much better. Better still seek casting instruction from a qualified instructor who is a member of the Association of Practical Game Angling Instructors (APGAI).

The Overhead Cast *(Fig 20)*
Of all the casting styles practised by salmon anglers

the overhead is the easiest to learn. This is because it only requires two power strokes, the back cast to lift the line clear of the water, and the forward cast to propel the fly line and flies out over the water to the part of the pool where we want to present them.

To execute this cast, first lower the rod so that it runs parallel to the surface of the water, then pull in a few feet of line so that it lies straight in the water. Keeping the rod in the same plane, point the rod tip to where you intend the line to land. Once this has been done the rod should be raised to between 20 and 30 degrees from the horizontal. Now with sufficient power lift the rod up to the position of execution to bring the line off the water and propel it behind you. The whole process should be unhurried with the rod being moved smoothly but powerfully to about the 11 o'clock position. As this position is reached the rod should be allowed to drift back with the line until it has arrives at the 1 o'clock position. We must keep the rod in this position until the line has had time to straighten out behind. When it does the tip of the rod will be pulled back, and at this point the forward power stroke is made. Again the rod should be punched forward against the weight of the line. The rod should then be stopped at about 10 o'clock and allowed to drift down and slightly forwards to accommodate the straightening line. Do not push the rod forwards, since this does not achieve extra distance. If extra yardage is sought pull some extra line off the reel before making the cast. (This extra line can easily be shot.)

During the back cast the extra line should be allowed to hang free below the reel. In order to stop this extra line going out during the back cast clamp it against the handle of the rod, with the forefinger of your right hand. The clamped line is not released until the rod is between the 11 and 10 o'clock position of the forward cast. The timing of the cast is very similar to the slow swing of a pendulum. It swings one way, briefly pauses and then moves the other way. One thing I urge you not to do is look over your shoulder to see what the line is doing. This is a common fault with beginners and should be avoided at all costs before it becomes a habit. Keep your eyes fixed ahead on where you want your fly to land.

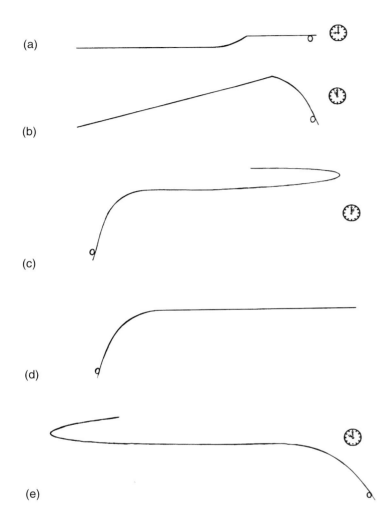

(a)

(b)

(c)

(d)

(e)

Fig 20 The overhead cast. (a) Rod pointing straight down the line. (b) Rod lifted progressively and positively to 11 o'clock position. (c) Rod tip allowed to drift back to the 1 o'clock position, but no further. As the line straightens out behind you will feel the tip of the rod being pulled back a little further. (d) When the tug on the end of the line is felt the rod should be punched forward causing it to bend against the weight of the line. The energy stored in the rod will now propel the line forward. (e) Rod should be stopped at around the 10 o'clock position and then lowered to around 9 o'clock as the line straightens and alights softly on the water surface.

The Switch Cast *(Fig 21)*

As with the previous cast we must get a few yards of line out beyond the rod tip before beginning. This cast is perhaps the most useful of all the casts for the spate stream angler. It requires less room to perform than the overhead and does not disturb the water for anglers fishing down behind, as the single or double Spey casts do. On a large river the immediate surface disturbance is of no consequence because the fish that we are intending to cover are usually well away from the commotion. This is a very important issue if we are fishing a busy association stretch. Who wants to fish down a pool where the surface of the fish-holding section has been disturbed by someone dumping line onto it while executing a Spey cast?

On performing the cast the line should first come to dangle below the rod. Next the rod should be raised to lift as much line off the water as possible, and at this stage we must pause. We must now describe an ellipse with the rod point, slowly at first, but gradually accelerating until the rod is in a position just past 12 o'clock. At this point the rod movement is brought to a halt. When the rod stops it will be in the position of execution, the position from which all casts are completed. After the rod

Arthur Oglesby giving a casting demonstration at the 1994 CLA Game Fair.

The position of execution. It is from this position that all casts are performed. If a long cast is to be made the reel should be brought up level with the side of the chin.

comes to a halt the line is allowed to fade and fall before the forward power stroke is made. The forward cast is generally made with a small, sharp flick of the wrist.

The Roll Cast *(Fig 22)*
This cast starts with the line lying straight and the rod in the horizontal plane. The rod should also be pointing along the line. To start the cast the rod is brought slowly back to a position just beyond the vertical. This brings it into the position of execution at which time the fly and line will come rifling back across the surface towards you. The fly and the majority of fly line that is beyond the rod tip should remain on the water.

When it can be raised no further the rod should be allowed to pass very slightly beyond the vertical to allow a 'D' loop to form behind. As the rod reaches this point we make the forward stroke. Arthur Oglesby at this stage of the cast instructs his students 'to break the rod with one quick snappy flick of the wrist', this action resulting in the rod sending the line rolling out above the water. The action is very similar to that used to make a rope roll out loops along the ground. The fly during the final stages of the cast is lifted off the surface by the uncurling of the line along the surface. Once we can perform this cast easily we can then move on to the single Spey.

It is absolutely essential that we become adept at roll casting before we attempt the single Spey.

Single Spey Cast *(Fig 23)*
When performing this cast it is essential to be 'ambidextrous'. The prime purpose of any Spey cast, whether it is the single or the double, is to keep the fly well away from the angler. Some anglers

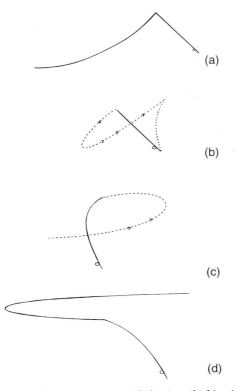

Fig 21 The switch cast. (a) Side view. (b) Line is thrown upwards over right shoulder. (c) Do not wait until the line has straightened before making the forward punch. (d) Line punched out high back over the water.

Roll casting to keep my fly and fly line away from the overhead cable above my head.

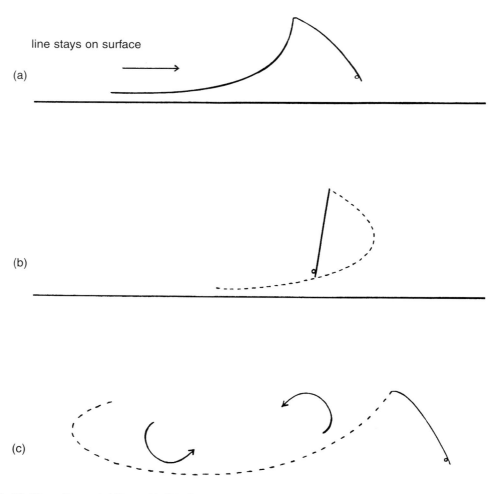

line stays on surface

(a)

(b)

(c)

Fig 22 The roll cast. (a) The rod is lifted to draw the line back across the surface. (b) Pass the rod slightly beyond the vertical to let the line form a 'D' loop behind. (c) The forward punch of the rod makes the rod flex forward as the line rolls out on top of the water.

think that it is the bank from which they are fishing that determines the cast used, but this is not the case, rather it is the wind that will determine which one is selected. If we are fishing from the left bank (remember the bank is determined by looking downstream) then with an upstream wind we will use the single Spey with the right hand uppermost on the rod, but if we are fishing from the right bank the left hand has to be uppermost. When fishing the left hand bank with a downstream wind we use the

double Spey with the left hand uppermost on the handle, and if we are fishing the right bank with a downstream wind we will use the double Spey with the right hand uppermost.

Some anglers shy clear of Spey casting, because they think that it is only a gifted few who can perform them, but this is not so – if done properly they are very easy casts to execute. In order to help me describe the single Spey cast I have decided to relate it to the left bank with an upstream wind.

Single Spey casting on the Spey. Not surprisingly it was on this river that this method of casting was developed.

Although the single Spey can be performed from the bank it is better to get into the water. The whole object of this cast under the conditions stated above is to place the fly upstream of the angler.

I have watched Arthur Oglesby give casting demonstrations at game fairs, and each time he has commented that he usually discovers it is the placing of the line upstream that his students find the most difficult. In order to place the line upstream it is merely a matter of lifting the rod point from the horizontal and bringing it around and upstream in one movement, an apparently simple motion. I remember asking him after his final demonstration of the 1993 Game Fair at Gosford Park if he thought it made much difference whether the forward taper or the belly of the line alighted first, when the line was placed upstream. He didn't think that it would make much difference so long as the upstream lift was made properly, the rod had the correct line rating and the line was allowed to alight on the water.

After placing the line upstream we can bring the rod round into the position of execution. From here we can deliver the forward power by trying to snap the rod to punch the line out over the water. If executed correctly the line should unroll above the water like an octopus uncoiling a tentacle. When trying for distance it is best to aim the line a little higher than one would for the overhead cast. It is a common misconception that the longer the rod the longer the line we can cast. On this subject Michael Evans, in a letter published in the *Salmon & Trout* magazine, wrote the following:

All Spey casts demand that the minimum amount of line is left on the water in preparation for the final punch of the cast, for maximum efficiency. With the single Spey the entire line is aerialized

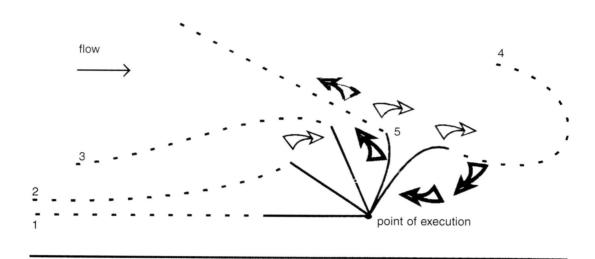

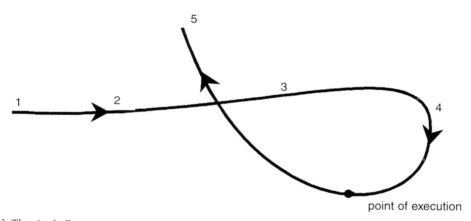

Fig 23 The single Spey cast.

and kept on the move as it is repositioned, and it is a simple matter to control the sweep to keep the bulk off the surface with just two to three yards alighting as the required anchor ... Distance, regardless of conditions, is maximized by achieving the optimum load of the rod spring and hence delivering maximum line speed. With the Spey casts you have a very short arc of rod movement available if you are to throw a tight loop on delivery ... recent work on the SpeyCaster rods gave me a better understanding of the optimum length of a double handed rod. A rod longer than 15ft gets progressively slower and harder to load quickly, but to

go below 15ft reduces the size of the initial D loop that can be kept airborne ... it is the strength of the rod spring and the caster's ability to load it, that dictates how far a cast will go, not the length of the rod.

In relation to the single Spey casting further than a double Spey he wrote:

A single Spey cast also has the advantage that the line is travelling faster throughout the cast and the weight of the moving loop can be used to increase the rod load which is what gives greater distance.

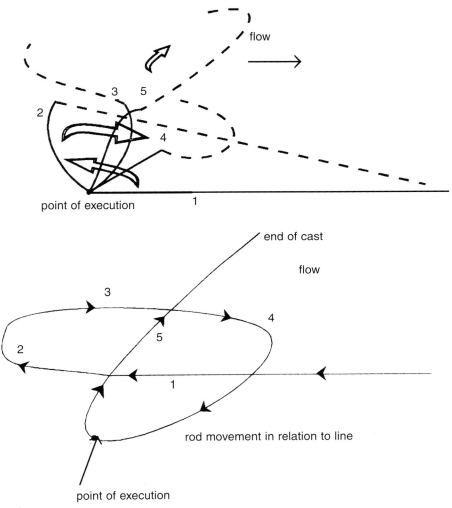

flow

point of execution

end of cast

flow

rod movement in relation to line

point of execution

Fig 24 The double Spey cast.

Double Spey Cast *(Fig 24)*

With this cast I have decided to describe it from the right bank with a downstream wind, as this will place the right hand uppermost on the handle of the rod, the most common scenario. With this cast the line must end up downstream of the angler so that the wind does not blow the fly into him. Start placing the line upstream in the same fashion as that used for the single Spey. Now bring the rod down and around so that the line riffles the surface on its way downstream. As the riffling comes to an end the rod should be getting raised into the position of execution.

9 TACKLING RUNNERS AND RESTERS

Although I feel that all salmon should be classified as running fish when they enter freshwater during their upstream migration to the spawning beds, for the purpose of this chapter I shall use the term 'running' to describe only those fish that are actually engaged in the act of swimming upstream.

PROBLEMS AND OPPORTUNITIES

A number of celebrated anglers inform us that running fish are virtually impossible to catch. Time and time again in the angling press we read that running fish are unwilling or reluctant to take a lure, though from my own experience I have not found this to be the case. The majority of my own fishing has been concentrated on the spate streams of the Scottish west coast, but when the opportunities have arisen I have been fortunate enough to be able to wet a line in some of the larger world-famous rivers on the opposite side of the country. In both types of river these fish are not bagged in as great numbers as resting fish, but nonetheless they still represent a good percentage of my annual catch.

If we approach the sport with an open, inquiring mind and adopt specialized methods of fishing for different fish, that is runners or resters, we can on occasions tempt a salmon or two. This is particularly pleasing when fish are difficult to come by, and when others who have preferred to stick to the old indoctrinated practices go fishless. When fishing for either running or resting salmon, I use two unambiguous methods that allow me to present my lures in front of one particular fish at a time. This is based on the thinking that the more we concentrate our efforts on catching one type of fish, the greater the chances of one taking hold. In saying this, though, any experienced salmon angler knows that there is no legal method of fishing that will guarantee the hooking of fish.

It is all very well fishing with a floating line and small fly when the water and air temperature dictate this is the best method, but if the water is flowing with an extra 6in (15cm) on the marker and running a touch coloured and we still use this method we will not be fishing in a fashion that gives us the best chance of a fish. Even though the salmon has excellent eyesight, small flies fished during times that are less than ideal will not allow us to maximize our chances. It should be noted that a great deal of what has been written about standard floating line methods and small fly techniques has been centred around the fishing experiences of those who fish and frequent rivers such as the Spey or Dee during the late spring or summer. The widely accepted and practised floating line techniques can be used in lesser rivers to good effect, but for best results they have to be fished when the fish are starting to take up residence in medium- to long-stay lies in between rises in water height. In medium and smaller rivers flowing 3–6in (7.5–15cm) higher than normal, with migrating fish rocketing upstream, a small subsurface fly fished with a floating line will on occasions take fish.

I have come to believe, through success, that a large fly fished deep during such times will produce better results. A large fly fished deep when the river is running a little above normal also appears to attract the more recent arrivals, while those fishing with a small fly at the same time seem to attract fish that have been in the river for some time. The number of 'fresh' salmon I hook in relation to red or stale fish when using a large fly fished deep at such times is approximately two to one, though the salmon, being such an unpredictable quarry, have on occasions behaved very badly. I have on some occasions taken the only coloured fish of the day, while others fishing small flies on floating lines took pristine 'bars of silver'. There do, however, seem to be 'accepted' methods that take salmon under designated conditions: for example, if the water is cold our lure should be large and fished deep and slow. At other times, especially when the water starts to warm up from late spring onwards, the orthodox small fly fished in conjunction with a floating line does well. These generally accepted methods, when fished during the times mentioned previously, do give sport, but both of these methods if fished at other times can produce sport from both running and resting salmon, particularly during the summer and early autumn.

I would suggest that running spate stream salmon are generally more easily caught than running salmon in larger rivers, where fish can enter and run without an increase in water height. Why the difference I have no idea, but it may be because the salmon that run the major salmon rivers are not so 'desperate' in their upstream migration, whereas the salmon that run the shorter and usually swifter-flowing spate rivers are more excited and determined to run upstream as fast and as far as possible during the time that the spate allows. Therefore in order to increase our chances of a fish in both river types we must choose where and how we are going to present our lures.

Running fish in any river do not swim very deep, usually no more than about 18in (46cm) down. Perhaps this is why a small fly and floating line on a larger river, where slow-running fish travel through relatively long medium-paced pools, works well. In smaller rivers, running fish seem more likely to take in the faster water at the head and tail of pools. No pools, however, seem to fish the same. I know one pool where the head stream is best, yet within 200 yards on the same river it is the tail of the next pool that comes up trumps.

METHOD FOR RUNNING FISH
(Fig 25)

By fishing with a floating line and fly of 'suitable' size for running fish I have had good sport when others fishing differently have had not a touch. My technique at this time is to fish with a fairly large fly, usually an Ally's Shrimp, tied on a number 6 low-water double, the overall size of the fly being about 2in (50mm). In addition I keep the leader on

Rough water on the Spey. Running fish, particularly grilse, are frequently taken from this stretch of water on a floating line.

the short side, 3 or 4ft (90–120cm), as this helps to keep my fly at the desired depth. Since the fish that I am intending to tempt with this approach are running, I am confident that my fly will be fishing at the correct depth, eyeball to eyeball. If the bait is at the same depth as the fish they seem more willing to take. This technique works well with fresh-run fish if fished right in the neck of the stream at the head of the pool, but in saying this I have also hooked fish in the tail of some pools using the same method.

Fishing with a fairly large fly in this fashion when fish are running has caught me many salmon, when others fishing a small fly at the same time (because the water temperature dictated this) failed to move a fish. Because I was hooking fish when practising this method I started to question the writings telling me that running fish do not take. From my observations and experiences the majority of running spate stream salmon that take a lure do so in the faster water at the head of the pool; however when the water starts to fall, but still flows with sufficient volume to allow the fish to run, the lip of a dam or tail of a pool can become more productive.

It is observing the fish that take at the tails of pools that has convinced me that running fish will take a lure. On many occasions, particularly during the autumn, I have watched salmon appear over the

lip of a weir and take my lure as it swung round in the current past their noses. They were swimming forward into the pool at the time they took, the whole affair being quite visible. Salmon that take in the faster, more streamy water at the head of a pool appear to reduce their running speed before doing so. It appears that they are assessing the pace of the current before pushing on up. Although some salmon will slow their running speed to a virtual halt, they still nevertheless continue moving forward. Some salmon will circle a few times, swim forward and drop back in the current, repeating the whole process a few times before ascending further.

Regardless of why they do this, they still count as running fish. On many rivers they must swim through this fast water, because it is this water that usually separates one pool from the next, particularly on smaller rivers. Running fish in the larger rivers are more inclined to take on the move in the slower middle section of the pools. The reasons for this difference in taking behaviour between a salmon running one type of river and a salmon running another is unclear. Possibly it is due to the fact that the fast-running water at the head of the pools in the larger east coast classics generally do not extend across the full width of the pools. The fish therefore do not have to run up through the main flow. In spate streams there may be some pockets of

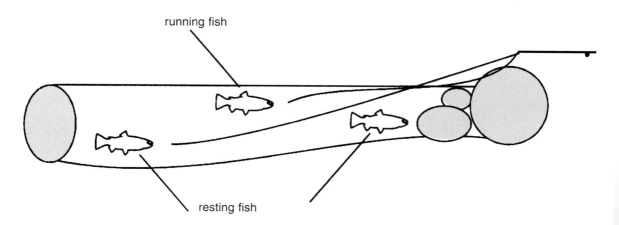

running fish

resting fish

Fig 25 Where and how to catch running and resting fish.

slow water in the neck of the pool, but very often the fish have to go through the fast water because they simply have no other choice.

When rivers are carrying extra water, particularly spate streams, most anglers will start fishing deep sunk lures, because they think that this is necessary in order to take fish. Before choosing one's lure or line density, however, we must decide whether we will be fishing for resting or running fish. If the river is at the maximum migration height the majority of fish will be engaged in running rather than resting. In order to tempt these running fish it is far better to fish the bait shallow, no more than 18in (46cm) as mentioned previously, while 6–9in (15–23cm) is better. Fish that are running are much more likely to rise to a bait fished above them than one that is below. If the bait is presented beneath the fish the chances of their seeing it will not be as good as for one fished higher in the water, the eye positioning of a salmon being designed primarily for forward and upward vision.

As well as fishing our lure at the correct depth we must also present it in the right place. In order to intercept running fish with this method it is best to concentrate one's efforts on the head and main body of the pool when the river is flowing at the maximum migration height, and on the tail of the pool when the water height starts to fall away. The ideal water heights for this method will be different for every river and must be learned through experience. On learning them we can then present our lures in the right place at the right time in the fashion described. When presenting our lure at this shallow depth we will be showing it to more fish than we would if we were to fish it deep, just off the bottom. When fly fishing this is best achieved with a floating line and medium-weighted fly or, alternatively, a slow sinker and lightweight fly. If spinning is the first choice the bait should be of a semi-buoyant Devon Minnow type fished in conjunction with a small anti-kink lead attached to the main line side of the swivel, the size of the bait or fly depending on the height of the water at the time.

When fishing a large east coast river running at normal height, with fresh fish running upstream every day, it is the temperature difference between the air and the water that determines the size of lure.

However, if we are fishing a spate stream it is the water height that dictates the lure size, something that many acknowledged experts fail to mention. Running fish that do take our bait are not always well hooked, with a lot being pricked and lost or only lightly hooked. They do not, for some reason, like to take a good hold of a lure, but instead prefer to nip or pluck at it.

METHOD FOR RESTING FISH

When rivers start to fall back and clear after a flood most anglers who choose to fish the fly will invariably fish a small one with a floating line. From my experience this does not seem to be the best approach at this time, especially if fish are still running in numbers. In the smaller, rain-dependent rivers there is an abundance of long, rough sections of water between pools. Most fish running up through these sections will generally have a moment's breather in the tail of the pool they have just entered. These fish will on occasion rise to a small fly fished on a floating line, but for the best chance of one providing sport it is better to present them with a large fly fished deep, right in front of their noses. I prefer to fish for these resting fish with a sinking line and large 1¾in (45mm) Waddington or tube. It is not the water temperature that concerns me at this time, but the water height and colour. As the water starts to clear and fall I will change down the size of fly to a size 6 or 8, but I would still fish it in conjunction with a sinking line, until the river falls right back to normal height and all fish migration stops, at which time I would start to fish the small fly and floating line.

My reason for fishing the sinking line for resting fish is related to my 'conservation of energy theory'. Let me explain. If you had just exerted a lot of energy you would want to get your breath back at the end of it and would be reluctant to move far until you had taken a breather. Any creature that exerts energy must have time to replenish the oxygen in its blood after strenuous activity and the salmon is no exception. Since I strongly believe that any fresh-run fish that takes a lure does so because its feeding instinct has not been fully

Fishing the River Bladnoch below Spittal Bridge. A large fly fished across the top of a weir such as the one shown is likely to produce a fish, even during the summer.

An angler hangs his fly in the head stream of a good holding pool. The fish cage is for gravid fish to be put in. They are then quickly moved to the hatchery and later stripped.

suppressed, I like to present my lure with this in mind and in a fashion that will optimize my chances of its taking it. If we hand these potential takers something on a plate, will they not be more inclined to take it than if they are forced to rise through three or more feet of water? If the lure is presented close to these resting fish it stands to reason that they will be more inclined to take hold of it. These fish are better takers than those fish that actually take in the process of running and, as a result, are also likely to be better hooked.

Different runs of fish, however, can and do produce fish that respond to different tactics, so for this reason it is best to decide whether you will be fishing for runners or resters and tackle up accordingly. I have also known small pockets of fish within the same run to react differently to the same approach (though at least one of them often seems willing to respond to the particularized method). At times the only fish that seems willing to respond to my fly has been the running fish, the resting fish ignoring all offerings, while on other occasions the only takes of the day have come from resting fish. From my records it would appear that summer fish, that is grilse, are more willing to take while running, while the autumn fish are more obliging while resting.

Although as described previously, running fish can be caught if approached in the right fashion, I prefer to fish for resting fish at the tails of pools and above the lips of weirs with a sinking line and large fly. This technique, when used during the summer and autumn, has caught me many salmon from the tails of pools when others who have been fishing with a floating line and small fly (because the water temperature 'dictated' this) have caught nothing. The technique of using a large fly and sinking line for fresh-run resting fish has outperformed the floating line and small fly so often that I seldom use any other method during the summer and autumn. I now only resort to the floater and small flies when fish have decided to, or have been forced to due to water height, take up residence in the main holding pools.

10 FLY FISHING WITH A FLOATING LINE

FLOATING LINE FOR SPRING AND SUMMER SALMON *(Figs 26–7)*

Many experienced anglers know that when the water is above a certain temperature, usually 48°F (9°C) and the air temperature is warmer by 4 or 5°, the salmon for some unknown reason prefer a fly fished close to the surface, and therefore they use a floating line to catch them. There is no doubt that fish do seem to prefer a small fly just under the surface when the water temperature rises above 48°F (9°C). Some regard this as the magic mark, but I am not so sure that the water temperature has to be this precise or that the fly to be fished has to be as close to the surface as some authorities suggest. One notable angler once said that if we do not see a taking fish break the surface when coming to our fly we must be fishing too deep. I would strongly disagree. If a fish comes to our fly but does not show, what are we going to do next time down the pool? Swim our fly nearer the surface, just so we can see the next one? I think not.

Seeing a fish roll on the surface with a classic nose and tail rise, then waiting for the fish to go down and the line to be drawn away beneath the surface is without doubt a great angling experience. More often than not, though, I have noticed that if the fly is too close to the surface some fish are inclined to roll over it, with no intention of taking hold. In any case, not all fish show as they take. I have hooked salmon on more than one occasion, using light trout tackle, when I have been fishing a small wet fly just under the surface during the evening for trout. I cannot recall any of these fish breaking the surface and in all cases the fly was no more than an inch or two under the surface. At the other extreme I have hooked salmon on deeply sunk

tubes after they have rolled on the surface and are moving back to their lies. The prime objective when fishing a small fly with a floating line is to achieve the correct swimming speed in relation to its size, not depth. If the fly is swimming at the correct speed in relation to its size, then the depth at which it will be fishing will automatically be taken care of by the current acting on the controlled line and fly – correct speed means correct depth. This equation does not hold true for a sinking line, however, unless one is a very competent angler.

The next question that must be answered is what size of fly to use. There has been a great deal written about this, some authors even going as far as producing a water temperature to fly size chart. These charts are good as a rough guide, but should only be used as such and nothing more. What I have never understood is why anglers will choose a fly for a specific water temperature while giving no consideration to the flow of the pool in which they are about to fish that fly. If the water temperature chart suggests the use of a size 8, it means a size 8 for that water temperature. What it does not say is that if the stream is a fast one we should be increasing the size of the fly to a 6 or, if a slow one, reducing to a size 10.

Size of fly is related to water speed as well as water temperature. If we were to fish a small fly in a fast current, even by carrying out the necessary mends and controlling the drag, its action would still be unnatural for such a small creature in such a current. Remember we are talking about water speed and not bank speed. This also means that as we fish on down the pool the size of the fly should also be changed to coincide with the change of water speed. Generally speaking I am inclined to start fishing the streamier, faster water at the neck of pools with a size larger than the accepted norm for any given water temperature and then change down as I approach the slower middle section. On nearing the tail, where the water starts to speed up, I will once again change up to a larger fly. It will usually be the same size that I used at the head, but this depends on the character of the pool and the pace of the current through its tail.

Water temperature charts, if used, should only be referred to as a guide for an eligible fly size for the main body of the pool and only when the water is running clear. After all, the size of the creature we are trying to represent, for example a small fish or shrimp, must be presented to the salmon at a water speed that it will believe as being natural for the lure's size. The size of a creature does not necessarily dictate the depth at which it can swim, however, and this is where I feel that a lot of people make a mistake – large does not mean deep, or vice versa.

Many anglers do not understand the principle of fishing a floating line with a small fly and merely go through the motions of casting and mending without giving any thought to what they are doing. I have watched anglers fish down a pool from head to tail, giving the solitary obligatory upstream mend

and not realizing that they are only fishing a small part of the pool effectively. By fishing in this fashion they are denying themselves many chances of tempting fish. Most anglers also do not appreciate that a river does not run uniformly across its width, some sections flowing faster or slower than others. In pools with more than the one main flow we must mend the line in accordance to every current that the line comes through. It is this aspect of line control that separates the skilful fly fisherman from the average angler.

Some anglers are very bad at putting an upstream mend into the line. This is because they lift their fly away from the place where it has started to settle and fish. Some people might think that at this stage in the cast it makes little difference. I think that it does. On many occasions I have hooked fish almost as soon as the fly has settled in the water, and on making the upstream mend found myself into a fish. It is therefore bad practice as far as I am concerned to move the fly on the upstream lift of the line. In order to keep the fly from being lifted during the upstream mend we can do two things; first of all we can cast a longer line than necessary, and at a narrower angle than the normal 45 degrees.

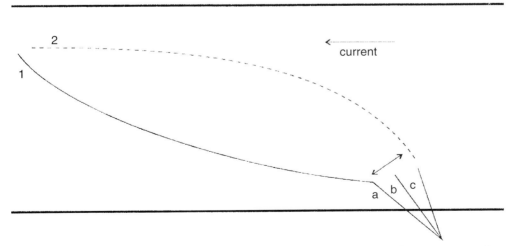

Fig 26 A long cast at a shallow angle prevents the fly from being lifted during the upstream mend. (1) The long downstream cast starts to belly. (2) Make a large upstream mend by moving the rod through a to c upstream is one continuous movement.

By doing this there will be more fly line beyond the arc of the mend than normal and consequently the fly will be less likely to be moved. The second method I use, especially if a short line (less than 25 yards) is being fished is the S mend. This technique, if done properly, creates a lovely snakey line, which gives it its name. If the river is narrow and the pool we are fishing has only one central flow down through it, a single S mend may be all that is required to keep the flies fishing at the correct speed. On a large river where the pool has two, three or more separate currents through it a succession of S mends will have to be performed to keep the fly's speed in check. We may also have to incorporate one or two downstream mends when the fly comes into dead water between flows.

All mends, but particularly the upstream mends or lifting over of the line, should, if done properly, be nothing more than the movement of the rod tip from a downstream to an upstream position, the whole process being a quiet, slow, semi-circular movement of the rod tip, from one position to the other. It is quite unlike the placing of the line upstream during the single Spey cast. The whole movement should not be hurried or jerky, as this will cause the fly to be moved, causing the length of

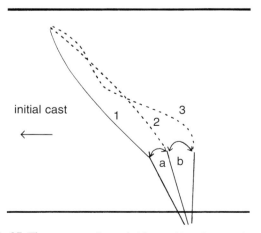

Fig 27 The upstream S mend. After making the initial cast (1), I put a small mend in the line (2) and then pull an extra couple of yards off the reel. Next I make a large upstream mend, releasing the extra yards at the same time (3).

the mended line to be reduced and therefore making the mend less effective. In order to keep the fly from being moved, the rod tip should be kept low and brought upstream in one continuous arc.

FLOATING LINE FOR AUTUMN SALMON

All too often, as soon as the first leaves begin to fall, many anglers abandon the floating line and small fly in favour of a sinker and large tube or Waddington. At times, particularly if the river is running high and coloured, or the water and air temperature are the same or very close, it will be this set-up that will be the most likely to get us a fish. Nevertheless, far too many anglers are over-keen in adopting the sinking line and large fly approach. I am sure this is because a lot of anglers who fish at this time of the year have little experience when it comes to fishing for autumn salmon, perhaps fishing only once or twice a year, and they therefore seek advice from others more experienced in fishing at this time. This is all very well, but very often the advice given is wrong or inappropriate, because they are told that when the leaves fall it is time to resume springtime tactics, large flies fished deep. Anglers may also read books or seasonable articles printed in the monthly publications, but time and time again that which is printed is for the type of approach necessary to maximize the chances of sport on the Tweed or Nith during some late autumn day. For the majority of anglers these rivers are just impossible to fish during the autumn, even if money is no object, with some beats only becoming available through dead men's shoes. For many it is the smaller and less well-known rivers that will be the only option. Therefore many who go in pursuit of autumn fish, may, for the majority of the time, be using tackle and tactics not conducive towards maximizing their chances. Those who persist with the sinking line and large fly regardless of conditions will take fish, but they are denying themselves many opportunities of better sport.

I am sure that the majority of autumn salmon anglers, regardless of the rivers they fish, suffer the reverse dilemma to that experienced by those who

Putting an upstream mend to help bring the fly slowly through the centre of the pool where the fish are lying opposite the burn mouth.

pursue spring fish, the question of when to change from one approach to the other. Many spring anglers are reluctant to go over to the floater, while many autumn fishers are over quick to do away with it. For many anglers the change from floater to sinker usually occurs with the first main runs of early autumn, or worse, come a date on the calendar. Changing from one approach to another on a specific date, like changing the clocks, is wrong.

It is a fallacy that early and mid-autumn salmon have to be pursued with a large fly presented deep. Throughout this period the weather generally starts to go through a change from summery to autumnal. This means that daytime temperatures on occasions will rise well into the 60s (15–20°C). Although the first night frosts can and do occur the air temperature will usually rise reasonably quickly once the sun has had a chance to get to work and it is therefore a mistake at such times to forsake the floater in favour of the sinker. Provided that the air temperature is significantly warmer than the water, a small fly fished just subsurface with a floater will gener-

ally produce more responses than a large fly fished just off the bottom, especially if the river is a bit on the low side. As long as the air temperature is higher than that of the water by at least 5°F (3°C) it is a mistake to opt for the sinker and large, deeply fished fly, particularly if the river is running clear after a spate or has been running at normal height for some time.

Although I am happy fishing with a 5°F (3°C) difference in favour of the air, I prefer a 10 °F (6°C) difference. When fishing with a 5°F difference I will opt for a 6 and then reduce hook size as the temperature difference increases. Provided that the air is warmer than the water, even when the water is very cold, say in the upper 30s (about 3°C), fish will still rise, at times through six of more feet of water. Many anglers believe that if the water is this cold fish will not rise to such a small lure. I have not found this to be the case with autumn fish though it may be so with spring fish. Possibly this is due to the fact that autumn fish are much more active than their earlier running cousins. If, however, the river is running

The unexpected godsend which accounts for the first fish of a week's holiday. Note its length. The reel is 4¼in (11cm) across.

coloured or the air and water temperatures have been very close together for a few days then I would prefer to fish with a sinking line and large fly.

The fact that it is possible to catch autumn salmon on a small fly fished near the surface when the air temperature is warmer than the water was brought home to me when my wife and I were fishing on the Mochrum Park stretch of the Bladnoch, a Solway river, during a very cold October week. Although there had been no rain for about a week, the river was still running a little above summer level and fresh fish were quietly nosing there way upstream between pools on every high tide. There was also a good stock of fish in the river with every holding pool having a good share of them. High pressure was dominating the weather situation with near cloudless skies along with light north-easterly winds during the day.

Daytime air temperatures during the week did not rise above 51°F, while nighttime temperatures

fell below zero, resulting in some sharp overnight frosts. In fact during the mornings the fly lines were freezing to the rod rings, with thin ice sometimes forming along the edges of some of the slower holding pools. Even by lunchtime the water temperature was still very low, 39°F, with an air temperature of 48°F. Initially I opted for a sinking line and a size 8 Ally's Shrimp tied on an Esmond Drury treble with a very long tail, the overall size of the fly being about 3in long. Over the next three days the water temperature fluctuated between 39°F and 41°F and the air between 49°F and 51°F. I took one fish and lost two others.

Although I had taken a fish I was not that happy with my lot considering the number of fish in the pools and I started to doubt whether or not fishing the sinking line and 'long' fly was the best method. True the water temperature called for a large fly, but the one thing that I did not bring into the equation when selecting the size of my fly at the time was the air temperature, even though I was monitoring it regularly. I was sure that I could get more offers from the fish if I used a different approach, but I didn't know what.

A possible answer came to me out of the blue, when I suddenly remembered part of a book that I had read where the author, Crossley, made reference to correspondence received from A. H. E. Wood describing how he used to fish in midwinter with a greased line and smallish fly, provided that the air temperature was significantly higher than the water temperature and how he would take fish on a small fly fished just under the surface. So next morning we decided to change tactics. I must admit that before tackling up I had some doubts. However, I remembered reading that if fish are hard to come by try the ridiculous and then the sublime. I had nothing to lose and having tried the ridiculous during the first half of the week and had some sport, it was now time to try the sublime.

I opted for a full floater and two Silver Stoat type flies tied on size 10 Esmond Drury trebles. I had

fished down the first two pools of our allocated beat for the day and had no response and was beginning to have some doubts about my change of tactics. When I was about halfway down the next pool a fish of about 10lb rose approximately a rod's length out. Backing up a few steps I covered it in the conventional fashion by letting the flies swing round out of the main flow, but there was no response. Holding the rod out at right angles to the flow on the next cast I let the flies hang right in front of where the fish was last seen to rise. The flies had only dangled and danced in front of the lie for a few seconds when the take came. Unfortunately the fish did not remain on for long, jumping and skittering along the surface on its tail causing me to lose contact, the hook coming away. Almost at the same time as my fish came off, my wife who was fishing down the next pool, shouted 'Fish!', a good one as it turned out of 15lb, which was duly landed. The next time down the pool she took another fish of 12lb. All three fish, including the one I lost, took small flies tied on size 10 Esmond Drury trebles

During the autumn many anglers make the mistake of fishing with too large a fly. A selection of summer flies will suffice provided the air stays warmer than the water.

that had their tying well within the bends. Without elaborating further another seven fish were taken and returned during the week using similar tactics. One interesting fact regarding all these fish was that they were hooked well back in the throat.

Although the other rods fishing that week caught fish with their sinking lines and large flies, the small flies fished just under the surface produced three times as many. By sticking to the sinking line throughout the week I am sure we would have taken another fish or two, but I cannot help thinking how on so many other previous occasions I had fished away with a large, deep fly when a small one fished just under the surface could have been a better choice. Since the incident described above I now fish with the floating line and small fly for autumn salmon whenever the air is warmer than the water, even if the water temperature is very low. Autumn salmon, unlike spring salmon, are much more active due to sexually induced anxiety, and therefore much more likely to come to a shallow fished fly.

One eminent angling authority has said in his books that when the water temperature reaches the magic 48°F (9°C) fish will move their attention from a large fly fished deep to one presented just below the surface. This is all very well, but nowhere in his book does he mention that the air temperature must be greater than the water temperature. I can only assume that because of this he must have missed many opportunities of a fish or two and in doing so denied himself the maximum pleasure from the sport. To neglect the air temperature as far as I am concerned is complete madness. If the temperature difference of the air is greater than the water by at least 5° (though I prefer to have at least 10° difference between them) the floating line becomes my first choice. So next time you go in pursuit of autumn salmon do not automatically reach for the box of tubes and fast sinker. Before making any choice of tackle and tactics reach for the most important item of tackle in any salmon fisherman's bag, the thermometer.

11 DIBBLING FOR SALMON

WHEN TO DIBBLE

Mention dibbling for summer salmon and most anglers conjure up the image of a rocky pool in a fast tumbling Highland stream. This is not surprising considering that most material written about the subject focuses on such rivers. There is no doubt that it is indeed a practice associated with such rivers, but it can also be used with a fair amount of success on many other rivers, provided there is an abundance of well-broken, oxygenated water. Most rivers have sections of rough, fast water in which the fish will temporarily lie. These are usually places where salmon will go to revitalize themselves, especially if the water temperature is high and the river is running at a low height. This is because fish become uncomfortable in the slow flow and from time to time feel the need to seek out the more highly oxygenated part of the pool. Some fish nevertheless may not move into and frequent the broken water during the hours of daylight, waiting instead until the light goes, when they feel much safer. This can be a good time to try dibbling, though generally speaking many dibblers seem to confine their fishing to the daytime.

When the main holding pools are slow and not fishable with conventional fly fishing methods, I will at times dibble for salmon. Many anglers who practise this method will tell you that it is only really suitable for fish that are starting to lose their sheen and have been in the river for some time, and there is no doubt that it seems to attract the less than fresh fish. In saying this I have dibbled with some limited success when rivers have been running with a little extra height for fresh fish which have been quietly nosing their way upstream between pools, particularly during the first and last light of the day.

At this time I will fish in the quieter dubs and pots, presenting my flies in front of and behind boulders, where salmon are known to lie. These lies can be virtually anywhere that happens to be just out of the main flow, particularly in the fast, rough water between pools. At times these lies will be in a calm eddy no bigger than the size of a doormat. Dibbling a fly at this time can be effective if you are patient and persistently present your flies through known hot spots. It is self-defeating to move from one spot to another while the fish are running – find your spot and stick to it. This of course is the difficult part, especially if you can see the fish's indifference to your efforts. Do not get despondent, though, very often a fish that has been covered and shows no interest will rise out of the blue and engulf your fly with no warning. I would rather this happen than cover a fish that rises time and time again with no intention of taking hold of the fly. Many theories have been put forward as to when salmon are most likely to come to a dibbled fly, some of which hold water while others do not, but I believe that success or failure is determined by the amount of dissolved oxygen available at the time.

METHODS OF DIBBLING *(Figs 28–9)*

There are two main methods of dibbling, both using two flies, a tail fly and a dropper. The first method is as follows. For maximum control a long double-handed rod of 15ft is best. This length enables us to cover more water, while remaining well back from the water's edge. Remaining out of sight is of paramount importance if we are to succeed, because on many occasions the fish are positioned where they can see everything. The flies are connected to the

Fig 28 Keep the rod point high and use a heavy tail fly to keep your fly in place when dibbling.

fly line, usually a floater with a 12ft (3.5m) level leader of 10lb. The dropper fly is connected to an 8in (20cm) dropper about 5ft (1.5m) from the end of the fly line. By making it this length we can keep the area of presentation free of nylon. This has two advantages; first, it prevents spooking the fish if it comes to the fly and happens to brush against it. If it does touch or feel the nylon it will shy away from the fly if it has not already taken it. A spooked fish will not rise to a fly a second time. Second the long dropper also helps us to fish the fly better, this especially being so with a long rod. By keeping the rod point high, the current cannot get hold of the nylon and pull it down and drown it, which would cause the fly to be pulled down into the water and away from the spot where we want it to dibble. When fishing in this fashion it also helps if the tail fly is heavier, since it acts as an anchor and stops any sudden gusts of wind lifting the nylon and moving the fly away from the surface area of the lie where we are presenting it. A sparse tying on a 6 or 8 Esmond Drury treble is ideal. When fishing this method of dibbling, the dropper size should be longer than the tail fly, and for best effect it should have 'character' so that it is clearly noticeable.

The basic idea when fishing in this fashion is to make the dibbled dropper fly skate, skitter and bob about, above, on and in the water. Some exponents of this style will tell you that it is important initially to plop the fly through the surface before dibbling it. The reason behind this approach is that the

initial splash will get the attention of the fish and as a result be much more likely to take. The fly should be made to behave in a fashion similar to the 'dapped' fly used by loch fishers. Instead of utilizing the energy of the wind, however, the dibbler controls the 'dancing' of the fly by rod actions. One method of achieving this, which requires a great deal of skill, is to raise and lower the rod point in such a way that will allow the fly to be 'batted' about by the waves in the stream. Alternatively, instead of fishing the water we can present the dropper fly through known lies by stroking it back and forth across the surface by casting and lifting.

The second method of dibbling again uses a 15ft rod and a floating line. The leader in this case should be tapered and about 9 to 10ft (2.7–3m) long. The dropper is tied some 3ft (90cm) from the end of the fly line. With this approach the dropper is the smallest of the two flies used, usually tied on a size 8 treble. The dressing of this fly is usually dark in nature with a good collar so that it can ripple the surface with ease. The tail fly, the longest of the two, is tied on a smaller treble, size 12 or 14. These flies are tied with an over-long tail, four to five times longer than the shank of the hook being used. The flies with this method are presented a little quicker than those used for the previous method and are cast a little squarer across the stream. After the cast the rod is raised to lift the dropper fly to the surface. When the flies swing round parallel to the bank raise the rod tip higher to work the flies further.

Fishing Polnessan Stream on the Doon. A well dibbled fly in this type of water will often produce a fish which has refused a fly fished in the conventional fashion.

At times this faster approach seems to work with fish that have refused the previous presentation method or with fish that have followed the flies round in the current and have needed that little bit more coaxing before taking. Those who practise this style tell me that most of the fish they take are on the long tail fly. But what is interesting is that on many occasions they see the fish following the dropper, before turning and taking the tail fly. Why this occurs is open to conjecture, but perhaps it is something to do with the chase aspect. They see one thing chasing something else, investigate and decide to become part of the hunt by grabbing the pursuing entity. Some exponents of the art will be saying that this is not true dibbling – perhaps it is not, but it does catch salmon.

Both these methods of fishing are not as easy as they first appear, because for the best part of the time we are fishing with only a small amount of fly line beyond the rod point, which means that the rod is never loaded. Accurate presentation of two flies with only a yard or two of line through the top ring and 10ft of nylon is not easy. We cannot cast in the normal fashion for obvious reasons, but instead have to make do by performing a half-hearted roll cast.

Sometimes fish will take the first time they are covered, almost as if they had been waiting for it, but more often that not persistent presentation is called for, many of them only coming to the fly after many hours. Our presentation therefore has to be such that it will not spook the fish. Hugh Falkus in his book *Salmon Fishing, A Practical Guide* states that 'provided it is covered properly and the fish is not scared, a salmon lie cannot be over fished'. In the context in which this was written I am in full agreement. Most anglers, however, do not seem to appreciate that this statement only holds true if the lie is covered with care – if it is, it can be fished all day.

When it comes to fly choice, shrimp flies with their long trailing feelers are excellent for both types of fishing. If you prefer the first method described these will be attached to the dropper, if on the other hand you choose the second method they are used on the tail. I like ones with a dressing that I can see easily and for this reason my first choice would have to

An autumn cock fish that fell to a large dibbled Ally's Shrimp, the hook being in so deep that the fish had to be killed.

be an Ally's Shrimp tied on either a size 6 or 8 low-water double hook. This fly has presence amongst the waves, because of its colour and overall size. I feel that the bucktail hair extending beyond the bends of the hooks, representing the shrimp's feelers, emphasizes and exaggerates the fly's presence, by scratching and cutting the surface of the water

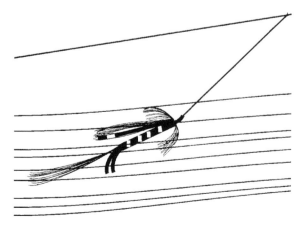

Fig 29 The action of the bucktail hair on an Ally's Shrimp clearly advertises the fly's presence.

every time that they come into contact with it. Some dedicated dibblers, on the other hand, will swear by the effectiveness of Elver-type flies, while others will favour a Collie Dog tied on a plastic tube.

Not all fish that come to the surface will have any intention of taking hold of our fly, many will rise very close, some nosing or brushing against it. Others will rise, but for some reason decide to keep their mouths well and truly shut. I recall a slightly stale fish in the fast, tumbling water above the Craig Pool on the Dalreoch stretch of the River Stinchar. Here the river turns with a left-hand dog-leg out of the tail stream of the Hairs Took. I was sitting pondering my next move after a long, fruitless day when I thought I caught sight of what appeared to be a fish doing a weak head and tail rise about ten feet out from the opposite bank, just out of the main flow. This is a difficult place to fish properly with any method, due to a large back eddy which causes an upstream flow in towards the left bank and is the sort of place often walked past. Remaining down on my knees I pulled about three yards of line off the reel and flicked my two-fly cast in the vicinity of the fish.

Now before going any further I must say that I was not tackled up for dibbling as both flies were rather on the small side. As soon as the flies landed

Dibbling for a summer salmon that might be lying in a shallow run at the head of a pool.

they were instantly caught by the upstream back eddy, so I raised the rod. As I did so the dropper fly started cutting the surface and had only travelled about twelve inches when up came the fish. It took me totally by surprise and I snatched the fly away. I thought that I had had my chance, but I decided to try again. As before up it came, but it had its mouth closed that and every other time that I moved it. I moved that fish eight times within an hour and each time its mouth was well and truly closed. Perhaps if I had persevered it would have eventually taken, but then again perhaps not.

A.H.E. WOOD – DIBBLING INNOVATOR

A.H.E. Wood of greased line fame knew and practised the technique. During a fishing trip to Ireland in 1903 he found the river he was to fish running very low after a prolonged dry spell. Although the pool he was fishing was full of fish they proved very difficult to tempt. While sitting down to ponder his next move he saw one fish followed by another rise to something floating on the surface and as he watched they continued to rise intermittently. He

soon observed that they were rising to a white moth. He then went to an eel-weir at the head of the pool where he found a number of fish resting with their noses up against the sill. Tying on a White Moth trout fly he positioned himself on the plank bridge over the weir. He then proceeded to dibble the fly over the fish while holding the gut in his hand. After a short time one of the fish rose to examine his fly, but for some reason decided not to take.

Wood reviewed the situation and came to the conclusion that the fish had been distracted by his feet, which were dangling over the edge of the plank, and so moving his position he dibbled his fly again. This time the fish rose more positively, but was pricked. He proceeded to raise and prick several other fish before he realized that because he was directly above them he was in actual fact pulling the fly out of their mouths when striking. Changing his approach and letting go of the gut at just the right time the fly was dropped into the mouth of the next rising fish.

It was this particular episode that set him thinking about the effectiveness of flies fished on or close to the surface. I finish the chapter with this question, is it possible that A.H.E. Wood was also the innovator of the dibbled fly?

12 NYMPHING FOR SALMON

WHY NYMPHING?

The easiest time to catch salmon is without doubt when they are fresh run and have arrived new into a pool. The longer that fish stay in a pool the more difficult they become to tempt, but though they may be more difficult, they are not impossible. Usually when the river starts to fall back after a spate anglers appear on the banks of most rivers, the majority of whom only ever fish during textbook conditions, when the river is most likely to produce fish, that is after it has turned and started to clear. As the river height starts to drop right back and the flow through the pools slows, many anglers seem to forget that fact that the salmon although no longer running are still present and taking up lies in the main holding pools. Many spate river anglers will not bother wetting a line during low water, preferring to wait instead until the river rises and turns once again. By adopting this approach they are denying themselves the opportunity of sport.

If the fish are in the pools they can be caught, maybe not so easily, but nonetheless sport can still be had if one is willing to put in the time and effort. As the water starts to drop and approach normal running height most fish migration slows, with salmon taking up residence in the deeper holding water to await the next rise in water. The longer these fish have to hang around between spates, the less likely they will be inclined to rise through five or more feet of water to take a small subsurface fly. During these periods of low water conventional fly fishing methods take the occasional fish, but in order to maximize one's chances it is best to exchange the salmon tackle for a single-handed rod and adopt a change of tactics.

The following tale of two anglers comes to mind. They arrived for a few days fishing at the Kirkholme beat of the Stinchar and found the river running beneath its summer low. Both anglers were well experienced enough to realize that conventional fly fishing tactics would be a waste of time. One tried a deeply sunk Dog Nobbler and soon hooked a fish, only to have it come off after a short struggle when the light trout hook straightened out. After this he tied on a Pheasant Tail nymph. To cut a long story short, over the next two days both anglers took five fish apiece and lost several others.

It is when faced with low water and bright overhead conditions that the single-handed rod armed with small flies and light leaders comes into its own. This is not to allow us to fish a small subsurface fly with light tackle, but instead to let us fish a small fly deep, with control and sensitivity, something that the longer rod does not facilitate.

The technique that I am about to describe can be performed with the double-handed rod, but the method is better suited to a light single-hander. Another reason for putting away the double-handed rod is that when using it many anglers for one reason or another seem to throw all caution and common sense to the wind. Many seem to think that salmon are not so easily spooked as trout – how wrong they are. If the single-handed rod is used, the same angler who thunders up and down the river bank with a double-hander will now adopt the cunning and stealth he practises when trout is the quarry. If the fish see you, you are wasting your time. Why the change of approach for one fish and not the other, I do not know!

Slow, almost stagnant pools, like the one shown, often fish well to a nymph.

THE NYMPHING TECHNIQUE
(Fig 30)

When fish have been lying up in a pool for some time they seem to become more and more indifferent to small subsurface flies with each passing day. However, if you have booked a week's fishing only to arrive and find the river running low, all is not doom and gloom – there are occasions when for some unknown reason fish will take a small deeply sunk fly fished close by.

One method of fly fishing during times of low water is a deeply sunk 'nymph'. It employs the same method as used and practised by trout fishermen who have unsuccessfully tried to tempt a trout by conventional presentation techniques. The method involves 'inducing' a response from a trout by pulling a deeply sunk nymph up, past and away from the fish. It is the lifting of the nymph at the correct time which seems to trigger the fish into taking, trout at times finding a nymph fished in this fashion irresistible. This method of fishing is called the 'induced take' and sometimes salmon that have been lying in a pool for some time can be tempted by presenting a fly to them in a similar fashion, on an eyeball-to-eyeball approach.

In order to present our fly properly it should be well weighted, with either copper or lead wire wound along the shank of the hook before the dressing is tied. In the slower holding pools small trebles are ideal for this type of fishing. If the lies are in a section of the pool that carries more pace, a single hook with a brass bead, as used for the gold-head flies favoured by some stillwater anglers, are ideal. I dress these goldhead nymphs on size 12, 10 or 8 International Sprite hooks. These hooks may be small and light, but they have a wide gape and are excellent hookers of fish. If the lie is in a deep, fast run I will use a small ¼in (6mm) or ½in (12mm) brass tube, thus enabling the fly to get down to the same depth as the fish relatively quickly.

If limited to only one type I would have to choose the goldhead. These give better results than the treble or brass tube version, not in hooking, but in the number of fish that are induced into taking. The goldhead dives head first and rises head first when fished in the correct fashion. I believe that the gold bead helps exaggerate the change in direction and I am sure that it is this action which makes the goldhead much more attractive to the fish than the treble or brass tube. Another fly style worth trying which produces results is a Cat's Whisker variant tied in the smaller sizes. Regardless of which style of fly or hook type one chooses, the dressings should be kept sparse for best effect.

My own choice of rod is the 10½ft Multi-trout made by Bruce & Walker. I find the rod is ideal for casting the small trebles or goldheads, though it lacks the power to cast the small brass tubes effectively. Perhaps I should invest in a single-handed salmon and sea-trout version specifically designed and better suited for the job.

When presenting the fly it should be cast well upstream at the end of about a 10ft (3m) length of 7 to 10lb nylon. This should be attached to the end of a floating line by means of a braided loop and secured with a half-blood-knot. The line should be cast up and across from where the fish are lying, so that by the time the fly 'drifts' downstream to where the fish are lying it has sunk to the correct depth. This is very important if we are to fish the fly properly and provoke a response from the fish. If the fly is not allowed to sink to the 'right' depth the fish more often than not will ignore it. They appear to be less interested in a midwater fly than one which is presented right down at nose level. It also goes without saying that it is essential when fishing the nymph to know the depth of the pool where the fish are lying.

I like a full floater as I feel that it gives better control and allows me to mend several times to ensure that the fly has sunk to the required depth before I start to fish the nymph. If the nymph is fished with a full sinking line it will not be so easy to fish it properly. A sinking line will be at the same depth as the fly when we start to bring it up and away from the fish. When fished at the end of a sinking line the fly will initially be pulled past the fish and not up and away, and it is the up and away motion which seems to be the triggering factor. For the fly to be fished in the 'induced take' fashion correctly we must use either a full floater or a floater with a braided leader of suitable density. When using both these set-ups we fish the fly by lifting the rod above our heads to raise the nymph towards the surface. In so doing it will rise in a much more natural and attractive fashion.

By fishing the fly like this we are much more likely to produce the desired response from the fish. Why fish seem to find a fly fished thus more attractive than a conventional overhead fly in low water I do not know, but perhaps it is because the fly coming closer and closer, and then suddenly rising away, triggers the salmon's predatory instinct. So often when spinning or fly fishing in the conventional fashion a fish will take the bait or fly just on the 'turn', that is, just as the lure kicks round in the current. If this turning of the lure in the horizontal

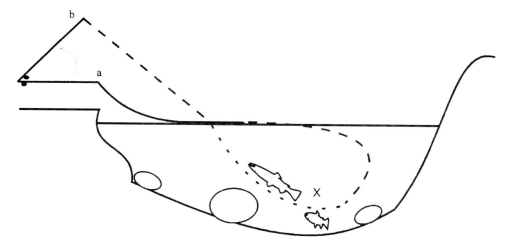

Fig 30 'Induced take' nymphing technique. The rod should be raised from position a to b in one continuous movement. If the rod is raised like this when the fly descends to position X the fly will rise towards the surface. This is usually when the fish will turn and take.

plane is so effective, why should a vertical change in direction be less successful? I am pretty sure that it is the evasive escaping action of the nymph or any other lure or fly fished in this fashion that is the fundamental ingredient in the success of these methods.

Many fish will follow the fly and take at the last minute, just when the rod cannot be raised any higher. These rises are pretty spectacular, with a great vortex appearing on the surface, followed by a good solid pull as the fish turns and starts to head back to its lie. Other fish will take just as the fly starts to rise in the water. This type of take is usually very gentle, the fish merely moving forwards and sucking it in. If anything is felt it is best to assume that a fish has taken, and to pull the hooks home at once. Not all fish that come to the fly will be hooked, but a few will be and it is these fish that make all the effort worth while.

DRESSINGS

The dressings that I have found most successful for this type of fishing are as follows.

Black Goldhead Nymph

Hook	International Sprite size 10.
Tail	A few black hackle fibres.
Body	Dubbed black seals subs.
Hackle	Small black cock.
Head	Gold bead.

Red and Black Drury Nymph

Hook	Size 10 Esmond Drury treble.
Tail	Few strands of red bucktail or hackle fibres.
Body	Black body floss (do not forget to tie in the lead or copper wire first).
Hackle	Small black cock.

Brass Nymph

Body	Undressed brass tube.
Wing	Mixed back and red bucktail or squirrel tail.

Pheasant Tail Nymph

Hook	Single long shank size 6.
Tail	Pheasant tail fibres.
Body	Mix of red, olive, and light ginger seal's fur.
Ribbing	Copper wire.
Thorax	Thicker dubbing of body material.
Wing case	Pheasant tail fibres tied in and brought over to form wing cases and then doubled down and back to form legs.

Cat's Whisker (variant)

Hook	International Sprite size 10.
Tail	Few strands of white marabou about half length of hook.
Body	Lime green chenille.
Wing	Few strands of white marabou.
Eyes	Silver beads.
Head	Black varnish.

13 THE DROPPED-BACK DROPPER

This is a very useful method to learn for summer grilse after the river has dropped and cleared. These fish are often the only chance of sport during the summer and in order to maximize our chances we must be willing to adapt and overcome the conditions. Grilse like to take up lies in the faster, streamier water that their heavier kin avoid. It is in these rougher stretches that we must therefore concentrate our efforts. In order to present our flies properly, a stretch with a good, streamy, well-oxygenated flow of 2–4ft (0.6–1.2m) is essential.

Although this method can be performed with the double-handed rod I prefer to use a long single-hander with a floating line. Unlike the technique of dibbling, we need to have enough line beyond the rod point to load the rod. With this method we initially present our flies by casting the line down and across the current in the conventional way. Initially the flies are fished in the standard down and across fashion, but when the fly approaches the vicinity of the lie we must raise the rod point to bring the dropper up to the surface so that we can bob and skate it across the top of the lie. It is therefore necessary with this form of fishing to know where the fish in the stream are lying.

We do not fish the water with this approach, but present our flies to individual fish in known lies. Although we could fish the water with this method in the hope that something will rise and take, it is best to present our flies to individual fish. A floating line is obligatory when presenting a fly in this fashion to allow us to control the lifting of it. The fly must be lifted at just the right time, which is something that takes a little practice. The basic approach is to lift the rod to raise the dropper fly to the surface and bob it in front of a salmon's nose for as long as possible, then let it fall fully onto the surface and be washed downstream past the fish. This can be achieved by either pulling some extra line off the reel, or by lowering the rod point. Both techniques of letting the fly 'fall back' work equally well, it only being a question of which method you prefer.

When raising the rod it may be necessary to lift it to full arm's length above your head, but this depends on how far away the fly is at the time. When it comes to flies keep them drab and on the small side – I like a small size 10 single or double on the point and a similar or larger size double on the dropper. At times of really high temperatures and low water I have reduced the size of my flies to 12 or 14. Many trout anglers fishing the early morning or evening rise with a team of small wet flies will hook salmon. When doing so they are usually totally surprised, but they shouldn't be because they are in actual fact fishing the correct size of fly for the prevailing conditions. A dark, drab fly seems to work best and for this reason I employ standard loch or river patterns such as Black Pennell, Connemara Black, Zulu (lightly dressed) and Greenwells Glory tied on either down-eyed bronzed trout doubles, Mustad Code 3852 or Sprite International wide gape singles.

Some anglers reading this might prefer to tie the above patterns on low-water salmon singles or doubles, feeling that the hooking ability of such small trout hooks is suspect, but I have not found them so. They may also prefer to use standard hairwing salmon patterns. By all means, I cannot think of any reason why they would be any less successful. The one thing that I must stress though is that it is essential to keep your flies small and dark.

When it comes to nylon I prefer to use a breaking strain of 6lb, but on occasions if there are some double-figure fish about I would increase it to 8lb. Under no circumstances would I go lighter than 6lb, doing so is not sporting and all you will do is leave your fly in a fish, along with a length of trailing nylon. If we use line heavier than the 8lb nylon the small flies used are much more difficult to control and will not fish very well. They will appear dead in the water and not give the semblance of life that is necessary to encourage the fish to take.

When a fish does come to the fly it will do so quickly, by rising and turning on it. If the fly is sitting on the surface the salmon more often than not will rise like a trout, turning and rolling over a dun or spinner, after it has floated past in the current. When fishing a fly in this fashion I have never had a fish that has taken by tailing back downstream and then heading and tailing upstream over the fly. In a few instances I have come across a fish that has risen from the bottom like lightning and exploded through the surface like a Polaris missile, these fish having taken a fly that had drifted downstream by only an inch or two after it had been bobbed. Usually, however, the fly will have travelled approximately 12–18in (30–45cm), but this depends on the pace of the current. Generally, any takes that do occur while the fly is on the drift are usually quite visible as the fish turns and boils the surface. If, on the other hand, the fly sinks after it has been bobbed and allowed to drift you may not see any sign of the take. As I said in Chapter 10, I have had salmon take small trout flies that were only an inch or two under the surface. In all these cases there was no sign that anything had occurred – it was only when the fish had moved back to their lies that I discovered I had one on.

Although a surface rise is pretty spectacular I prefer not to see it. This is because my weakness, I must confess, when fishing with a single-handed rod, is to strike by reacting to the surface disturbance, instead of waiting until the fish is felt. Possibly the reason I do this is because I use the same rod for most of my trout fishing. It is a great mistake to strike the instant that the disturbance is seen, as the fish at this stage has not yet mouthed the fly. Do nothing until the fish is felt and then lift into it.

I have pondered this method and must admit I am at a loss to explain why salmon will sometimes take a fly fished in this way. I do not think that it is merely the presence of the fly in the fish's window of vision that stimulates them into taking. If it was there would be few fish left to catch. Perhaps it is the 'getting away' movement which triggers this unconscious and instinctive predatory response.

This type of water is ideal for fishing a dropped-back dropper, the fish in this stream tending to lie in the edge of the rough water down the right-hand side of the photo.

14 BOMBERS, DOLLIES AND SKATED TUBES

DRY FLY FISHING

Dry fly fishing for one reason or another has never been very popular with UK salmon anglers. The main reason for this might be that many anglers in this country are conservative in their approach and show an innate disregard for anything new. It could of course also be due to the fact that very few fish are ever reported being taken by this method in the river reports section of the monthly periodicals. Every now and again you hear of someone taking a fish that was steadily rising to a hatch of mayfly, or that was taken on a skittered sedge pattern intended for sea-trout or brown trout. River anglers shy away from the dry fly for salmon, but the very same when fishing a loch will quite happily dapp or bob a dropper for them. Some might be saying that dapping or bobbing a fly is not true dry fly fishing. I don't disagree, but if these flies are on the surface when a fish takes them then the fish was taken on a 'dry fly' as far as I am concerned.

Although widely used in America and Canada and rivers of the Kola Peninsula in Russia, the dry fly has never been accepted here. Through experience the Canadians have discovered that for the dry fly to be productive it is best utilized during times of clear, low, warm water. It is documented by some leading transatlantic experts that the method is best employed when the air is warmer than the water by 5 to 10° and with a water temperature in excess of 60°F (15°C). No doubt some UK anglers are asking when they ever get such water temperatures. If so it would appear that they seldom if ever use or carry a thermometer, since during the height of summer I have often fished with water temperatures in the sixties (15–20°C).

During times of low, warm water most British anglers will be using tiny wisps of flies, fished just subsurface with a floating line. By fishing flies that are just subsurface it would appear that we are heading in the right direction, but when I put together information kindly made available to me from various sources across the pond it emerged that perhaps we have been fishing too deep!

Why British anglers show reluctance to go all the way and fish flies on the surface I do not know, but it seems that few salmon anglers in the UK are willing to practise this art. Those who regularly take fish probably feel that they have no need to develop new techniques, while those who catch the occasional fish, in wanting to maximize their chances, only stick to the old tried and tested methods. The Canadian and American anglers, on the other hand, appear to be more adventurous when it comes to trying out new ideas and techniques which is probably because rod fishing across the Pacific for Atlantic salmon is still in its relative infancy, there not being the same pressure on them to use so-called 'traditional' methods. Any British angling authors who are not seen to be towing the line generally end up being labelled as eccentric and are shunned at every possibility.

The Atlantic salmon shows no great fear of venturing to, or through the surface, something that is obvious if you sit on the banks of a holding pool of any river for a period of time where fish can be seen splashing and jumping about. Anyway, they are not called *Salmo salar*, the leaper, for nothing. Since the fish show no restraint at coming to the surface, why not place a fly on it? As I mentioned in Chapter 12 it was observing and hooking salmon which were rising to surface moths that provoked A. H. E. Wood into subsequently fishing his flies as close to the surface as possible whenever he could.

A selection of Bombers and Yellow Dollies.

Now before going any further I should say that I have not caught hundreds of salmon on the dry fly, nor am I ever likely to do so. It has given me the odd fish during conditions considered by others at the time as being next to impossible. What I have discovered with my limited experience is that the dry fly seems to be more productive with grilse, that is fish which have only been away from the river for a short period of time. I am not sure, but I suspect that it is due to the fish's lingering memory of its ravenous river feeding as parr.

For many years I ignored the dry fly approach, but I now use it when the opportunity arises. The first time I tried it was when fishing from the right bank of the association water on the Spey at Grantown, in the fast, rough water under the Old Spey Bridge, a good holding section of water. After

persevering with it for about half an hour a fish rose from the depths to grab my fly. As it happened it took me totally by surprise, and as a result we quickly parted company. On reflection I do not think that the water was very low or very warm at the time, as some anglers were worming, something that is not permitted unless the river is above a certain height. I got some funny looks, but I did raise a fish. Since then I have used the dry fly with some success on one or two clear-running spate streams. If the water is roily it does not seem to work for some reason. Since I do most of my dry fly fishing during times of low water I use a single-handed rod, with either a double taper or weight forward floater and 6lb degreased leader. It is important to degrease the nylon to stop it causing undue surface disturbance.

THE BOMBER *(Figs 31–2)*

When it comes to flies my first choice is one which has accounted for many thousands of salmon, the Bomber. This is the dry fly favoured by many American and Canadian anglers for Atlantic and Pacific salmon, my philosophy being that if it is good enough for them, it is good enough for me. The dressing of the fly is as follows:

Hook	Low-water singles size 10 to 6.
Tail floats	White deer hair or bucktail.
Body	Spun and cut deer hair. Can be orange, grey, brown, white, black, or red.
Body hackle	If brown body use cock grizzle, if not use matching body colour cock hackle.
Front floats	White deer hair or bucktail.

This fly can either be fished up or downstream to individual fish, or alternatively we can fish the water. I have found that the upstream method is best executed to individual fish by adopting the tactics of dry fly fishing for trout and as such one should stay well back from the water's edge and off the sky line. A stealthy downstream approach should be used at all times – it is no use pounding up and down the river bank, all you will do is disturb the fish. Remember we are fishing in low, clear water. Once we have taken up our position of attack we can start to lengthen the line. This should only be done behind the fish's field of vision – do not false cast line above where the fish is lying, as this will almost certainly frighten the fish. When we have enough line out the fly should be cast above the fish and allowed to drift down over it unhindered. Sometimes a fish will rise at once, but more often than not many hours of delicate casting are necessary to provoke a response. As is so often the case with this approach the angler gives up long before the fish takes interest.

Although deer hair is a very buoyant material I find it best to give it a good coat of silicon floatant before commencing. Dry it well before starting, since there is nothing worse than seeing an oily silicon slick coming off a fly. (I do not know if this

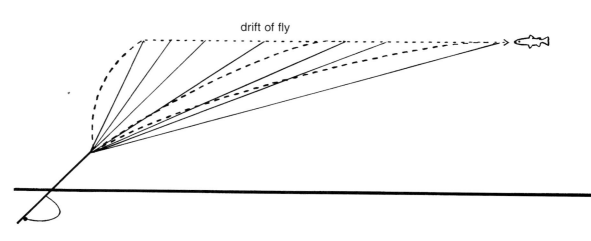

Fig 31 By mending and feeding line the fly can be made to drift on a parallel path the length of the pool.

would actually put a fish off coming to a fly, but I feel that it is better to give them the benefit of any doubt.)

One technique that sometimes works if two fish are lying relatively close to each other is as follows. When one fish seems semi-interested, that is, starts showing increased fin activity, rises or turns away, it is sometimes worth a change of presentation by placing the fly between the two fish. Very often this will provide the additional stimulus and provoke the 'interested' fish into rising and taking it. I learned this tactic when fishing for trout and I am sure that it has something to do with greed – the fish must have it, even though it doesn't really want it. By offering the fly to another salmon could it be that we are provoking the same emotional response? Another little trick that I sometimes use is to cause the fly to drag just as it approaches the fish by pulling in a few inches of line. Some fish will rise quickly and take with a terrific wallop, head and tail down on it, while others merely rise and gently suck it in, like a trout with a dun.

The two main methods of fishing the water are by dead drifting or skating the fly. Both are best employed by casting a long downstream line. When fishing a fly in dead drift fashion we must constantly make upstream mends and shoot extra line at the same time, to enable our fly to travel the length of the pool without dragging.

It is a technique that takes some practice, but once perfected we can dead drift our fly the entire length of most small salmon pools with ease. The skated fly is much easier to fish, as after making our cast we do not have to feed line. We fish the fly in the conventional across and down fashion and let the current do the work. We may, however, have to put in a downstream mend or two, especially if the pool is a slow one. Both methods can also be employed to great advantage in the one cast, especially if there is a known lie. The fly can initially be drifted down just above the lie, then at just the right time we can skate it. This can be done by either pulling in some line, raising the rod tip or by putting in a downstream mend in the line. It is also worth letting a dead drift fly skate across the remaining width of the pool when it comes to the end of its travel, as sometimes a fish will follow it round in the current and take just as it comes to the

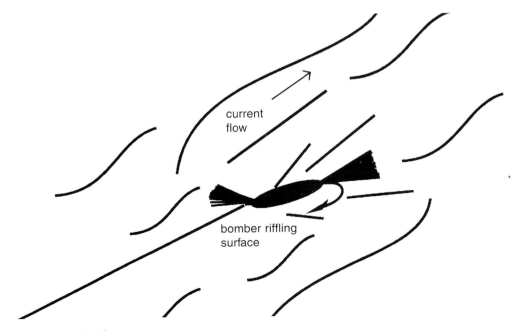

current
flow

bomber riffling
surface

Fig 32 Skating the fly.

dangle. With any of these methods it is important that the fly leads the nylon and fly line down the pool at all times.

THE DOLLY

One angler, Derek Knowles, has probably had more consistent sport with the dry fly for salmon than anyone else. So much so that he developed his own fly, a Yellow Dolly. The dressing is as follows.

Tube	Red plastic, from ¼ to ⅝ in (6mm to 15mm).
Body (rear)	Collar of stiff yellow bucktail, trimmed and flared.
Body (front)	As above but black hair.

The flies were called dollies because they are said to look like little dolls. The overall size after trimming varies from ⅛in to ¾in (3–18mm). Small out-point treble hooks are used at the business end. These flies should be fished high in the water and it is therefore advisable to grease the dolly. I know some anglers who will also grease the nylon, but this is a practice I do not favour.

The flies produce more fish long after a spate has run its course. They must be fished with a floating line, but can be cast either up or downstream, at the end of a long leader. As with the Bomber, drag can also be induced or they can be left to the whim of the current. If the fly skitters the surface there seems to be a better response from fish, possibly because the disturbance simulates life. The secret to success with this method is to stay out of sight and be patient. On many occasions fish will rise to the fly without taking hold of it. These fish should be left for a period of time and tried again a little later in the day. When trying them again do so with the same fly as before, but if that fails change down or up until you get a response. Sometimes, however, it does not matter what you do – they will treat your offering with the utmost contempt.

THE SKATED TUBE *(Figs 33–5)*

Another fly that can be fished on, or rather through, the surface that salmon sometimes find hard to resist is a 'skated tube'. The reason I have included this type of fly fishing in this section of the book and not along with the chapter on dibbling is that all flies outlined in this chapter stay either on, or in the

Fishing the Spey with a floating line and small fly. On occasions, however, a Bomber fished in the rough water at the neck of a stream can sometimes move a fish that has refused a small subsurface fly.

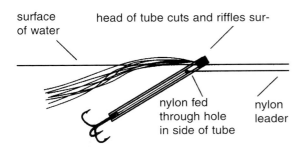

surface of water

head of tube cuts and riffles sur-

nylon fed through hole in side of tube

nylon leader

Fig 33 Skating the tube.

surface layer of the water. The flies are never total-ly submersed or lifted clear of the water, (apart from when we are casting them of course). Both the Bomber and Yellow Dolly are used almost exclu-sively when the rivers have fallen back during the summer months and are starting to show their bare bones. The skated tube, though, can be used when the water is cold or warm. When choosing the size of fly the same guidelines still apply that we use for conventional floating or sinking line tactics – the warmer the water the smaller the fly. With this method, even when the water is warm, above 50°F (10°C), a fly in excess of 3in (75mm) is complete-

ly acceptable. A Collie Dog tied on a modified plas-tic tube is ideal for this type of fishing. The pattern is tied in the conventional fashion, but prior to start-ing a hole must be made in the body of the tube so that the nylon can be passed through and secured to the treble. This is essential so that when we hold it against the current it planes across the width of the pool, cutting a positive 'V' through the surface as it does so. It swims hooks down.

Owing to the size of flies involved it is best to use a double-handed rod with this method. By using the long rod our flies can then be fished in the con-ventional step and cast fashion, which will enable us to fish the entire pool with ease.

Alternatively we can dead drift the fly down-stream. When it approaches the part of the pool that we intend to fish we simply stop mending and feed-ing line, hold the line against the handle of the rod and let it come round in the current. This is a par-ticularly good method if the fish we are intending to cover are under overhanging trees or bushes. One of the most productive ways of fishing a skated tube is to strip it back across the width of the pool and fish it square on to the fish. By presenting a fly in this fashion we can cover all the lies in the pool effec-tively.

To do this, cast square across the pool and then

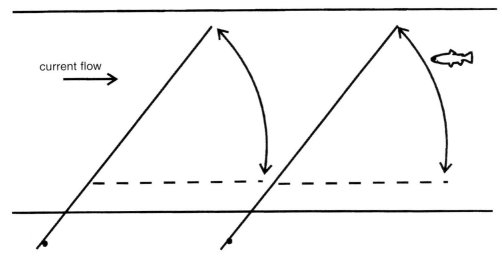

current flow

Fig 34 Fishing cast and step fashion.

strip in line at a good rate of knots by pulling in a yard or more at a time. In a fast flow the current will belly the line, but do not worry about this as it helps to keep the fly swimming fast. If the flow is almost non-existent it may be necessary to put a downstream mend into the line to help. From my experience of this type of fishing, a fly fished fast seems to provoke more responses than a slow one. Never think that your fly is fishing too fast with this approach as I have never yet found a salmon that can be out-paced. At times a great wake will suddenly appear behind the fly as a salmon moves to intercept it. If you see any sign of a fish do not stop stripping in, because if you do the chances are that

the salmon will stop following and turn away – and they seldom come back if presented with a fly again. The instant you see any indication of a fish following, speed up your retrieve as this often makes the salmon move up a gear and take with conviction. Needless to say, like any other method there will be a number of fish that merely roll in the vicinity of the fly without opening their mouths. I believe that the fish that do this have no intention of taking the fly. Any fish that do take, though, are generally well hooked, right at the back of the throat. This I think is due to the hooks being suspended low down at the rear of the tube.

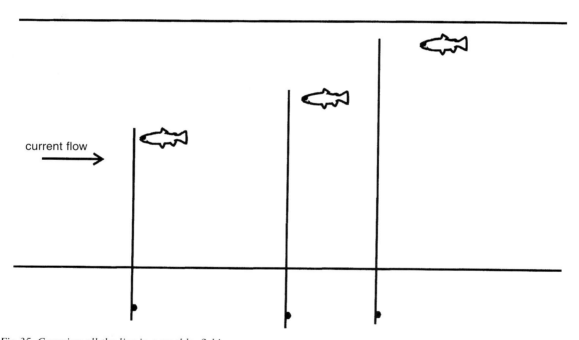

Fig 35 Covering all the lies in a pool by fishing square on.

15 FISHING WITH A SINKING LINE

WHEN AND HOW TO USE THE SINKING LINE *(Figs 36–40)*

Most anglers only use a sinking line when the water and air temperatures are close to each other, that is early or late in the season. The sinking line can also be very effective, however, during the summer and early autumn when the river is fining down after a spate and still carrying a few extra inches.

At this time fish will be quietly nosing their way up through the slacker, quieter water just out from the sides. Initially it is detrimental to wade, as we would be wading in the very section of water that is most likely to provide us with a fish. To start with keep well back from the water's edge and cast only a short line covering the water immediately in front. After this has been fished out make the next cast from the same spot, but this time shoot a little extra line. Eventually, after about three or four casts, all the water within casting range will have been covered. It is now time to take a step or two down the pool and repeat the whole process. This technique has provided me with sport when other anglers have gone fishless, possibly because they have been more interested in wading than fishing.

When the water starts to fall a little further the extra 'reach' and water command of the longer double-handed rod now comes into its own. One technique that I use if wading is not possible or desirable is to cast the line out at a shallow angle

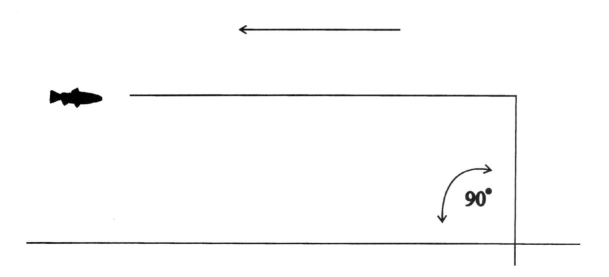

Fig 36 The 90-degree approach.

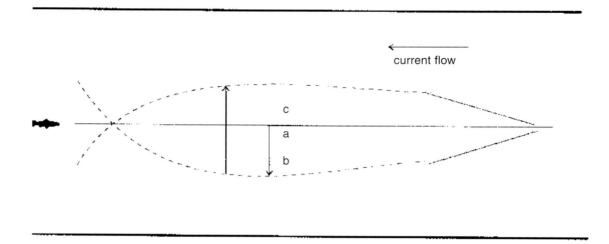

current flow

Fig 37 Fishing on the dangle. (1) Just before the line comes to position a, swing rod in towards position b (your own bank). (2) Prior to the line coming to b, swing the rod round to position c (midstream).

and then hold the rod out at right angles to the flow.

A better method if wading is possible, particularly when the fish are running up through the deeper middle section of the pool, is to wade in well above where they are lying, and then prior to the fly coming to the dangle move the rod round in towards your own bank. As the fly comes to the end of its swim move the rod back out into a midstream position. By doing this, the fly can be made to swim enticingly back and forth in front of the fish for an almost indefinite period of time.

This method also works very well in the faster streamier water in the neck of the pool where the current is a lot faster. By adopting this technique we can present our flies to the fish much more slowly and in so doing stand a much better chance of tempting fish from these faster-flowing, streamier sections. If the fly is fished too fast in the rough water in the head stream the fish are inclined to swirl at the fly in a half-hearted fashion, many only being lightly hooked and lost after the initial pull. For this reason alone it is beneficial to wade in well above the stream, even if it means wading in the tail glide of the previous pool. This should only be done, however, if the streamier water in the neck of the pool in which we are intending to fish is more

productive at the height of water than the tail of the pool which we intend to fish from. In many cases there are many yards of thin, streamy water between the tail of one pool and the head of another, but if the tail of one and the head of the other are relatively close to each other then we must give consideration to other anglers who might want to fish the tail of the pool we intend fishing from.

Another approach that I use and find very effective when fishing over a lie in a slow midstream position with very little flow is as follows. After the cast has been made the rod should be held out almost at right angles to the bank, then brought round into a downstream position to allow the current to form a belly in the line, which will draw the fly abruptly past and away from the fish. In saying this the fly should not be brought through the lie too quickly. It is the change in direction of the fly and not its speed that is the critical factor with this method. This sudden change in direction and speed can sometimes provoke a response from a fish that has not responded to the standard approach. There is no need to either feed line or give slack when a take comes as the fish is usually just on.

Regardless of the size of river being fished I opt for a Wet Cel II double taper line. Some anglers

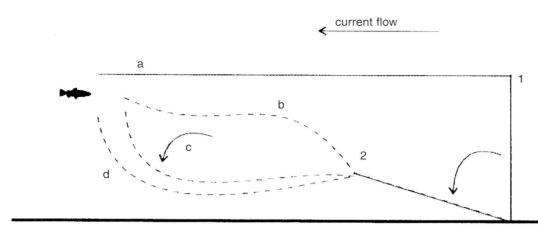

current flow

Fig 38 The accelerated fly. As the line is initially running parallel to the flow, the fly hovers enticingly in front of the fish and as the rod is moved from position 1 through to position 2 the current takes control of the line at b. This means that the fly will momentarily stop fishing until the current puts a belly in the line at c, at this point the fly will once again start to fish as it is pulled across and away from the lie. The take generally comes somewhere between c and d.

might think that this line is too high a density for small rivers, but since we are only working with about 10 to 15 yards of line, the depth at which the fly will be fishing will be no deeper than the same fly fished at the end of a full Wet Cel I. If the fish are lying at the far side of the pool and will not respond to the usual cast and mend, try a slightly squarer cast without mending. Again with this method the fish will generally take just as the fly accelerates away from them. If the water is very cold, or the section of water that we intend fishing is deep with a strong current through it, one technique of getting the fly down to where the fish are lying is a variation of the 'S' mend that I described in Chapter 10 (Fig 27). Initially perform the cast exactly as you would for the floating line, but not quite as square. Now double mend the line in the fashion described and take a step downstream. You will have to be quick with the mends before the water drowns the line.

Another successful method of taking salmon on the fly that is fast catching on among many spate stream anglers is the *Booby Shrimp*. The idea with this method is to fish a fast sinking line right down on the bottom with a buoyant fly ballooning above.

The density of the line must be such that it will sink quickly and settle either on, or just off, the bottom of the pool in which we are going to fish. In order to achieve the desired Booby effect it is essential to use a short leader, usually no more than 2ft (60cm) in length with a fly of neutral density. If the fly has negative buoyancy you are wasting your time. A deer hair fly tied as a shrimp imitation works quite well, though a better construction method is to use an ethafoam body, fly bodies made in this way working perfectly.

When fishing in this fashion it is best to wade and get well in above the lie, as shown, and cast a long line. The idea is for the fly to dance and dart about right in front of the salmon's nose. If you want to add a little extra life to the shrimp you can lift and draw by raising and lowering the rod point, which sometimes proves irresistible. The method works well in slow, deep flows, but is also excellent for taking temporary resting fish which are running and have just come up over the lip of a weir. During dry weather, when the river has fallen right back this method is also worth considering. It is a gentle, relaxing way to spend time trying to tempt a fish – you do not have to keep casting as this would defeat

The Tweed at Melrose showing its 'skeleton' during a summer drought. In such low water a fly fished with a sinking line would continually get hung up on the bottom. During the autumn, with an extra two feet on the gauge many Tweed anglers will use nothing else.

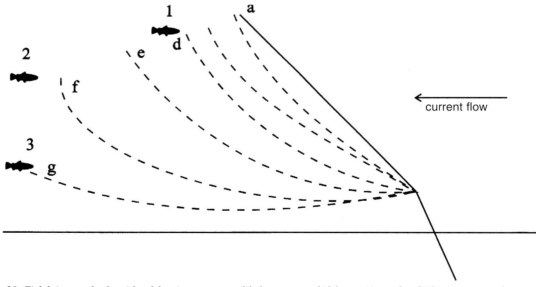

current flow

Fig 39 Fish lying on the far side of the river are more likely to respond if the cast is made a little more squarely across the pool. The take of fish 1 will come between d and e. Fish 2 will take at f as the fly moves away. As the fly approaches f a couple of extra yards of line can be pulled quickly back through the rings, providing an increase in fly speed as it moves off upstream. When the fly comes to the dangle position g and no response has occurred, pull in another couple of yards fairly quickly. This action can sometimes be enough to make a fish move forward and take, particularly if it has followed the fly round and for some reason decided not to take.

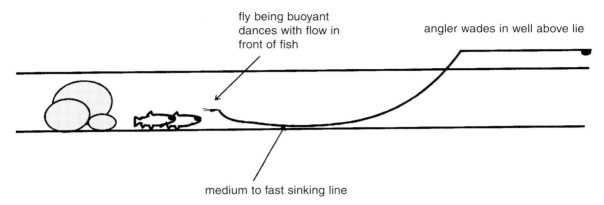

fly being buoyant
dances with flow in
front of fish

angler wades in well above lie

medium to fast sinking line

Fig 40 Fishing the Booby Shrimp.

the purpose. Some conservative fly fishers I know have scorned me when fishing this method, saying that it is not 'true' fly fishing, but they have soon changed their ideas after seeing me extract fish from right out in front of them which had ignored their previous offerings.

WHAT TACKLE TO USE

All of the methods described work equally well in dubs and pots, as well as streams and pools, the only difference being that a shorter line must be fished, hence the advantage of the longer rod to enable the line to be controlled through the fish-holding section of water. Brass tubes, aluminium, or Waddington-shanked flies in the range of 1–2in (25–50mm) are ideal, with the hair extending well past the bend of the treble. In some cases this can make a 1in (25mm) tube effectively a 2in (50mm) fly, a Garry Dog or a Willie Gunn being the first choice. A 2in fly might sound a bit on the large side, but I would only start off fishing this size just as the water starts to fall and clear, changing down size as the water falls and clears further. Anyway if I was spinning at the same water height I would be opting for a 2½in (60mm) Devon Minnow.

I recall an article that I had written – and had published in a monthly periodical on fishing in this fashion during the autumn with a 2in (50mm) brass tube. The editor had removed the dimensions and

tube material because he thought that it might be conducive to foul hooking, but let me assure you that if the fly is fished properly you stand no greater risk of foul hooking a fish than with any other method. The nylon should be 20lb or heavier if fishing a 2in (50mm) tube and no more than 5ft (1.5m) in length. If the water is running high and coloured then reduce the length to about 3ft (1m). When the water starts to fall and clear increase the length of your leader to about 7ft (2m). When fishing a 1in (25mm) tube or Waddington I would fish nylon of 15lb. It is no use fishing with nylon any lighter than this to give the fish a so-called sporting chance as there is nothing sporting about leaving a hook in a fish.

Incidentally, during the autumn, even when fishing smaller flies, I have not found fish being put off by the 15lb nylon. This heavier nylon during the 'back end' allows me to cope with the assortment of leaves of which there is always an abundance, as I find that the heavier gauge cuts its way through the discarded foliage well, allowing the nylon to get down into the flow and resulting in more effective fly control. This means that my flies are fishing through the holding water for a longer period of time and as a result increasing my chances of a fish. Lighter nylon does not do this and only results in more time having to be spent removing leaves from the hooks.

The tubes that I use are the Slipstream type as distributed by Veniards, as they have a very slim profile which allows them to get down quickly in fast, streamy water. As for hooks, my preference is the outpoint trebles made by Partridge, code number X1BR, GSRX8 or Rob Wilsons's CS9. These hooks are not the cheapest, but they are excellent. As far as patterns are concerned, a fly with yellow, orange and red at this time of the year is preferred, because all three colours in one shade or another are present in the colouration of the spawning livery of autumn fish. If, as some acknowledged experts claim, colour is of little consequence, then why does the spawning livery of the fish contain these three colours? Everything in nature is there for a reason, so if colour plays no part then why does the salmon undergo such a drastic change in skin pigmentation? This is why my first choice of fly during the last few weeks of the season contains one if not all three colours.

16 BACKING UP

There are many stretches of river where the conventional across and down approach is just not possible due to the lack of pull from the current through them, so the angler has to change his tactics and try to present the fly to the fish from behind. These slow pools are generally deep in nature; as the old saying goes, still water runs deep, and for this reason wading is unnecessary when backing up. In fact a great deal of the water that fishes best with this method is impossible to wade in any case, due to the physical circumstances. On many of the pools that I fish with this method the river bed quickly falls away into the depths, only a short distance out from the bank. Sometimes it is impossible to fish a pool by backing up, as to do so properly you will need to have the pool to yourself. On some association stretches this is virtually impossible due to the number of other anglers wanting to fish at the same time, but if you are fishing a private beat there is usually a better chance of being able to do so, especially if you are allocated your own stretch or pools.

Many fly fishers ignore deep, slow water, and do so at their loss. These deep slow pools, regardless of river size, generally hold good numbers of fish, especially during periods of low water, not to mention the number of resting fish that take up short- or medium-term lies during times of high water. In any case, regardless of water height, any fish that tenant these pools more often than not become the attention of the worming and spinning fraternity and so seldom or never see a fly. I think that most resident fish which are covered time and time again with the same lure or bait soon become contemptuous of it and scorn all similar offerings. Yes, I know of instances where anglers have persisted with a fish and been successful (I have done so myself) but these fish only amount to a very small percentage of the total numbers taken. I feel that on the whole an

Pools with very little pull through them are often walked past by many anglers fishing the fly. A backed-up fly pulled quickly upstream over a fish from behind can at times be very effective.

angler's best chance of taking a resident fish, or any fish for that matter, occurs the first time the fish are covered that day. If it does not take on the first throw then I feel that the chances of success dwindle thereafter at an exponential rate. Nevertheless, these fish, if shown something that looks and behaves completely differently from what they have previously seen may be excited into responding. Taking this into account gives the adaptable fly fisher an advantage over those who stick to the more preferable streamy sections.

Some authors claim that this method only works on a few rivers, but I have found that backing up takes fish on many rivers from Strathspey to Ayrshire. By fishing in the manners described later in the chapter I have taken fish in every river in which I have used it. I am not saying that I have taken fish every time, but I do take fish from them regularly throughout the year. A number of anglers that I have discussed this method with say that it is only of any use in cold water – not true, this is one of the best methods I know of taking fish lying deep in the main holding pools during the summer months, particularly on the larger east coast rivers of Scotland. On many of these rivers the holding water is well out of casting range. However, if a boat is available with a ghillie or boatman backing up, can be quite productive if the boat is rowed or motored upstream at the necessary speed after the line has been allowed to sink to the proper depth. A good boatman will know the depth of the pool and where the fish are likely to be, thus saving time covering water which might not hold fish. I have found that backing up from a boat works well on the Tay.

METHODS OF BACKING UP

Many years ago, before I ever thought of writing a book, I used to read vast amounts of literature on many aspects of fly fishing. The one thing that stuck in my mind was just how few pages there were devoted to the subject of backing up, considering this was a favoured and tested method on many slow-flowing rivers. I was surprised to find that the authors who did cover this topic only touched upon it very briefly. There was the odd diagram and a little text, but usually there was no more than a page or two at most. It also appeared that the majority who wrote about the subject, with one exception, only regurgitated selected bits and pieces of what other eminent authorities past and present had already written. I was also amazed to find that no one had made an attempt to explain the technique in detail, and needless to say no one covered the subject material to my satisfaction. The one thing which I did discover was that every author stated that the main object when backing up was to bring the flies over the fish from behind.

The Standard Method *(Fig 41)*
The angler starts at the tail of the pool and casts square across. If the water is deep he may put in an upstream mend to allow his flies to sink that bit further or, if very slow, put in a downstream mend to help create some belly in the line. He then waits until the current takes hold of the line and then starts walking upstream for a few steps. This is all very well in practice, but it is fundamentally flawed, as the fly will only cover fish properly, that is from behind, for a very short period of time. The reason for this is that during the early stages of the fly's traverse across the pool it is being pulled downstream head first by the current, creating a downstream belly in the line. As this happens the angler starts walking upstream against the 'pull' and starts taking some of the belly out of the line, and as he does so the fly will turn at right angles to the flow. During both these stages of swim the fly cannot come over the fish from behind, because during the initial stages of its travel it is pulled towards any fish by the current, then across them when the angler starts to walk upstream. Although fish can take the fly at any stage of its travel through the pool we are only presenting it 'correctly' for about a third of the time that it is actually fishing. Since the aim is to bring the flies over as many fish as possible from behind I feel that this is not the best approach.

An Alternative New Method *(Fig 42)*
As before, we start at the tail of the pool. With this method, however, we do not wait until the current

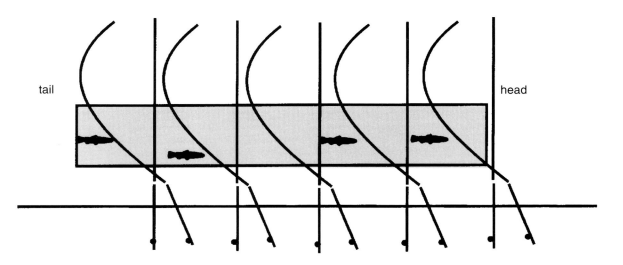

Fig 41 The standard method of backing up. The angler waits for the current to belly the line, then walks upstream a few steps. The fish in the shaded area are only covered properly for about a third of the time that the fly is being fished.

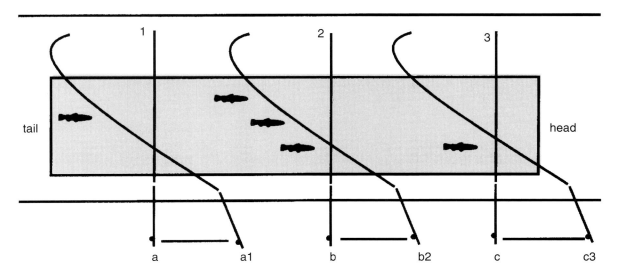

Fig 42 The alternative backing up method. As before, start at the tail of the pool at a and cast straight across to 1. Do not wait for the current to belly the line but walk upstream as soon as possible to a1. Do not stop walking until the fly comes to the dangle. Repeat the process at positions b and c, working your way up the pool.

starts to belly the line before walking upstream. Before the line shows any signs of bellying and coming round with the current, we start walking backwards upstream. The distance walked generally depends on the length of line being cast: with this method the angler does not stop walking upstream until the fly comes to the dangle. By doing this we are not casting as often and hence are causing less disturbance. When the line starts to swing into the side a few yards of line can be pulled or stripped in. This can sometimes bring a response, particularly during high water from a fish which has either followed round and is unsure, or from a fish lying close in against our own bank. By continually walking upstream as described, the belly in the line will be reduced to a minimum. It is important that we do not let too much belly develop, as this will result in the flies fishing in the same way as with the conventional method. The alternative method if done properly allows our flies to come over more fish from behind.

When fishing in this fashion it is essential that we use the correct line – a normal medium or fast sinking line will not do. I use a Wet Cel II 'Uniform Sink' because the tip of this line sinks first, unlike other conventional lines where the belly sinks first. The Uniform Sink allows the flies to get down quickly so that we can start walking back upstream almost as soon as the line alights. Although the fly during the early stages of its swim still behaves in a similar fashion to the fly in the standard method described, it does not do so for such a long period of travel. This means that the fly is fishing correctly for longer. Some anglers might think that a sink tip might be better suited, but I do not, because the floating section of the line will cause unnecessary disturbance. If you do not fancy the additional expenditure of a line that you might only use once or twice a year then you can purchase an extra-fast sinking braided leader and attach it to your standard sinker. Although it does not present the flies in exactly the same fashion as the 'Universal' line, it is the next best thing.

During the traverse of the flies from one side of the pool to the other, the rod point should be kept low. This has two advantages: first it helps keep our flies low in the water, and second it helps to keep us more in touch with what is happening at the other end of the line. If you do fish with the rod tip high your flies will rise in the water, something you do not want with this approach. Also, like any other method, it is best to try the pool from both sides if possible because very often light falling on a lure from a different angle will bring a response from a fish where there was none previously.

FURTHER COMMENTS

Backing up can be performed with either a single- or double-handed rod, the prevailing conditions at the time dictating which. If we are fishing a wide pool, or during times of high water where a large fly is needed, the double-hander is best, but if we are fishing a narrow pool when the water is running clear a single-handed rod with small flies will be sufficient.

The main disadvantage with both methods described is that the line comes over the fish before the fly, which may put some fish off. However, it is the sudden appearance of the fly in the fish's window of vision from behind that seems to stimulate any 'taking' fish to move to the fly.

17 THE STRIPPED FLY

With salmon being so highly unpredictable in their taking behaviour it sometimes pays to present our flies in a fashion that contravenes the accepted tried and tested methods for the prevailing conditions. For the majority of the time we strive to present our flies to fish as slowly as possible, whether we are fishing with small flies during the summer or large ones early or late in the season. With the 'stripped' method we use a large garish fly, usually 2in (5cm) or more pulled quickly across the pool close to the surface.

Do not think that a 2in (50mm) fly is too big, I have seen salmon come and grab a 6ft (1.8m) length of orange nylon rope that had been washed downstream from somewhere and ended up becoming attached to a trailing branch of a tree. Not only did the same salmon have one go at it, it had several. When it comes to fly patterns I do not think it makes all that much difference which you choose with this style of fishing. Some anglers who regularly fish the stripped fly prefer their own flies to have Jungle Cock cheeks incorporated. They believe that by fitting these the fly has a more illuminated presence, like a car's headlights down a dark country lane. The whole object, regardless of whether Jungle Cock cheeks are used or not, is that the fly's complete passage across the pool is clearly visible.

This method of presenting a fly is particularly successful when fishing in low water during the summer months, especially during bright overhead conditions, when a small subsurface fly is often ignored. It is surprising the height of water a salmon will rise through to take a fly fished in this fashion, even during the brightest conditions. In addition, the stripped fly takes both fresh and stale fish from slow flowing pools or fast, streamy water throughout the year, provided that the air is warmer than the water by at least 5°F (3°C). This type of fishing is not for the idle because it requires many casts to be made, many more than would normally be required if fishing the pool in a conventional down and across fashion.

TACKLE AND TECHNIQUE *(Fig 43)*

Before I describe the technique I must first highlight the tackle necessary that will enable us to perform this style of fishing properly. Since we will be using a large fly it is essential to use the double-handed rod. This is because the single-hander will just not cope with the size of flies used. The flies I use for this style of fishing are tied on low-water doubles and Waddington shanks. The hair used in both cases should be cut long enough to be taken well past the bends of the hooks, my first choice of colour being hot orange or bright yellow. In fast flows I like to use flies tied on Waddington shanks fished in conjunction with a sinking line, the density of line depending on the pace of the current in which the fly is to be fished. Although some anglers might think that Waddington shanks fished with a sinking line will fish deep, this is not necessarily the case. If they are retrieved at the 'correct' speed they will not sink deep. The slower you strip in line the deeper they will fish. In order to keep them fishing at the desired depth of 2–3in (5–8cm) beneath the surface a relatively quick retrieve is necessary. Since the pace of current at the head of a pool is generally faster than it is in the middle, the speed at which your flies will have to be stripped back may vary from cast to cast. This is not as daunting as it may first appear.

Stripping in on a slow pool. The rod in the photograph is being held too low.

When I am fishing this method and asked by other anglers how I can tell when my flies are fishing at the correct depth I ask them if they can see my fly's passage across the pool – a 'yes' answers their question. (Thankfully I have yet to experience a myopic individual.) In the slower 'dead' pools I will use flies tied on low-water doubles. Again the same principles apply, the only difference being that I will use a neutral density line instead of a full sinker.

The length of leader used will depend on the height and colour of the water – if it is low and clear I use one of 12ft (3.6m) of 12lb, if on the other hand the river is high and turgid I will use a 15lb line shortened to about 6ft (1.8m). To fish all the different types of pool properly, three sinking lines are necessary, a Neutral density for slow water, a Wet Cel I for medium flows and a Wet Cel II for fast,

streamy water. I know one or two anglers who swear by the floating line for this type of fishing, but I don't. On a smooth, glassy glide a floater is inclined to leave a bit of a wake, when the only thing that should leave a wake if any with this style of presentation is the fly. The fly should be presented square across the pool and stripped back across the flow at such a rate to stop the current forming a belly in the line. If this happens the fly will not swim square on to the fish.

For this technique to work properly it is essential that the fly comes across the fish side on. By keeping the rod point high we can help control the passage of the fly across the pool and it also helps to keep the majority of the line off the surface. Stripping line back is not difficult, but to do it correctly both hands must work together readily. The whole process starts with the index finger of the right hand securing the line against the handle of the rod. Next the left hand takes hold of the line and pulls down to the left thigh in one continuous movement. When this point is reached the index finger of the right hand once again clamps the line against the handle, then the left hand comes up to take hold for the next pull. The whole process is repeated until the fly is brought back across the pool to the place where we want to make our next cast from. Left-handed angles should read 'left' for 'right' and vice versa.

As the line starts to shorten it is best to stop stripping and move the rod point upstream. When the fly has completed its swim the tip of the rod is raised further and brought into the position of execution for a single Spey cast. This is a better method of fishing out the cast than merely raising the rod point to the vertical. Since the line is always fairly taut any fish that take generally draw the hooks in well past the barbs. Some anglers will swear that it is essential to feed slack line to fish that come to a fly fished in this fashion, though that is their choice, not mine. Not all fish turn in the opposite direction to that is which the fly was moving when they take. This is something that is absolutely essential for good slack line hooking. I do not intend going into

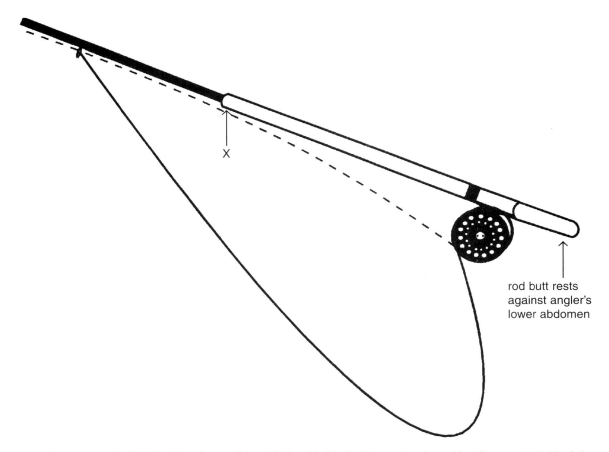

X

rod butt rests
against angler's
lower abdomen

Fig 43 Presenting the fly. The index finger of the right hand holds the line against the rod handle at point X. The left hand comes up to take hold of the line at X. Then it is brought down to a position between the knee and thigh on the outside of the left leg. After the 'pull' the right index finger once again secures the line against the handle until the left hand comes up to take hold of it again.

A silver prize safely ashore.

the different principles of hooking fish here, as I do so at depth later in the book.

Any fish coming to the fly are usually very visible, making this method of fishing very exciting. Sometimes a wake will be seen behind the fly, while on other occasions a dorsal fin will be seen cutting the surface like a cruising shark. Generally, though, the first indication of an interested fish is a flash of silver as it turns on the fly, or a small white flash suddenly appearing as the fish rises vertically and opens its mouth to engulf it. I can remember one fish which went ballistic, shooting four or more feet into the air, though I have also hooked fish that showed no sign of taking. These fish took my fly during the quiescent period of stripping in line, when the fly was briefly stationary, and when my left hand was coming up to take the line for another pull. It was only when I started to strip in line again that I realized a fish had mouthed my fly. It is imperative, regardless of what visually occurs, not to respond. If you do the rod will only remain straight, wait until you feel the fish.

I know of a ghillie who has been experimenting with plastic tubes by forming a vane on the front end. He forms these vanes by applying a hot knife blade prior to tying on the wing. At the time of writing he has not had many opportunities to fish these 'vane' flies and as a result they are as yet unproved, though I am sure that given a decent swim they will soon establish themselves. The idea behind these flies is that they will dive when retrieved and rise when not. It is also hoped that they will wobble and weave from side to side when fished conventionally while held against a flow. By behaving in this fashion it is hoped they will more closely represent the erratic movement of a darting minnow.

18 MICROFLIES

Anyone who books a week's fishing on a spate river is taking a great gamble, as more often than not the river will be running low, even during a wet year. If the gods are favourable and there is rain in sufficient quantity you might perhaps get one or two days fishing with the river running at a good height. The absence of rain, although undesirable, need not spoil a week's sport. Even when spate rivers flow in a skeletal state they can still produce an odd fish or two to anyone who is willing to put in the effort and fish carefully and stealthily. There is no doubt that the longer fish are in freshwater the more difficult they are to tempt. This is because during times of low water they generally frequent the deeper holding pools and keep their heads down. As one ghillie put it they become 'glued to the bottom'. These fish nonetheless can still be caught if we are willing to try an unconventional approach.

One method that works in low water is the use of very small weighted flies, fished deep. These can be presented with either a slow sinker or sink tip line, depending on the depth of the pool being fished. For a stealthy approach it is best to use a single-handed rod. The fly should be cast across the pool and given time to sink. When it has reached the appropriate depth it is then worked back with short, sharp pulls. Another method employed is to let the fly sink to the bottom, then after a short period of time work it back with a sink and draw retrieve, with positive pauses between each draw. The flies can also be fished upstream, but they must be retrieved at such a rate that you can keep in touch with them.

The dressings of the flies are very simple and sparse, consisting of only a ribbed body with a few strands of hair tied in around the tail. The dressings of the original flies tied by Peter Smith, who wrote an article which appeared in an edition of *Trout & Salmon* are as follows:

All Black

Hook	Size 16 outpoint tube fly type, eg Partridge code types X1 BL, X3 BL or CS9 BL.
Tail	Black squirrel or stoats tail.
Body	Black floss ribbed with oval silver.
Head	Black varnish.

Red and White

Hook	As above.
Tail	White cock hackle fibres.
Body	Red floss ribbed with oval silver.
Head	Black varnish.

Chinaman

Hook	As above.
Tail	Black squirrel or stoat's tail.
Body	Yellow floss ribbed with oval silver.
Head	Black varnished.

Peter tells me that he still uses these flies as his 'main weapon' when fishing in the north-west of Scotland.

I know of an angler who fishes my local association water with small flies fished similarly to the methods described above. Through the years I have watched him coax out many fish, especially on occasions when other anglers had given up all hope of a fish. The flies he uses are conventional Silver Stoat's Tails tied on small size 10 and 12 Partridge X2B or Esmond Drury trebles. If the water is very low he will use size 14s. I have watched him put this method to good use in the main holding pools when the river has been blessed with some extra depth and is running a touch coloured. Going from what I have observed these tiny flies appear to produce the 'best' occupant from the pool. It has always amazed me why a double-figure fish, or any fish for that matter, that has ignored everything including shrimp and worm finds these miniature temptations irresistible.

The River Findhorn fining down after a summer spate. This river has been called the most beautiful river in Scotland, on which I reserve judgement. It is probably the most satisfying to take a fish from, however.

Presenting a small fly to tempt summer grilse from the Spey. The river on this occasion was running with an additional three inches on the gauge and fish were running up the slack water to the mainstream side of the rock where Mary is presenting her flies. Just after this frame was taken she hooked and then landed a 7lb fish from the very spot shown.

Two anglers fishing from the casting platform on Clach Na Strone Pool on the River Spey. They would give themselves a better chance of a fish if they got into the water immediately in front of it. By doing this they would keep themselves out of the sky line.

Fishing down the Long Pool on the Strathspey Angling Association water of the Spey.

Two summer fish from the Spey. The top one shows the rounder head of the hen fish, while the bottom one shows the smaller, sharper head of the cock.

Ghillie John Thompson of Castle Grant Number 1 Beat Spey casting down the Slop Gachrach Pool.

Fishing a pool on the Kincardine Beat of the Spey.

A silver prize from the Cower Craig Pool just upstream of Aberlour.

Mary Keachie playing a summer fish from The Battery Pool on the Stinchar. She hooked the fish on only her third or fourth cast of the day.

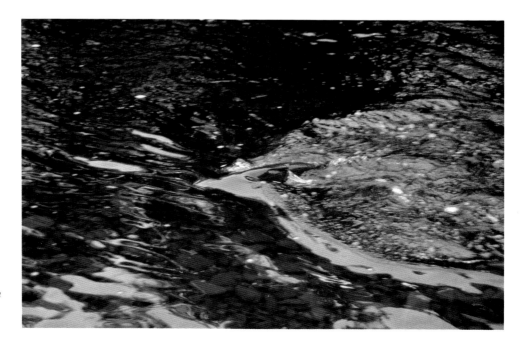

A fish being drawn towards the shore for beaching.

A visiting angler fishes down Polcrain Pool on the Spey.

Summer on the River Doon in Ayrshire.

Well pleased with two summer fish from the Spey, both taken on a fly.

Presenting a fly in a deep, narrow run between the Craig and the Hairs Took Pools on the River Stinchar.

A marvellous array of flies, but do we need such a collection? Any one of them fished properly would probably tempt a taking fish.

19 HOOKING, PLAYING AND LANDING

HOOKING *(Figs 44–6)*

There has probably been more written about hooking salmon on the fly than any other aspect of the sport, but much of this has been merely regurgitated literature from past authorities. Today, anyone taking up salmon fishing and reading books on the subject finds that there are as many ideas on the hooking of a salmon as there are books relating to the topic, and will find themselves confused and not knowing which practice to follow. Some contemporary anglers, including me, are starting to question the methods preached and used by those still adhering to the old techniques.

When a salmon comes to a fly the two main practices are to either feed slack or tighten as soon as a fish is felt. The first of these I question in some detail, because as soon as we give the fish slack line, its likelihood of ejecting it instantly rises to 50 per cent. The majority who fish in this fashion strongly believe that the fish need to be fed line in order to secure a good hook hold. The logic behind

this idea is that the current will pull the fly into the corner of the fish's mouth. This is all very well, provided that the fish does not turn in the same instant as taking the fly; however, a lot of fish that decide to take our fly will usually follow it round and take it either by turning away or towards the angler, or by taking hold of it and continuing on upstream before tailing back downstream with the current.

We can now look at the first case, the fish that turns away from the angler when given slack line. Some of these fish will stand a good chance of being hooked, the line being pulled downstream by the current dragging the fly into the right-hand side maxillary bone of the fish's jaw.

However, if the fish turns towards the angler, then the chances of the fly being pulled out of the fish's mouth will be greatly increased, because as the fish turns and heads downstream the current will start to pull the fly out of the fish's mouth, particularly if it is still open. If these fish are hooked at all, it is usually in the lower or upper lip, and as a result the hooks frequently come out.

Feeding slack line to a fish that has taken and moved forward in the same instant will only hook the fish if the current is strong enough to pull the line downstream before the fish starts to tail back in the current. If the current is strong, however, the hooks may be pulled in while the fish is still moving forward, but if the current is slow, then the fish may start to tail back at a faster rate than the flow, and if this happens the chance of the hooks being pulled out of the salmon's mouth will greatly increase. The overriding factor with the slack line method is the way in which the fish takes our fly – this and this alone will determine whether or not it will be hooked and it is this uncertainty that makes me shy clear of using it.

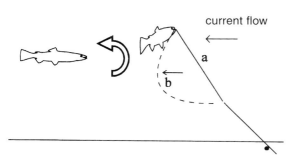

Fig 44 The fish that turns away from the angler.

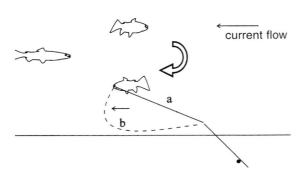

Fig 45 *The fish that turns towards the angler.*

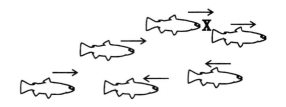

Fig 46 *The fish that takes and moves forward at the same time.*

Fish that move forward, suck in your fly and then keep moving forward before tailing back downstream in the current are the very devil to hook, because the chances are that they will have ejected your fly before they have tailed back far enough for it to register as a pull on the line. It is very difficult to detect these takes, because very often the fish will merely suck the fly in and carry it forward in a pocket of water between its open jaws. The only indication that the angler gets with this taking behaviour is a feeling similar to that when the fly comes into a slack dead section of water. If you suspect that this type of take has occurred then start pulling in the line at a good rate of knots, feeling for the fish as you do so. If it has closed its mouth you will feel the fish and the rod should be lifted into it, but if the fish keeps its mouth open the chances of hooking it will not be good, because all we will be doing is pulling the fly out of the fish's open jaws. Watch the two or three yards of line that you have just pulled in and don't let it get tangled around anything, because if you do feel the fish, and tighten into it, it generally disappears quickly once it realizes what is going on.

Practitioners of the slack line method point out that if the water temperature is on the low side, during the spring or late autumn, the fish will come to and turn on the fly in a much slower fashion. This I can accept and if there is a time to give slack then this is it, but many who fish the slack line method also do so during the warmer summer months. This

I cannot accept, because this is when we should in actual fact be lifting into the fish, and not feeding line, because the fish will be rising to the fly much more quickly due to the warmer water temperatures. Many anglers who fish for grilse complain that they are very difficult to hook. If they are the same people who are in the habit of giving line then I am not at all surprised, because these fish usually rise and snap at flies in a trout-like fashion and so should be tightened into. I do not know of any trout anglers who feed line!

My own preferred method of hooking salmon is to tighten by lifting the rod progressively into them. Until someone can prove to me that a salmon takes a spinning bait differently from a fly then I am quite content to lift the rod and pull the hooks home as soon as I feel the slightest resistance. Anyway with the small modern outpoint trebles the force needed for them to penetrate beyond the barb is minimal and the force transmitted along the line that tells the angler that a fish has mouthed his fly is usually enough for these hooks to take hold. At this point I merely lift the rod until I feel the weight of the fish. I see no logical reason for feeding a fish slack that already has taken my fly into its mouth, and given it a good tug. I have yet to meet anyone who, when spinning for salmon, pulls a yard or so of line off their reel at the moment of the take. The governing factor that determines how well fish are hooked with any method employed is the direction in which it moves or turns after it has taken the fly. Since we seldom see the take there is no 'one' right way or wrong way, there is only the preferred way.

Without any doubt, if the fish turns away from the bank from which the angler is fishing, the fish will

Some anglers will fish with the rod tip held high. I do not favour this method.

be well hooked, but if it turns towards the bank or moves forward in the same instant, then the chances of it being hooked well will not be so good. I can recall fishing one day late in the season on my local river when a run of fish came into the stretch I was fishing. I hooked, played and lost five fish, all within the space of a few hours. At the time I put it down to just bad luck, but on reflection four of the fish that took turned towards me and were on for only a very short period of time. The final fish of the day turned away from me and was only lost at the very last minute, when the hooks came away, just as I bent down to tail it out. This instance in itself might not prove much, but since then I have been more observant when it comes to the direction in which a fish turns or moves in relation to where I am fishing from. I have come to the conclusion that the only way to deal with most fish is to lift the rod progressively into them immediately they are felt. Most of the fish which turn towards me after taking the fly, if tightened into at once, are nearly all hooked in the top left-hand side of the mouth, whereas the ones that are tightened into that turn away from me are

almost without exception hooked in the corner of the right-hand jaw. In both cases the hooks very often have to be cut out.

Some fish will merely pluck at the fly, and as far as I am concerned this is connected with the feeding instinct. I believe that this occurs when fish are very fresh run and still have their feeding instinct

The moment of the take as the line is lifted off the water.

Playing a summer grilse on the Spey.

Almost ready to beach.

The fish heads upstream.

The fish is drawn ashore ready to be tailed out.

Safely ashore. If you are intending keeping your fish take it well away from the water's edge before killing it.

intact – they are merely touching and tasting; this type of taking fish is very difficult to hook.

One method that works reasonably well is to keep the dressing well within the bend of the hook, a solution which came to me one day by pure chance. I had been fishing away most of the day and was becoming very frustrated, because I had hooked and pricked a good number of these 'devils'. I tried all sorts, changing up, changing down, tightening and yes, feeding slack line, but all to no avail. After a while I went full circle and returned to the fly that I had started the day with, a small Silver Stoat's Tail tied on half an inch of biro refill. After tying the treble to the line I pushed the hook right into the end of the tube. The bends of the treble were now hard against the end of the tube. Next time down the pool I took a fish of 16lb, firmly hooked in the roof of the mouth, and lost two others during play. The only difference now was that the hooks were within the hair, whereas before they

Fishing with a high rod point and loop.

Fishing 'off the reel'. With this method the rod point should be kept low, to allow the fish to take line easily. After a few yards is taken the line is clamped to the handle of the rod, to set the hooks.

The fly line coming to the dangle. There are probably more fish hooked and lost from this taking position than any other.

had extended about half an inch beyond the end of the tube.

The one take that I have not mentioned yet is the one that occurs when the fly has come to the dangle below the angler. If the fly comes to the end of its swim and merely hovers with the force of the current, any fish that do take at this time are usually not well hooked. I suspect that they have followed the fly round and for some reason remain uncertain right up to the last moment whether to take or not. The take if it does come is generally a tentative one, with the fish being very lightly hooked on the end of their nose. One method that I now use to overcome these tentative takes on the dangle is to increase the fly's water speed by pulling in a yard or so of line before the fly gets to the dangle. This action usually results in the fish being well hooked, possibly because it arouses the fish's predatory instinct as it sees the fly escaping and heading off upstream. By speeding the fly up and pulling it away from the fish we usually get a much more positive response.

Not all fish respond to the fly in the same fashion – the four fish that turned towards me in the incident described earlier all took in a similar way, but this I think is extremely rare. I have witnessed fish from the same group reacting to the fly in com-

pletely different fashions, with some turning away and others turning towards me. I have tried to tabulate results from my diaries to see if the different takes fall into a specific pattern in relation to light conditions, time of day, freshness of fish, or clarity of the water, but there appears to be no consistency.

I have tried all the other methods of hooking fish. One is the rod point held high to create droop, with line held between index finger and the rod handle being released the instant a fish takes. Another method tried was holding the rod at the point of balance, with the handle tucked under my arm, the theory being that by the time I had felt the fish and moved the rod into the standard position the time delay between one position and the other would be enough for the fish to turn. One technique used was fishing off the reel. This method allows fish to take line directly from the reel and then, after perhaps a yard or more has been pulled off, the line is clamped against the handle and lifted into them. Bill Currie uses this method with great success and describes it as 'letting the reel speak'.

I have discovered that the last two techniques work relatively well when fishing with the sinking line and large flies early or late in the season, but after thirty years of fishing for salmon on the fly I

Mary playing a spirited fish which took an orange Waddington on a cold late autumn day.

prefer to tighten as soon as I feel the fish. Each method works well at times, but no method seems to work all the time and it is therefore just a question of trying each technique, and sticking to the one that most often produces the desired results. Tightening at once is my choice, because for me the hooking-to-landing ratio is far greater using this technique than any of the other methods described and tried. I like to use methods which I have confidence in and by tightening into fish as soon as I feel them I have landed over 70 per cent of all fish hooked, whether they took small flies fished just subsurface on a floater or a two-inch tube on a sinker.

PLAYING *(Fig 47)*

The whole object of playing a fish should be that the fight can be brought to a conclusion as quickly as possible, the fish being played but not played with. It is extremely bad practice to play a fish for longer than is necessary, this bad habit merely turning the taking of a fish into a game for our own personal pleasure. Salmon fishing is not a game, it is a field sport that usually ends in a creature's death. The salmon I catch are killed quickly and as humanely as possible, ending up on someone's table and so becoming part of the food chain. The anti-fishing fraternity will argue that we are causing the fish needless suffering, but a quick, humane death at the hands of an angler is in my opinion better than being eaten alive in the clutches of a seal.

For some reason, many novices when they hook their first salmon are over-cautious and do not put enough pressure on the fish, perhaps feeling that if they bend into it they will be more likely to lose it. Very often quite the reverse is true since by not applying pressure the chances of the hooks coming out will be greatly increased. The length of time that a fish is played will generally be determined by the condition of the fish, the water temperature and the pace of the current in which the fish is being played. It might be assumed that a fresh-run fish will give a better account of itself than a stale one that has been in a pool for some time but this is very often not the case. If the water is at such a level as to allow fish to run, the chances are that any fresh fish taken at this time will be tired by having to come up through rough water or by having to ascend a number of obstacles. These fresh-run fish, however, when rested up in a pool for a short time will be a very different proposition.

Stale or resident fish at the back end which have left the lower holding pools and are running further upstream will also be tired, perhaps more so, since they will have lost much of their reserves over the previous weeks or months. The first salmon that my wife ever hooked was one of these tired, stale fellows and it did not give a good account of itself, merely wallowing about and going belly up after a short time. It was very much an anti-climax, because she had read books praising the great fighting prowess that these fish have and watched salmon fishing videos displaying fish ripping yards of line from the reel. This was not to mention listening to my own tales of epic battles! (Her next fish thankfully was a different story.)

The water temperature also affects the way that a fish fights, not so much because the fish is a cold-blooded creature, but because of the amount of dissolved oxygen available at a given time. Fish taken when the water temperature is high put up much less resistance than a fish hooked in cold water. This is evident in the way that spring or autumn fish fight when the water temperature is either just starting to warm up or cool down. During periods of low warm water any fish that do get caught do not usually fight to their full potential and can generally be landed relatively quickly compared to a similar-sized fish caught at a time when the water temperature is that little bit cooler. This is of course assuming that both fish came from the same pool at the same height of water and had rested before being hooked.

The pace of current in a pool will also determine the playing time. If a fish is made to fight both current and rod it will tire quickly, but if there is no current to speak of the only thing that the fish has to fight is the energy stored in the flexing of the rod. These fish take more time to tire, which means that

the chances of losing them will increase in relation to the time for which they are being played. The playing of a fish begins the instant that the rod is raised and bent against it. No two salmon are exactly the same when they come to being played and so each fish should be treated on its merits. Some authorities who have put pen to paper have given playing times to the pound weight of fish, for example a minute to the pound. This statement is absolute nonsense. The playing time of a fish does not depend on its size as some might think, but on a unique set of circumstances that affect both the fish and the angler.

Before an angler even wets his line he should be looking for a suitable place from which he can play and land his fish. As soon as the rod bends under the weight of the fish the angler should be starting to make his way to the place that he previously decided to play it from. By adopting this approach of preparing and clearing likely looking landing spots I have been able to successfully land fish that would have been very difficult, if not impossible, to land otherwise. I remember one particular occurrence when I cleared away a lot of long grass from a small sandy bay before fishing down a pool. I was asked at the time by my wife Mary what I was doing, to which I replied 'this is where I am going to land my fish'. Although I got a strange look, within the hour I had beached my fish. So often I have seen anglers get themselves into trouble when this could easily have been avoided, if only a little thought had gone into selecting and clearing a suitable place to make their stand, prior to fishing down the pool.

Having hooked our fish and got to the spot from where we have decided to play it, the next thing that happens generally depends on how the fish reacts. One author of a book that I started to read said that if a fish ran downstream on its first run, the likelihood was that it was not fresh. I had never read such rubbish and needless to say I have still to finish the book. Most of the fresh fish that I have hooked, or seen anyone else hooking, have almost without exception run downstream. Is this not the natural response from a fish that has just come from a 'safe' pool and is fighting for its very life as an unseen force pulls against it? This downstream run is no more than a bid for self-preservation and nothing to do with the freshness of the fish. Resident fish that have been in a pool for some time when hooked do not generally try to leave the pool in which they are hooked. Possibly this is because they are very familiar with the underwater geography and know all the places of safety within the pool.

If fish are hooked near the tail of the pool they will more often than not try to leave it and get into the fast, streamy water below. There are two main ways of dealing with this situation; one is to hold the fish hard and try to stop it, and the other, usually the more successful way, is to simply ease up on the pressure. Easing up on the pressure may not seem the logical thing to do, but if we analyse it more closely then in fact it makes more sense than leaning into the fish. As I explained earlier it is the pulling of the line that causes the fish to panic, and not the hook. On easing up the fish generally perform an about turn and head back into the main body of the pool, on occasions to the very lie from which they came. I have tried both methods and by far the more successful is easing up.

Many anglers seem to think that in order to exert maximum pressure the rod should be raised to or beyond the vertical and bent until the rod creaks. This is in fact a common misconception, since the maximum pressure is in fact exerted when the rod is at a much lower angle. The following experiment was carried out using my Bruce & Walker 15ft Expert and a spring balance. The spring balance was anchored to a suitable point and the rod butt

held at various angles to the horizontal. The rod was then bent until no more pressure could be exerted. Maximum pressure of 8lb was registered when the butt of the rod was at an angle of 30 degrees to the horizontal, while minimum pressure was measured when the butt of the rod was at an angle of 120 degrees to the horizontal, 2lb. The best angle of the rod is therefore somewhere between the 60 and 90 degree position, as this will allow the rod to act as a cushion and absorb the lunges of the fish, especially during the later stages of the fight when the fish is at close quarters.

The pressure exerted on the rod when held at different angles

Angle of rod (degrees)	Pressure
30	8lb
45	5lb 3oz
60	3lb
90	2lb 8oz
120	2lb

Once we get the fish back into the main body of the pool, we must try to get below or opposite the fish so that we can keep it on the move by continually trying to pull it off balance. If we do not do this it will just sit in the current expending very little effort. By continually upsetting its equilibrium it must fight in order to stay out in the current and by so doing will be contending with both the rod and

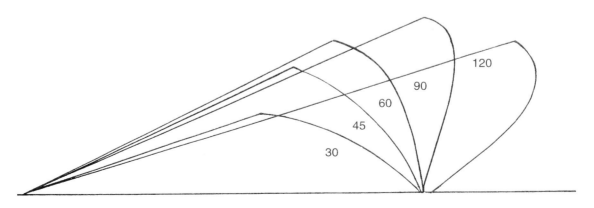

Fig 47 The pressure on the rod at different angles.

Mary tempts fate by keeping her rod tip too low as a heavy fish boils the surface.

flow. Do not let a fish get its head down and 'sulk', always try and keep its head up. The whole object of playing a fish is to let it run when it likes, and then work it back in again. By doing this the fish will very soon tire and start to wallow about on the surface. Usually the first sign of a fish becoming tired is the tail appearing out of the water as the fish performs a slow, semi-submerged underwater cartwheel. Once this occurs it will not be long before it starts to show its belly. Shortly after this it will go belly up and lie motionless on the surface – the time has now come to land our prize.

LANDING

The two most widely used landing aids on the market today are the landing net, and the mechanical tailer. When choosing a net make sure that it is of a reputable make. The best landing net is the type with a fixed head, though the Gye type, where the head slides down the shaft, comes a close second. When it comes to tailers I have an inherent distrust of them, but I do know of some anglers who swear by them. Again, choose one from a reputable company, as the cheaper makes on the market have a

tendency to fail just when you need them most.

My own preference when it comes to landing fish is to hand tail them whenever possible. When hand tailing a fish there are two commonly practised methods. The first of these is to grip the fish around its tail wrist with the index finger and thumb positioned towards the tail end. The other, and the one that I prefer, is to place the index finger and thumb so that they are positioned on the torso side of the wrist, which I feel gives a more secure hold. This is because clasping a fish in this way means you have a little 'extra' fish to grip if it starts to object and struggle. With the thumb and index finger positioned towards the torso it will not be so easy for it to slip out of your grasp. If on the other hand you place your forefinger and thumb at the tail end of the wrist and the fish starts to slip, you do not have very much wrist left to re-establish your grip. It will therefore not be long before your fingers start sliding up along the outer edge the tail, and when this occurs it is impossible to maintain your grasp. In order to tail our fish it must be completely played out and lying quite motionless, for if it is not, as soon as it feels your touch it will react by thrashing violently. If it does so do not panic, simply let the fish calm down before attempting it again.

When playing a fish keep the rod tip up. By doing this it acts like a spring and absorbs any lunges that a fish might make.

Sea-trout are a bonus when salmon are scarce. This one fell to a worm below the Old Spey Bridge.

When tailing out a fish it is best to place the index finger and thumb on the torso side of the tail as shown. If the fish is a large one it is better to push it ashore before attempting to lift it.

Do not attempt to lift a fish ashore by letting the handle take the strain, it is far better to slide your hand down the shaft as shown. By doing this your net will last longer.

Another technique used where there is a shallow shelving bank is beaching. This, like tailing, must only be attempted when the fish is completely played out. To beach a fish we start by drawing it slowly towards the bank. As the fish approaches it should be kept on the move until its head is brought out and onto the bank. At this stage it is a simple matter of quietly walking up behind the fish and lifting it out. The fish can then either be lifted out by hand tailing or, in the case of a large one, by pushing it up the bank and then lifting. When beaching a fish it is best to place oneself downstream of it and get into the water, so that the fish's head can be pulled up onto the bank by bringing the rod round in towards the bank on which the fish is being landed. By approaching the fish in this fashion the pressure from the rod will continue to keep the fish's head ashore.

In places where tailing or beaching is not possible a net can be used to great effect, but it should only be used by someone experienced. I have seen many fish lost by anglers who were in too big a hurry to get their fish ashore, or were trying to get their fish into the net from the wrong position. When netting a fish it should be played out and belly up, something many anglers seem to forget. Having a net seems to encourage anglers to try to net out fish that are still full of fight and a long way from being beaten.

To net a fish successfully it is best to get downstream of it and submerge the head of the net before making any attempt at bringing the fish over it. The fish, if played out, can then be drifted over the rim of the waiting net by gently easing back on the pressure and letting the current do the work. When the fish is over the rim of the net it should be lifted in one positive movement. Once it is in the net do not try to lift the net ashore by letting the handle take the strain. Slide your hand down the shaft and lift the fish ashore in the mesh of the net by transferring your grip to the rim. This will save you bending the shaft of your net and stop the shaft from revolving. If this occurs the net head will spin and as a result could possibly dump the fish back into the river. Netting a fish takes skill and only comes with practice.

I can recall the first time that my wife Mary acted as ghillie. We were sharing a rod on a medium productive beat of the Stinchar in Ayrshire when I got into a fish in a difficult place. We were fishing a pool called the Dangart, a pool which sits on a right-hand bend and has a good, long, heavy stream at its head. The tail, which is very deep, has many boils and swirls on the surface, indicating the boulders and 'nasties' that lie beneath. It then turns slowly along the left bank creating a fast glide at its tail. A lot of the pool is unfishable from the left bank due to the bank erosion of some previous winter spate and it also goes vertical, straight down into deep, swirling water.

The section of the pool that we were interested in was where the head stream starts to slow as it flows into the main body and runs down the right-hand bank around the bend. In order to fish this part of the pool properly it is essential to wade and wade deep. This is difficult because there is a gravel bed down the centre with the bottom falling away on both sides into deep water. Deep wading is necessary here if you are to present your flies properly to fish lying on the inside bend under the opposite bank. As I waded into position, fish were showing along the run on the far side and, making my way carefully down the central gravel shelf, I lengthened line. It was difficult to cover fish properly, but by S mending my Wet Cel II as soon as it landed I was happy knowing that my flies were fishing reasonably well in the vicinity of where the fish were showing.

After about a dozen casts my line went tight. What a situation, deep water to the sides and front. Slowly edging back upstream I gingerly made my way out and back along the bank in order to get opposite the fish. The fish, however, had other ideas and headed for the tail of the pool. Since I could not follow it all I could do was stand my ground and after some crafty manoeuvring I managed to make it about turn. As it did so it headed for the far side, where it exhibited itself in a flurry of spray. After a further few uneventful minutes it went belly up and was ready for the net. It was a dreadful place to land a fish, no shelving banking or back eddy, only deep swirling water. Hand tailing was totally out of the question.

'OK', I said to Mary, 'you net it'. The first

A 12lb fish that fell to a Yellow Belly.

attempt at netting was not successful, the fish objecting violently by splashing and thrashing the surface. After it had calmed down I said 'right, place the net in the water and then when the fish is brought over the rim, lift'. This time it was tossed in the air like a pancake. 'Oh dear', I thought! 'Right, let's forget the net', I said. 'See that small clearing among the grass, when I get its head into that you pick it up'. 'OK', she replied. In came the fish, up slid its head, so down went Mary. 'Have you got it?' I asked. 'Yes', she replied. On hearing this I about turned and started to make my way up the banking.

On reaching the top I turned around to see how she was getting on, only to discover that she had not tailed the fish, but had instead picked it up the only way a mother knows how, by cuddling it in both arms. The fish, however, was not falling for any of her charms as it kicked and jumped it's way out of her grasp back into the water, only this time not attached to the hook. This is a true and accurate account of a pantomime that generally occurs when someone lacks the necessary experience. Since the incident mentioned Mary has mastered the art and netted numerous fish for me, in fact she now nets fish better than some ghillies I know.

Since many rivers now have their main runs of fish entering them during the autumn it stands to reason that many will be hooked that are long past their best. Even many new silver bright fish bearing sea lice running into the rivers at this time will be heavy with milt or roe. These fish on occasions are all too easily caught and because of this we should exercise some self-restraint and take only what we need. There is no use filling the freezer with fish that are only days away from spawning. The decision to kill a fish used to be chiefly a matter of one's conscience, but a recent case in 1991, where a ghillie was convicted of possessing 'unclean or unseasonable' fish in 1991, should make anglers think twice before administering any last rites to fish full of roe of milt. The conviction was overturned by the Appeal Court in 1995, but since the initial case went to court there has been a great deal of controversy regarding the term 'unseasonable'. Until the case came to light most anglers regarded 'unseasonable' fish to be either kelts or baggots caught early in the season, or any other fish caught out with the legal rod season. According to Lord Justice General Hope, the residing appeal judge, however, salmon could only be described as being 'unseasonable' when either their milt or roe could be stripped by pressing the fish's belly gently towards the vent. This decision consequently means that any fish, whether new into the river and bearing sea lice, (which can occur in the late autumn), or stale coloured fish that have been in the river for some time, if killed, could render the angler responsible liable to prosecution.

If we intend returning any fish we catch then we must use a safe method of landing. Any fish that is to be returned should never be beached on rough gravel or stone as these will cause skin damage and allow infection into any open wounds that may have been inflicted. I only beach fish that I am intending to return on soft mud. Netting fish also causes skin damage, specially if the mesh is of the knotted variety. Nets with knotless mesh are not so lethal, but they still graze skin and remove protective mucus, therefore nets should only be used as a last resort. The best method of all, if the fish lies quietly, is to unhook it while it is still in the water, but this is not always possible. The next best alter-

native is to gently hand tail the fish out on to a soft, grassy patch where the hooks can be quickly removed with the aid of forceps.

When handling fish do not cause any blood loss; if it bleeds heavily, knock it on the head. Some anglers have their hearts in the right place and intend returning their fish, but during the process of returning them they keep them out of the water longer than necessary, perhaps to take a photograph. If you must have a photo of your prize get someone else to take it while you are removing the hooks or, better still, as you return it to the water. Keeping fish out of the water for longer than necessary is inhuman. Be particularly careful when handling them; don't squeeze them, since if you do, you may hear a squeal coming from a burst air bladder which will cause the fish to die. I should point out that the 'grunting' from a dead fish is caused by expanding gases and not a burst air bladder; the two should not be confused.

When returning fish never 'throw them back' – they must be held in the water in the recovery position, with their heads facing into the flow and supported upright by placing one hand under the pectoral fins and the other around the wrist of their tail. Keep them in this position until they regain their strength; when their energy returns they will give a strong kick and swim off. The recovery time needed seems to vary from fish to fish, but the one thing that I have noticed is that if they are not ready they will not swim away. Under no circumstances push a fish back and forth in the flow: this does not speed up the recovery time and doing so will only open the gill covers in the wrong direction and tear the gill filaments, causing them to bleed. If the gills are damaged the fish will die.

Finally if you decide to keep your catch knock it on the head before doing anything else, and this includes removing the hooks.

20 SPINNING TACKLE

A long rod enables you to keep your back straight. There is nothing worse than trying to straighten up after many hours fishing hunched over the handle of a rod.

Although I prefer to fish with a fly rod there are times and places where this is just not possible due to water conditions or the bank being lined with trees or bushes. In these situations it is time to bring out the spinning tackle. When it comes to choice of rod I prefer one of 10ft for a number of reasons. A long rod means that you do not have to stoop while retrieving a lure while with a short one you have to bend in order to keep the rod point down to retrieve the bait properly. Short rods only pain the lower back and none of us are getting any younger.

Through the years I have noticed that by using a long rod and staying well back from the water's edge, particularly when fishing medium to small rivers, I have caught fish that I do not think I would otherwise have taken.

Some years ago when I used to spin with a short rod I saw a lot of fish following the lure round out of the current in towards the bank that I was standing on, and then at the last minute turn away as they caught sight of me. By watching fish respond in this way to my presence I began to question the effectiveness of a short rod. When I started using the longer rod and kept well back from the edge out of sight, more fish continued to pursue and grab my lure, at times intercepting the lure only inches from the bank. Another advantage of the longer rod is that it enables me to stick the tip section through any obstructing foliage and flick my choice of lure to any likely looking sections of water where a salmon may be lying. By being able to do this I have caught fish that I am certain I could not have hoped to have taken with a short rod. In saying this I have ended up getting myself into some terrible messes and on more than one occasion I have been unable to follow lively and spirited fish that have decided to leave the pool.

On small rivers some anglers might prefer to fish with a small rod of 7ft or 8ft, I do not. Many small spate streams, particularly those in the south-west of Scotland, have a run of fish known locally as greybacks. These are late season, heavy, fresh-run

fish from 15 to 30lb. These fish fight like tigers and anyone who has ever hooked one of them in a fast-flowing river will know the strength and stamina that one is up against. It is these fish that many autumn salmon anglers dream of catching.

BUYING A SPINNING ROD

When it comes to purchasing a spinning rod buy the best that you can afford at the time. For some unknown reason many anglers seem to subject their spinning rods to more punishment than they would ever think of administering to their fly rods. Some might be thinking that this could be a good reason for buying a cheap one, but a cheap rod will not last as long or stand up to the punishment. I have two, a Hardy 10ft Fibalite which I use for fishing smallish rivers with a fixed spool reel and a Bruce & Walker 10ft Multispin which I use with a multiplier for

Spinning a Devon Minnow through Kenmure Pool on the River Tarf.

rivers such as the Tay or Spey. If anything, I am inclined to cosset my rods, but a friend whom I regularly fish with is not as caring and subjects his Multispin to all sorts of things, which at times make me cringe. I have seen his rod take some punishment through the years and that in itself is a good advertisement for its build quality, a cheap rod not being able to stand up to the same level of abuse!

SPINNING REELS *(Figs 48–9)*

There are two types of reel available, the *fixed spool* and the *multiplier*.

Fixed Spool

For all of my spate stream salmon spinning I prefer a fixed spool type. These fixed spool reels, as the name suggests, operate by keeping the drum onto which the nylon is wound stationary. They operate on the bobbin principle, where an arm, a bail arm in this case, revolves around as well as up and down the drum. By moving the bail arm in this fashion the nylon is wound evenly onto the drum. This puts down one layer at a time over the entire width of the drum, so that when the lure or bait is cast the nylon peels off easily.

When buying a reel pick one of reputable make. I have used a Mitchell 300 now for almost twenty-five years. It lacks some of the features found on some of the more modern reels, but I am happy using it and this is important. The one thing that I do find a little bit of a nuisance is the drag adjustment control, which is positioned on top of the drum. This adjustment control sometimes proves to be a bit of a drag (pardon the pun), especially when I have to adjust it quickly if a fish starts to splash about on a short line during the final stages of play. My wife uses the rear drag version of this reel,

A selection of modern fixed spool reels and multipliers, the size of the river and lure being fished dictating which type is used.

which is excellent. Other makes of fixed spool reels worth considering are Abu and Shimano. Regardless of which make you decide on, I would recommend that you purchase at least two other spools.

In order to be prepared for most water conditions I would suggest that you load each of the spools with the following breaking strains – 8lb, 12lb and 15lb. By having spools loaded with different gauges of nylon we will able to cast a wide variety of bait weights easily in different heights of water. A small lightweight bait fished with a heavy gauge monofilament line will not fish properly and will appear less attractive.

The one major problem with fixed spool reels is the amount of line twisting they produce. One way of overcoming it to some extent is to wind the nylon from the spool to the drum so that the line comes off the spool in the same rotational direction as the bail arm. This is not a perfect method, mainly because of the fact that the spool and the drum are generally of different diameters, resulting in an occasional phase difference. However, this method does help to eliminate some twisting.

Before starting to transfer the nylon from the spool to the drum of the reel, tie the nylon to the drum of the spinning reel by using the same knot that I described for attaching the backing to the drum of the fly reel (*see* page 53). Since the diameter of the nylon is smaller than the backing it is a good idea to use more than one overhand knot; I use three, one placed on top of the other. This gives a good head for the loop to be pulled up against. Once the knot is secure the spool can be filled. In order to

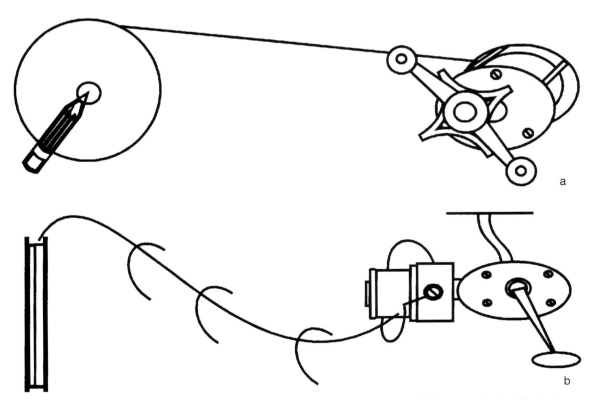

Fig 48 Spinning reels. (a) The correct method of loading line onto a multiplier reel. (b) One method of eliminating line twist with a fixed spool reel is to wind the nylon off the dispenser in the same rotational direction as the bail arm of the reel.

allow the line to feed off the drum smoothly we must load the correct amount. Too little nylon and the lure will not be cast with ease, while too much will cause the line to peel off the rim of the spool too easily, causing coiling, which will result in tangling. For best results the spool should only be filled to about ⅛in (3mm) from the edge of the rim.

The first patented reel to use this style of line retrieve was the Illingworth, invented by and named after Alfred Holden Illingworth. As far as I am concerned this type of reel is possibly the main reason for so many people taking up fishing. More often than not the first rod and reel that someone buys, or gets a go with, is a spinning outfit equipped with a fixed spool reel and this is an ideal way of introducing someone to the sport. After being instructed in the basics of how to use this tackle most people very quickly become familiar with the mechanics of casting, and in no time at all are fishing lures relatively well through fish-holding water. I believe that if newcomers are to become 'hooked' it is imperative that success comes early. I introduced my wife to the sport using a spinning rod with a fixed spool reel and she quickly got the hang of it with initial success coming quickly, and from then on it was difficult to get her to put the spinning rod to one side and start persevering with the fly. However, it is important not to become glued to only one method of fishing.

Multiplier Reels

When fishing a large, wide river with a spinning rod, the multiplier reel is without equal. These reels allow a lure to be cast substantial distances, much further than could be achieved with a fixed spool type. They are also less prone to line twist. This is due mainly to the way that the line is wound around the drum. Unlike the fixed spool reel where the line peels off the side of the drum, the line on a multiplier feeds directly off and on to a rotating drum. When winding nylon on to the reel put a pencil through the centre hole of the spool and position it so that it runs square to the drum of the reel and take the nylon so that it comes from the top of the spool. This means that when the nylon gets wound on to the drum of the reel, the spool will rotate in a clockwise direction, in other words wind the nylon off the spool onto the multiplier reel in the very fashion not recommended for loading a fixed spool reel. In addition, keep the nylon under tension during the transfer process. Although the amount you load is not as critical as when loading line on to a fixed spool reel, the nylon should be taken to about ⅛in (3mm) off the lip of the drum.

The main advantage that the multiplier has over

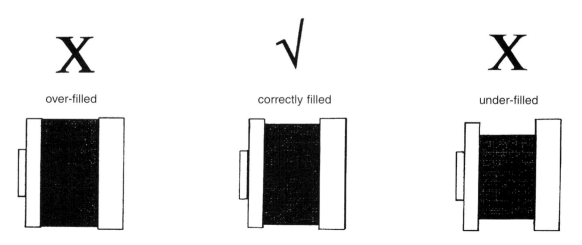

Fig 49 Fill the spool with the correct amount of line to ensure trouble-free casting.

A fish on the multiplier from the Barjarg beat of the Nith. This fish, although fresh run, was showing a small patch of UDN on one side of its head.

a fixed spool reel is that any loss of nylon does not affect the ease with which the line comes off the drum, in other words we do not lose any distance when casting. Multipliers come in many shapes and sizes. When buying choose one that will take a good amount of line, 200m (220yards) or more of 18 to 20lb. Also, purchase one of reputable make such as Shimano or Abu, both of which are excellent and will give many years of service. My own choice is the Ambassadeur models 6001 C and the 6501 C-3. These are the left-hand wind versions of the world famous 6000. When it comes to left- or right-hand wind models it is really a question of personal choice, though personally speaking I can see no advantage in winding with the right hand.

SWIVELS *(Figs 50–3)*

The swivel is one of the most important items of spinning tackle. Its main function is to provide a rotating link between the main spinning line and the lure. Basically, a swivel consists of two independent rotating spindles with their bearing points contained inside the same housing. If we were to fish without one on our line it would very quickly become a nightmare to fish with and control. This is because as soon as any slack appears in the line, it will try to form itself into loops and coils which strongly attract each other. When this happens the only solution is to disconnect the swivel and lure and walk the line off the reel out across a field and then rewind it slowly back onto the reel. By having to do this we are wasting fishing time, which on a spate stream is sacrilege as on some rivers the water only remains fishable for a very short period of time. Any 'spinning' lure which is retrieved will have a tendency to cause some twisting of the line, this being true even of lures which wobble. However, a spinning lure like a Devon Minnow, which is designed to rotate through its own axis is particularly bad and will very quickly kink and

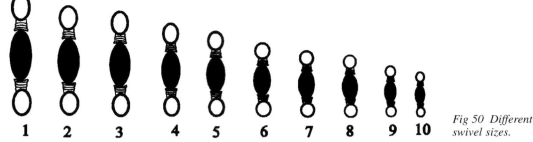

Fig 50 Different swivel sizes.

twist the line if a good-quality swivel is not used.

There are three types of swivel generally available: *ball bearing, barrel* and *roller*. The first of these is without doubt the best, but is however very expensive, while the barrel type has the annoying habit of picking up suspended matter between the casing and the spindles, which restricts its action. I prefer the roller type as they are a fraction of the cost of the ball bearing and seldom become sticky due to suspended matter. If a swivel does become jammed the rotating action of the spindles will very soon become impeded. Due to the laws of mechanics no swivel is perfect and cannot operate without some friction having to be overcome. The test of a good swivel is how good it is at stopping line twist when a lure is retrieved in a fast flow. A fast flow has more energy than a slow flow and therefore any

stickiness between the rotational parts and the body will have to be reduced to a minimum. In order to achieve this the best swivels have very little lateral movement of the eyelet. This is because in a fast flow the lure will rise and fall with the buffeting effect of the current, causing the spindle of the swivel to follow the lure. When this happens the eyelet in relation to the body of the swivel will change, meaning that the rotational plane of the spindle will also change and not run true in the hole in which it is rotating.

This means that the spindle will rub against the inside casing, creating friction, which will needless to say cause line twist. Since there is no guarantee of the lure staying in line with the rotating spindle it is best to anchor one end of the swivel, and this is best done with the use of a pierced bullet and a wire

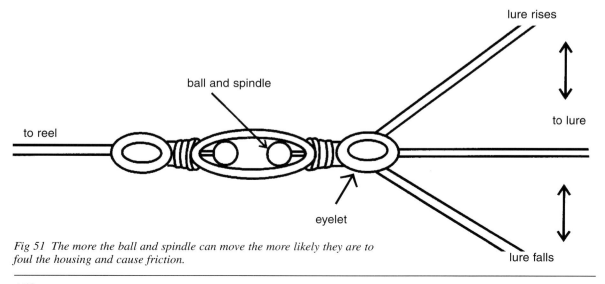

Fig 51 The more the ball and spindle can move the more likely they are to foul the housing and cause friction.

clip, for example a Hillman lead-type anti-kink weight. Lead bullets are no longer legal so we have to use the modern zinc equivalents. Size for size they are not so heavy, but they still do the job. There is no need to buy all the different sizes available – I buy only four sizes – 10, 8, 6 and 4 sixteenths. These four sizes are adequate for covering all the conditions you are ever likely to encounter.

SPINNING LURES

There is a bewildering assortment of spinning lures to choose from. With modern manufacturing techniques tackle companies have not been slow to exploit the angler's constant search for the ultimate lure. Some lures have stood the test of time, while others have quickly fallen by the wayside. It is not my intention here to highlight all the types of lure available, because I would need an entire book on the subject alone, but I will cover the ones that I have found to be the most effective.

10/16	8/16	6/16	4/16

Fig 52 Anti-kink weights.

Devon Minnow *(Figs 54–5)*

The Devon Minnow without any doubt is unequalled in spinning lures as a fish catcher. Why this is so I am really not sure, but I suspect it is because of the stroboscopic effect as the Minnow revolves around its own axis, this especially being so with a brightly coloured one such as a Yellow Belly. There has been much speculation as to exactly what these Devon Minnows represent since their spinning action is too quick to simulate an injured fish. One of the most popular beliefs is that the lure was originally designed to resemble a squid. It has even been suggested that contemporary anglers fish it the wrong way round on the mount, but

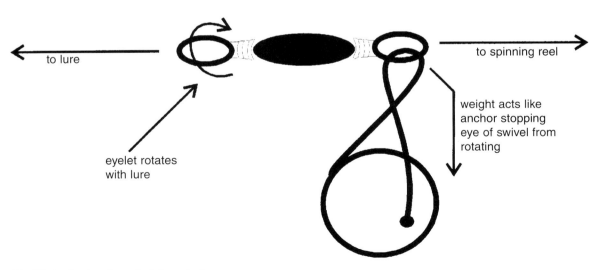

to lure

eyelet rotates
with lure

to spinning reel

weight acts like
anchor stopping
eye of swivel from
rotating

Fig 53 Anchoring the end of the swivel.

regardless of which way it should be fished it is excellent at provoking fish into taking.

Devon Minnows are made from a wide variety of materials such as metal, wood and plastic, and they come in many shapes, sizes and weights. This means that we can choose the type which is just right for the conditions. Although I now only use a spinner in

very high and dirty water a small lightweight Minnow fished slow, just subsurface, can be a very effective lure for summer salmon. For most of my high-water spinning I use a Minnow which has a plastic body, with either a lead or copper core. In a fast flow I am happy fishing with a conventionally shaped Minnow, but in a slow current I prefer one

When spinning in dirty water periodically check your swivel and anti-kink weight, as these often pick up suspended rubbish, which if not removed will almost certainly impair their efficiency.

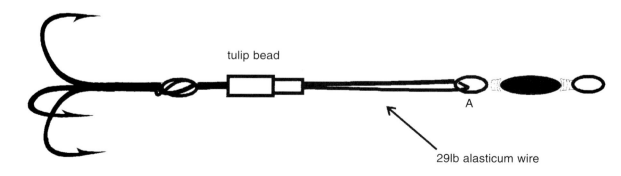

tulip bead

A

29lb alasticum wire

Fig 54 How to make a trace. (1) Cut a length of wire and pass through eye A of the swivel. (2) Push a tulip bead onto the wire. (3) Pass each end of wire through different sides of the hook eyelet by about 2in (5cm). Next turn both ends in the same direction around the shank. (4) Now holding the treble hook carefully, put a needle through eye A and twist until the wire goes tight.

with a bulkier body such as the Severn or Sprat style. Through the years I have come to favour the ones manufactured by Gordon & Griffiths and Bruce & Walker, in sizes ranging from 1½ to 3in (40–70mm) in length because both makes have fins that are integral parts of the body. By being part of the body construction they do not break off easily if they become stuck up on something. I also like the metal minnows with their large elephant ear-like fins. These fins can be bent to make the Minnow fish slower or faster depending on the current. I like these when using the multiplier reel as they are of sufficient weight to be cast on their own.

The business end of the Minnow is the trace. Some tackle shops will sell these as individual items of tackle, though the trend with many tackle dealers now is to sell them with the Devon Minnow shell as part of a complete set-up. This is why I make my own. These traces are easily manufactured and can be made for a fraction of the cost of the shop-bought items. Another reason I dislike the shop-made traces is that the wire is usually only secured around the shank with the minimum of turns – I like my turns to be wound down the entire shank of the hook. However, the main reason why I don't like using the shop-bought traces is that they tend to be over-long, the swivel in my opinion extending too far beyond the front of the Minnow. The further the swivel pro-

trudes past the front of the Minnow the more it will be inclined to hinge and foul around the main line when being cast, similar to what happens with a tube fly if the treble is not secured by means of a rubber sleeve. If only one eye of the swivel protrudes out of the front of the Devon the treble does not become caught up so often. Time spent in sorting out unnecessary tangles will needless to say result in fewer fish lying on the bank.

The Devon Minnow is a good hooker of fish if taken end on. This is due to the trace and treble hooks rotating with the shell, which means that not only do the hooks pull into the flesh of the fish, but they screw their way in as well. If the fish takes hold of the Minnow side on, however, then there are occasions when it is possible for the hooks to remain outside the salmon's mouth. I have witnessed a salmon grabbing hold of a Devon across its flank, hanging on for a period of time and participating in a tug of war until someone tried to scoop it out with a net. Needless to say at this point it let it go.

Flying Condom
The Flying 'C', as it is more commonly known, originated not in Ireland as many think, but in France. In saying this it was the Irish salmon fishers that popularized its use. The lure is really a variation

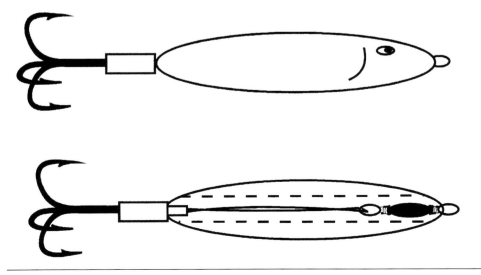

Fig 55 The modified Minnow trace with only one swivel eye protruding.

Spinning for salmon during a summer spate on the Stinchar.

of the Mepp's spinner, the only real difference being a flexible rubber tail, similar to those found on the Phantom Minnows of old. The main advantage they have over the Mepp's is that they are available in a wide variety of weights for the same size of blade, the most popular sizes being 10 and 15g. They are available with either a silver or brass blade along with a number of silicon rubber tail colours, the most popular and productive colour being red. I like a silver blade in clear water and a brass one when the river is running the colour of unmilked tea. They are best fished without an anti-kink weight.

These lures are great attractors of fish, but they are bad hookers and as a result many fish come off within a short period of mouthing them. There has been many reasons put forward for this, but I suspect the reason is that the fish go for the rotating blade rather than the flexible rubber tail, where the treble is situated. One angler that I struck up a conversation with on the Swallow Braes beat on the River Doon told me that he had started to incorporate an additional flying treble between the original treble and the blade. From what I observed at the time these modified 'C's did not seem to swim as cleanly or look as tidy as the unmodified version, but they certainly worked, because almost to prove

When selecting a lure many anglers choose one for its colour and not its size.

the point of the increased hooking capability he quickly extracted a bright sea-liced 9lb fish. Yes, it was hooked on the flying treble.

Toby Spoon

These spoons are among the most popular spinning lures available and they are excellent attractors, especially for running fish, but they are infamous hookers. Through the years some ingenious methods have been devised to increase their hooking ability, the most popular of which being an additional split ring. Although this adaptation is

favoured by many anglers I prefer to secure the treble so that it remains fixed in a horizontal plane. This can be done by removing the split ring and attaching the hook by means of Alasticum wire. This keeps the hook in line with the spoon and provides much better hooking. Tobys come in a wide assortment of colours such as, black/gold, green/gold, blue/silver, and black/green. In addition they are available in mono colouration such as silver and copper. They range in weight from 7 to 28g.

Generally, however, I only bother to fish these lures on wide rivers and only when they are carrying additional water and running coloured. For this

Colin MacKenzie, the ghillie at Smithston on the River Doon, fishing a Rapala down Murphy's pool.

reason I tend to use just the heavier sizes. When fishing from the bank they should be cast well downstream and retrieved slowly up the pool, a technique that will be explained in Chapter 21. Their action through the water is similar to that of an injured fish, wobbling from side to side. Like the Flying 'C' these lures are best fished without an anti-kink weight being fitted.

RAPALAS

These are fish-shaped plugs with a diving vane attached at the front. They come in three types,

sinking, floating and jointed. The first two come in silver/black, gold/black, gold/orange and peach to mention but a few, while the jointed come in gold, silver or peach. They come in sizes ranging from 2 to 5in (50–125mm). Colin MacKenzie, a young ghillie whom I have much respect for, uses these lures almost to the exclusion of anything else and in my opinion he is without equal fishing this lure. Rapalas are highly successful lures for salmon but are very expensive. The Rapala is best fished in a similar fashion to the Toby and for best effect should be tied to the nylon with the knot recommended by Normark. A diagram of the knot is included with each lure.

WHAT LURE SHOULD I USE?

There are many other lures available, such as Blair Spoons, Quill Minnows, Broken Back Minnows, Irish Minnows, Bucktail Spinners and Phantom Tails – each have their devotees. I think, however, especially for newcomers to the sport, it is best to restrict yourself to a small selection of spinning lures, such as the ones I have highlighted. If you do so you will not go far wrong and will save yourself a great deal of money and effort in trying to find the 'magic' lure – there is none, so forget about finding it. It is better to have a good stock in various weights and sizes of three or four types, than have a box full of everything. Far too often I have seen anglers constantly changing lures as they go up and down a pool. They seem to think that by showing the fish something different every time they cover it they will eventually show it something that it will like. This is nonsense, if a fish is in a taking mood it will take almost anything, but if not, it will take nothing. By changing lures at every cast all they are doing is wasting valuable fishing time because spinning is generally best when the river is high, which means that the highest proportion of fish being covered at any one time will be running fish and any that see our lure will probably only see it once before moving on into the next pool.

21 THE SECRETS OF SUCCESSFUL SPINNING

Some fly-only anglers have a superior attitude towards spinning. Why, I have no idea; perhaps they feel that spinning is beneath them and that the fly is the only method worthy of taking a salmon. This attitude is all very well, but in so thinking they miss many opportunities of a fish. When fishing at times or in rivers that facilitate the use of the fly rod then by all means use it, but do not make catching salmon more difficult by using the fly rod under inappropriate conditions. Many rivers are impossible to fish with the fly due to the distance that a lure must be cast, or due to the surrounding terrain, for example overhanging branches. It is all very well saying use the Spey cast, but in order to perform it we still need room to move the rod. On some small rivers this is just not possible due to dense tree growth, and in these places a spinning rod comes into its own. Many of these difficult places hold salmon because of the very shade produced by the overhanging branches. Notwithstanding, many of these 'difficult' places are often walked past by anglers favouring the easier, more open pools instead. In so doing they are missing many opportunities of sport. In addition, there are times when it is extremely difficult to present a fly properly, especially when rivers are swollen with flood water.

Regardless of location or size of river, the spinning rod in the hands of a skilful angler will take as many, or dare I say it, more fish than the fly fished at the same time. Anyone can walk into a tackle shop, purchase the necessary fixed spool reel and spinning rod, go down to the river and with the minimum of instruction cast a lure across the pool – and they may even catch a salmon. Their success, however, will probably be short lived, as they have just happened to be in the right place at the right time, when a 'daft' fish had a go. The skilful angler with a spinning rod

on the other hand will consistently take fish from 'his' stretch of river time and time again. The secret of reasonably consistent success regardless of the method used is local knowledge, but in saying this the knowledge is of little use if the angler cannot control his lure properly. It is the controlling of the lure that is of paramount importance when fishing for salmon. When spinning, competent lure control starts even before the lure hits the water.

SPINNING WITH A FIXED SPOOL REEL

Choosing the Correct Tackle

When spinning relatively light lures, that is less than 15g, in medium to small rivers, a fixed spool type reel is best. However, before starting to fish we must select the correct spool loaded with the breaking strain of monofilament to suit the weight of lure. For most of the time nylon of 12 to 15lb will be more than adequate. On the other hand, if the river is running low and clear, we should use a small lightweight lure, 10g or less. When fishing with these small lightweight lures, nylon in the 8 to 10lb range is better suited, it being no use using the same 12 or 15lb we used for the heavier lures. If we do the accuracy and the distance of the cast will suffer. Like fly fishing, a small light lure tethered to the end of a thick line will not fish properly, as it will not rise and fall in the water in a lifelike fashion. For any lure to be successful it must be fished properly.

Some might think that 15lb is a bit on the heavy side for fishing smallish rivers, but I don't. I do not see anything sporting about leaving a treble hook in a fish just to say that I gave it a so-called sporting chance. As for lures you would not go far wrong with a selection of Devon Minnows ranging from 1¼ to 2½in (30–60mm) of medium weight. There is also no need to purchase every colour going, three colour combinations being quite sufficient. When the water is running coloured I like a fluorescent Yellow Belly, of Saturn Yellow and Emerald Green.

The colours and sizes of lure I use for different conditions

Water Temp °F (°C)	Lure Appearance	Lure size, in	Lure Colour
44 (6.7)	Dirty	2½	FL YB
44 (6.7)	Coloured	2½	FL RB
44 (6.7)	Clear	2¼	BL GLD
46 (7.8)	Dirty	2½	FL YB
46 (7.8)	Coloured	2¼	FL RB
46 (7.8)	Clear	2¼	BL GLD
48 (8.9)	Dirty	2½	FL YB
48 (8.9)	Coloured	2¼	FL RB
48 (8.9)	Clear	2	BL GLD
50 (10.0)	Dirty	2¼	FL YB
50 (10.0)	Coloured	2	FL RB
50 (10.0)	Clear	2	BL GLD
52 (11.1)	Dirty	2	FL YB
52 (11.1)	Coloured	2	FL RB
52 (11.1)	Clear	1¾	BL GLD
54 (12.2)	Dirty	2	FL YB
54 (12.2)	Coloured	1¾	FL RB
54 (12.2)	Clear	1¾	BL GLD
56 (13.3)	Dirty	1¾	FL YB
56 (13.3)	Coloured	1¾	FL RB
56 (13.3)	Clear	1½	BL GLD
58 (14.4)	Dirty	1¾	FL YB
58 (14.4)	Coloured	1½	FL RB
58 (14.4)	Clear	1½	BL GLD
60 (15.5)	Dirty	1½	FL YB
60 (15.5)	Coloured	1½	FL RB
60 (15.5)	Clear	1¼	BL GLD

Abbreviations: FL YB = Fluorescent Yellow Belly; FL RB = Fluorescent Red and Black; BL GLD = Black and Gold.

Note: Water height is considered high (over one foot) in all cases.

Since most manufacturers do not produce Minnows in this colour I buy unpainted shells from various sources and paint them myself using enamel spray paint. One source of unpainted shells is Lakeland Lures of Cumbria. (For best effect you should give the shells a coat of white matt paint first.) Another excellent colour combination that works well, once the water starts to clear a little during the autumn, is a fluorescent red and black, as found on the Devon Minnows manufactured by Gordon & Griffiths. One interesting statistic which comes to light after checking my diary is that 75 per cent of all hen fish taken when spinning fell to a fluorescent Yellow Belly, while 68 per cent of all cock fish taken when spinning fell to the fluorescent red and black. As the water starts to fall and clear do not forget to go down in size. It also pays to select a less colourful lure as well. An excellent colour combination to use at this time is black and gold, a combination which has probably caught more salmon than any other.

Preparation for Casting

Once we have chosen the correct tackle for the conditions we must decide where during the prevailing water conditions the salmon are likely to be lying; having established this we can then set about casting our lure. However, before doing so we must take note of the riverside terrain so that we can decide in what fashion we are going to cast it, that is forehand or backhand. In some cases there is no such decision to be made as the surrounding banking facilitates any method. In many instances, however, particularly on the smaller spate streams, the bankings are overgrown. Having taken note of any offending foliage and vegetation we must now decide in which fashion we are going to propel our lure to the desired spot. We must also decide how much effort is going to be needed for the lure to travel the required distance. This might all sound very simple, but the hand-to-eye co-ordination required for the forehand cast is different from that needed for the backhand cast. The distance and accuracy of the cast depends not so much on the effort used, but the timing of its release. In saying this the weight of the lure must be such that it will flex the rod. This energy must be transferred back into the lure when the rod is flexed forward to propel the lure out across the water. Accurate casting depends on both the flexing of the rod and the timing of the release of line – if these are 'right' the accuracy of the cast will be assured.

Forehand Cast *(Fig 56)*

Suppose that we wish to place the lure directly across from where we are standing using the forehand cast. Initially the rod will be held out to the right (assuming that we are right-handed) and a little behind and beyond the parallel to the bank on which we are standing. The lure at this point should be hanging about 2ft (60cm) down from the top ring and at right angles to the bank. If the rod is flicked forward with an upward movement with just the right amount of effort, the lure will initially rise away from the vertical to approximately 45 degrees to the plane in which the rod tip was prior to the cast being made. This upward movement means that the rod will start to flex and store energy much earlier than if the rod was merely moved through the horizontal plane.

In addition the weight of the lure being pulled forward will flex the rod even more, the maximum flexing of the rod occurring just prior to the point of movement, when the lure has reached the position to be cast, and the line is released. The rod will flex provided the line is secure, after which the lure will be propelled forward by the momentum introduced by moving the rod and the stored energy contained within the flexed fibres of the rod material. If the line is released too early the lure will land upstream of where we intended it to go, and will also fall well short of the distance we are trying for. If, on the other hand, it is released too late, it will land well downstream only a few yards out from the bank. A very bad forehand cast executed by releasing the line too early will result in the bait landing near our own bank and in extreme cases it may even land upstream amongst the vegetation. At the other extreme if we let the line go too late then the bait will land downstream of its target. If let go very late it will almost certainly find itself caught up in the bankside vegetation downstream of where we are standing or worse still up a tree.

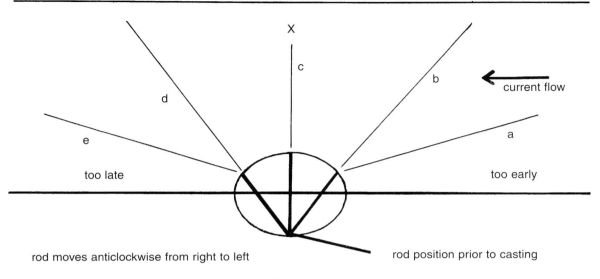

Fig 56 The forehand cast. For the lure to land at X it should be released between b and c.

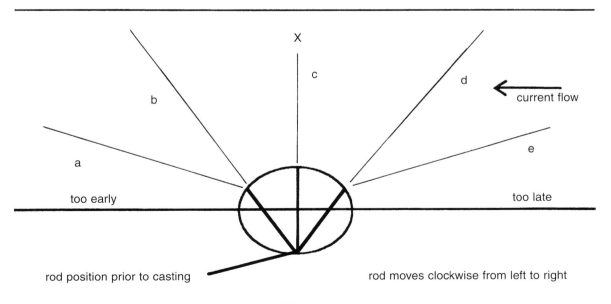

Fig 57 The backhand cast. For the lure to land at X it should be released between b and c.

Backhand Cast *(Fig 57)*

The backhand cast starts as previously, with the rod parallel to the river bank, but this time the handle of the rod is placed across the lower torso with the lure once again hanging at 90 degrees to the rod tip. The initial forward and upward movement of the rod will lift the lure so that it will rise in the same plane in which the rod is being moved. As the rod is moved forward further it will be flexed by the weight of the lure. With this cast, however, if the line is let go too early the lure will land downstream from where we are standing. Like with the forehand cast if we let it go over early it will fly into the banking , usually only a few feet downstream from where we are standing. If the line is released late then the bait will land upstream from where it was intended to go. When let go even later the lure will shoot upstream from where we are standing, which could be very dangerous for another angler if he happens to be standing fishing down the pool behind us.

Accuracy of the cast can also suffer if an anti-kink weight is placed on the main line side of the swivel, this being due to the bolas effect of the anti-kink weight and the lure working against each other. To accurately place a lure with this type of set-up takes great skill. The casting techniques described previously help to overcome this effect by starting the lure movement as close to the plane in which the rod is moving as possible. If the rod is kept moving through the plane parallel to the bank from which we are casting, the lure and weight are usually initially propelled forward through the air in a path that runs parallel to our bank. However, since both the weight and the lure are usually of different loads and aerodynamic shapes, it stands to reason that one will start to slow down faster than the other. At this point one will try to overtake the other and this will reduce the momentum of the forward motion, and hence the accuracy of the cast. With the casting technique described the lure usually leads the anti-kink weight out over the water and because of this it is inclined to pull the weight along behind, which means that one is not working against the other.

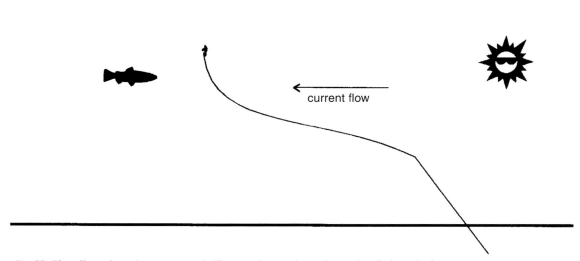

current flow

Fig 58 The effect of sunshine on a pool. The sun shining down the pool will show the lure as a silhouette. The fish will also be dazzled by the light, so they will come short.

Presenting the Lure *(Figs 58–9)*

Once we can place a lure accurately we can fish it through known salmon lies, the main problem now being that we must present the lure in a fashion that will provoke a response from the fish. The lies frequented by fish will depend on the height of the water at any one time, and it is because of this that we must be able to present a lure in a variety of ways through the many varied places that salmon will lie. The lure must be controlled through each lie so that it will fish in a fashion that will provoke a response from the fish. In order to do this we must be able to fish our lure so that it swims enticingly past the fish. The speed of the current needs to be considered and we also need to ask whether the lure will need to be retrieved and whether the pace of the flow is sufficient to bring the lure nicely through the lie without turning the handle of the reel. The speed at which the lure comes through the lie must also be contemplated. Will the lure be more likely to produce fish if brought over it end or side on? All these points must be given consideration. In addition some salmon lies will only bring about a response from the fish in residence when the lure is brought across them in a particular fashion. Why, I have no idea, but perhaps it is due to the light or flow conditions through that particular lie at the time. Taking all these points into account we must be capable of controlling the lure at all times if we want to become successful at spinning for salmon.

Sunlight can either be a friend or an enemy, depending on its position in relation to the pool. If the sun is shining down the pool the lure will appear in silhouette. It is better where possible to present our lure so that the sun illuminates it from the rear. This is particularly beneficial if the water is a touch coloured, as what light does manage to penetrate the murk will help to highlight it, particularly if the lure is brightly coloured.

Although this aspect of sun position is being related here to spinning the same also applies to fishing a fly.

For the reasons given previously we must be able to cast and control our lures in many different

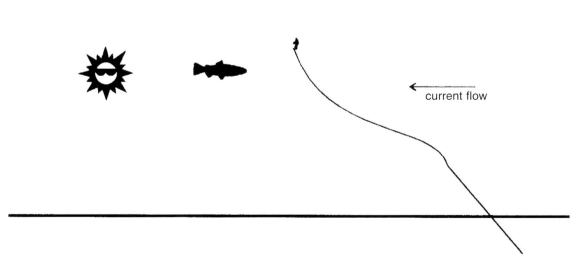

current flow

Fig 59 When the sun shines up the pool there will be a better chance of tempting the fish. This is because the lure will be illuminated as it passes in front of the salmon.

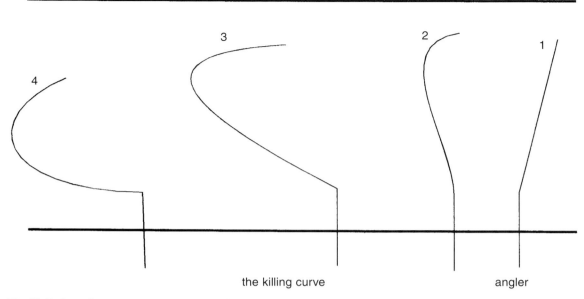

Fig 60 Fishing the Devon Minnow. (1) Initial cast upstream. (2) The current starts to belly the line. (3) Current now fishes the line and pulls the lure head first downstream. (4) Lure starts to kick around in the current.

ways. Lure selection and control cannot be fully learned from a book or article, only from practice. If we can cast a lure accurately we will catch a few salmon, and with each fish will come a little bit more experience, and that will in turn lead to more fish.

Fishing the Devon Minnow *(Fig 60)*

Start at the head of the pool and cast across and upstream. With reference to Fig 60, the angler casts to position **1** as indicated. As the current takes hold of the line a belly will be created at position **2** The angler should only turn the handle on the reel to keep in touch with the lure, the current doing all that is necessary. Initially the lure will be travelling head first downstream, but as the current takes additional hold of the line, as indicated by line position **3**, the lure will start to change direction and fish at right angles to the bank that we are standing on. As the line is swinging round to position **4** the lure will start to swim at right angles to the bank that it is being fished from. It is during the change in

direction between **3** and **4** that a fish is most likely to take.

The middle section of the pool should be fished in similar fashion, but instead of casting the lure up and across, it is best to cast it straight across. This is because the current here will not be as fast as that in the head of the pool. If we do cast the lure upstream it will have a tendency to get stuck on the bottom before the current has had a chance to take a hold of the line. When fishing these slower sections it may be necessary to turn the handle of the reel a little in order to keep the lure up off the bottom. The lure should only be controlled by the angler, not fished, as this is done by the current bellying the line. The tail of the pool, however, can be fished by casting up and across. Always be on the lookout for fish showing in the tail of a pool, as these are generally good takers.

Over the years I have noted that some fish on entering a pool only show their backs, while some will slap the surface of the water with their tails. These tail-slapping salmon for some unknown reason are very good takers and should be covered at once. Any delay and the fish will almost certainly have moved on up into the main body of the pool, where they are not so keen to oblige. It is watching these fish that makes me think not all the fish we catch have been resting, as I have observed these tail-slapping salmon actually take lures as they ran into a pool.

A good place to fish and keep an eye on, particularly in smaller rivers, is the lip of a weir. Again, if any fish are seen cover them at once, even if it means running along the bank, but be careful and never go in front of another angler. Some fish will take like a tiger, while others will take so softly that it feels as if a leaf has become impaled on the hook. The technique I explained above is very effective and has accounted for many fish. I suspect that it is due to the lure appearing suddenly in the fish's window of vision and then as suddenly changing direction and heading off upstream, thus triggering the salmon's predatory instinct.

Fishing the Flying 'C' *(Fig 61)*
These lures, unlike the Devon Minnow, should not be fished with an anti-kink weight as this will impede their action. In addition, they are not as versatile, and do not like fast, rough water. The buffeting of the water can stop the blade revolving, so for this reason I prefer to use them only in the slower main body of the pool. If fished here they are highly effective for fresh fish if presented across their noses. Alternatively, we can cast them upstream and wind them back quickly downstream past the fish. These lures are without equal for upstream spinning.

Fishing the Toby Spoon *(Fig 62)*
The Toby, being a spoon in design, is best fished downstream and retrieved against the flow. When fished in a slow flow it is best to wind it back relatively quickly, but if fished in a rough stream or run a quick retrieve will be detrimental, because the lure will rise and plane on the surface. When fished downstream and wound back the spoon suddenly appears in the fish's window of vision from behind. This is a good lure for running fish, but in a lot of cases they merely snap at it without taking a good hold.

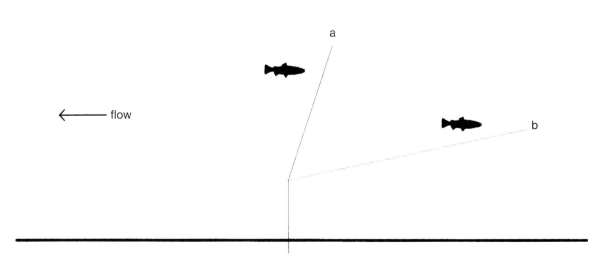

Fig 61 Fishing the Flying 'C'.

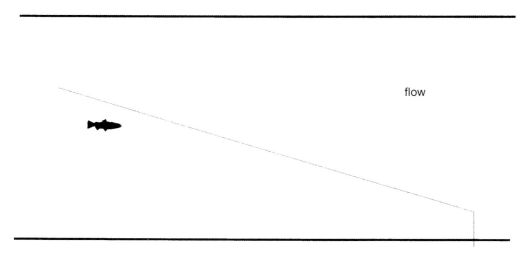

flow

Fig 62 Fishing the Toby Spoon.

Fishing the Rapala Plug

As I mentioned previously there are two main types of Rapala: the floating and the sinking. For most of the time the floating type is all that is needed because it can be fished in a variety of ways. We can either cast it across and retrieve it so that it kicks round in the current, or fish it down and retrieve it against the flow like the Toby. The rate of retrieve and the speed of the current will dictate what depth it fishes at. If we are intending to cover running fish we can fish it high in the water or, alternatively, if we are after resting fish we can make it dive deep. In order to fish these lures correctly it is necessary to have a 'feel' for what is happening at the other end of the line. All too often I have seen anglers buy these lures and not have a clue how to fish them properly, presenting them in such a fashion that anything which grabs hold of them must be an obvious 'suicide' case.

To fish the floating plug deep in a strong flow very little winding of the reel handle is necessary, the current controlling the depth and not the rate of retrieve. This is due to the action of the water pressing against the diving vane at the front end. On this aspect, if we wish the same depth in a slow flow we have to wind it back quickly and in this case a sinker is better suited. With a floating Rapala we can cast it to an alternative upstream position in the water and dead drift it down to the lie by keeping the bail arm open and allowing line to peel off the drum. When the plug gets to the required position the bail arm is closed so that the plug comes to the end of its travel. At this stage it will start to dive as the water acts on the diving vane and forces it down.

MULTIPLIER CASTING AND LURE PRESENTATION

Multiplier reels are not for the faint-hearted. You either love them or loath them, but for fishing a heavy lure of 15g or more in a large river they are ideal. When fishing large lures in such rivers I would recommend nylon of 18lb minimum. Before we can cast a lure effectively the brake must be adjusted to suit. If it is set on the light side the lure can be cast considerable distances, but at the same time it can produce some horrendous tangles. These occur when the line starts to come off the drum faster than the lure is taking it out, known as 'backlash'. Backlash tangles are virtually impossible to extricate, the only solution being to cut away the offending 'birds nest'. On the other hand, if the brake is set over-tight it will be difficult to achieve any distance.

When using a multiplier reel on a large river the tip should be kept up as shown. This allows the lure to swim that little bit deeper and not close to the surface, as some might think.

This setting up of the brake must be done with the rod, line and lure assembled. To adjust the brake hold the rod at approximately 45 degrees to the horizontal and disengage the spool by pressing the release function button. Take note of how fast the lure falls to the ground. If the lure goes into free fall the brake will need adjustment. Re-engage the spool and wind the lure back to within 6 or 7in (15–17cm) of the top ring. Now disengage the spool, but keep your thumb against the drum to stop it rotating. Adjust the brake control and remove your thumb, and keep doing this until the lure descends slowly. Now adjust the control further so that the lure only descends if the rod tip is flicked up and down.

Next we must adjust the drag. In the handbook I received with my Ambassador it describes how this can be done in two different ways. The first involves tying the end of the line to a set of spring balances, which are anchored at one end. At this stage the drag adjustment is set to maximum. Now raise the rod to approximately 45 degrees and apply pressure. Slowly reduce the drag setting until it starts to slip and the scales read approximately one third of the breaking strain of the line being used. Another method, if a spring balance is not available, is to attach the line to a secured object and apply pressure until the line looks as if it is just about to break. The drag is then set to a point just prior to this. Of the two methods I have described I prefer the first as it is more accurate.

Since the reel sits on the rod with the rings facing up, a multiplier set-up is only really suitable for forehand casting. Although the backhand cast can be used it does not give the same level of control. Unlike with the fixed spool reel, the cast should be aimed high. As the lure starts to descend it is a good idea to provide some additional braking by the use of the thumb. When using a multiplier set-up I prefer all the weight to be in the lure, unlike with the fixed spool arrangement where the anti-kink Hillman-type lead provides the weight. If anti-kink weights are used with a multiplier they make accurate casting that bit more difficult.

When presenting my lure with one of these reels I like to keep the rod tip up and let the current bring it round, as when fishing a fly. It is also advisable to keep your thumb 'hovering' just above the drum, which, if a fish does take, can be brought down to set the hooks. By keeping the rod tip up my lure can fish deeper than if held low like with the fixed spool reel when I am fishing smaller rivers. If the lure occasionally nudges the bottom I don't mind too much, but if it continually gets caught up I know it will need changing for a lighter one. It is the weight of the lure that will determine its depth and not necessarily its size. Since these reels do not have the same flexibility as the fixed spool variety they do not lend themselves to many different styles of presentation, only really being suitable for across and down casting. However, with a little practice we can fish a Devon Minnow in the fashion shown in Fig 60.

When playing a fish on these reels we must use a technique known as 'pumping', because of the gear mechanisms within the reel. To do this lower the rod tip towards the fish, winding as you do so. Now put your thumb on the drum and raise the rod, the whole process being repeated until the fish is played out.

22 A FISH FROM THE SPEY

Rather than write about a day's fishing when things went according to the book, I have decided to recount a few hours of a week's fishing of the 1994 season on the Strathspey Angling Association water at Grantown. From the end of 1993 there had been much speculation about the increased numbers of fish that would run the river in 1994 since this was the first year that the main summer grilse runs would not be decimated by the nets in Spey Bay. As it turned out some beats had done better than previous years, while others were down.

The fishing year up to the beginning of July on the association stretch at Grantown had got off to a slow start, with snow on the Cairngorms keeping the water at an unusually high level. Even during the first two weeks of July, the time that my wife and I were fishing the river, the notice board outside Mortimers tackle shop indicated the river fluctuating between three and six inches above normal summer level.

We arrived at our cottage on the Saturday, where we quickly unpacked and then made our way to the Old Spey Bridge. We found the river running at a level that allowed worming on the association stretch below the New Bridge. Two visiting anglers were fishing below the Old Bridge when we arrived, trotting worms down through the pool. Within a few minutes of our arrival a sea-trout around the 2lb mark was hooked and quickly landed. During our visit, however, we did not see any salmon splashing about beneath the bridge, an unusual occurrence for this pool. From our vantage point on the bridge we did see an angler rise a salmon to a large, bright yellow and orange Waddington fished fast across the middle of the pool, just downstream of the bridge. As it transpired this was one last ditch effort from the angler, as he

had fished hard all week using small, conventional summer-style flies to no avail. When speaking to him afterwards, it emerged that he did not know that a fish had moved to his fly.

There were all sorts of theories being put forward as to why the association water was short of fish, while the two private beats, Castle Grant and Tulchan estate, were taking good catches. Some locals were saying that it was because the water was still a touch on the cold side due to the snow melt coming down from the mountains. During our seven days fishing I monitored the water temperature regularly, and it was always in the high 50s or low 60s, with the air temperature 5 to 10°F higher. Whatever the reason I am certain that it was not water temperature that was stopping the fish running into the town water. As it happened, by the end of the following week the two private beats mentioned previously had accounted for fifty and 100 fish respectively. The association water that week, the first in July, only managed eleven. Since we generally take our tickets from Thursday to Thursday there was always time for things to change – always the optimist! As it transpired, by the end of the second week there were still very few fish being taken from the association water, sixteen if I recall correctly.

Thursday came so we bought our tickets, but rather than fish all day, because of the bright overhead conditions we decided not to fish until after tea. After tackling up at the Old Bridge we made our way down to the long pool. We fished the top third of the pool two or three times, during which time we saw a few fish. Although the water was running four inches above summer level I felt sure that fishing small size 8s and 10s with a floating line was the order of the day. Even though most other anglers who had fished all the previous week with conventional summer flies had failed to move fish, I was sure that if any fish were to be taken they would come to flies fished in the classic summer style. After a couple of times down the pool I was starting to have my doubts. Needless to say we did not have any offers that we knew about.

Friday morning came and once again it was bright overhead, so we once again decided to go touring and leave any fishing until after tea. Come late afternoon however, some cloud arrived bringing with it some fine drizzle. As for the previous evening we tackled up at the Old Bridge, and the river this time was flowing with three inches on the gauge. I decided that a change of tactics was called for, because it was obvious from what I had seen on the previous Saturday evening and had experienced myself that using small flies fished just under the surface was not working. I kept the floating line, but instead of reaching for my box of summer flies I brought out my box of tubes and connected a Collie Dog with a 5in wing tied on a 1¾in aluminium tube. Mary stuck to small flies.

Once we had tackled up we decided to try our luck upstream. Some anglers were already fishing some of the fast, rough, streamy water between the two bridges and I have heard anglers saying that they have taken grilse from these rough stretches. Nonetheless I do not like these stretches of fast white water, preferring instead to try the deeper holding pools instead. It was about 7.00 p.m. when we reached pool 23, Clach Na Strone, and although the drizzle had stopped it was getting very dark with heavy black clouds coming down the Spey valley.

The Clach Na Strone is a very famous pool not perhaps in numbers of fish caught, but by the frequency of times a photograph of it has featured in some monthly fishing periodical. Generally most photographs that demonstrate an angler fishing show him standing on top of the concrete platform. This, as far as I am concerned, is a bad way to fish this pool, since by standing on top of the platform the angler is in full view of any fish. To fish the pool correctly from the platform side involves wading and this should be done by getting into the water either on the inshore or mainstream side of

the platform, depending on the height of the water and how the fish are running into and through the pool. The depth of water on both sides is not deep, just coming up past the knees in places, though the wading on the mainstream side of the concrete is the easiest going. If, however, the fish are running up along the mainstream side of the platform then keep to the inshore side.

The first time I fished this pool I made the same mistake that so many anglers make and fished down the pool standing on top of the concrete. It was not until I noticed fish running up through the slack water only about six feet out from the mainstream side of the platform that I thought about my approach. Keeping low and off the skyline will always increase your chances of a fish, regardless of which pool you are fishing.

As mentioned previously I had selected a Collie Dog to fish with and my idea was to fish it fast, either by casting it square across and letting the current swing it round, or by casting it at approximately 60 degrees across the pool and stripping it back. I made my way to the large stone at the head of the pool so that I could cover the neck properly. Within a few casts a large reddish fished rolled just out of the main current. Perhaps my fly had disturbed it, I don't know. I covered it a few more times before moving down to the casting platform, but it did not show again. When I reached the upstream end of the platform I decided to stay in the water to the mainstream side of it, as I had not seen any fish running up the slack water immediately in front of it. Casting a long line out across the pool and stripping the fly back at a moderate pace, I detected what appeared to be a soft take. At this point I was about half-way down the length of the platform. As it happened, when I raised the rod there was no 'weight' of fish to bend it. Perhaps other anglers might have thought it had been a piece of weed, or an over-ambitious trout. I was certain, however, that a salmon had moved to my fly.

At this point the heavens opened and down it came. I had left my jacket on the porch of the hut, and since I had only two or three more casts left before I had fished out the pool I decided not to bother going for my jacket. What a mistake, within a few minutes I was soaked, but I did touch a fish.

Having fished out the pool I waded ashore to take shelter in the hut until the rain eased. Within twenty minutes the rain had stopped and the sky started to clear a little, though it was still dark for the time of day. Since I had moved a fish to the Collie Dog I decided to fish down the pool again, but before doing so I removed the Collie and replaced it with a smaller fly. The one I chose was a predominantly yellow and orange hairwing version of the Willie Gunn tied on a size 8 treble. The overall size of the fly was about 1½in, with the hair extending beyond the bends of the hooks. When fishing the Collie Dog I did not have to bother about mending line to control the fly's swim since I was stripping it back. With the smaller fly I was about to fish, I would have to mend and control the line in order to make it swim at the correct speed during its traverse across the pool. Although the main flow in this pool is down through the centre, the line needs continual correcting by mending a number of times to keep the fly swimming at the correct speed through the deeper, fish-holding central part of the pool.

Again I started in at the large boulder at the top of the pool. Here it is only necessary to cast a short line and put in a single upstream mend, then, when the fly swings out of the main flow, the rod can be held out at right angles to enable the fly to be hovered on the inside edge of the main stream. This approach is very useful in the neck section of this particular pool, but on this occasion it proved fruitless. I fished on in this fashion until I got opposite the top of the concrete platform. Again on reaching the platform I remained in the water. In order to fish the main body of the pool a long cast is necessary to initially place your fly in the slack water on the opposite side of the central flow. To bring the fly through this section of the pool two, three and, depending on the height of the water, even four upstream mends are sometimes necessary. I started

fishing down the remainder of the pool carrying out corrective mending as required. When I was about two casts from where I had had my Collie Dog touched earlier I waded out a shade further to help slow the passage of the fly.

Next cast should do it, I thought. As the fly approached the same spot of water where something had briefly made acquaintance with my Collie Dog earlier I felt that unmistakable pull of a fish taking and turning down. On lifting the rod the line jumped off the surface, leaving behind it a spray of water droplets. I was into a fish. The fish, on feeling the rod bend against it, came to the surface where it skittered and splashed violently for a number of yards. I do not like it when they do this as it is usually a sign of a light hook hold.

Keeping the same pressure, I lowered the rod tip, which seemed to work as the fish went deep, making a run to the far side of the pool. My main intention at this point was to try to get opposite, or downstream of it. There was no way that I could do this while I was still in the water so I headed back to the concrete platform. Once on top of it I was then able to position myself more advantageously and I was now in a position to apply side pressure on the fish. On applying pressure it turned and headed towards the tail of the pool, however, fortunately, it decided to turn and came back up along the side of the platform. Soon, after a few short dashes to the edge of the nearside current, it tired and went silver side up. At this point I drew it towards me, and Mary netted it out – a fine fresh-run fish of 7lb with one solitary sea louse still attached to its flank.

Not the biggest fish from the Spey, but considering how few there had been all week I was happy. The following Monday we took one fish each of 7lb and 6lb. What were they taken on? Would you believe small size 10 summer flies fished just under the surface. What a fickle fish the salmon is.

23 A DAY ON THE STINCHAR

During the first week of August, localized pockets of rain saw most of the Ayrshire rivers in spate, though not all at the same time. During this week I was religiously on the phone 8.00 a.m. sharp to Dalreoch Estate to find out if any of the rain that north Ayrshire was enjoying was finding its way down to the Stinchar valley. On Monday, Tuesday, and Wednesday I was informed that the river was not up, while on Thursday morning, much to my surprise I was told that there had been some rain in the early hours, and that the river was at the six-inch mark on the gauge at Colmonell Bridge. I called back just after 6.00 p.m. to be told that it had risen to four feet during the afternoon and was just starting to drop back. If there was no more heavy rain then the following day should be good and I had no hesitation in booking one rod for the Friday.

On driving south we passed over the Ayr, which was running big and brown. A little further on we caught sight of the Doon, which was up but not dirty. I slowed as we drove over the bridge at Colmonell and the water looked in fine order. On arrival at the lodge around 9.30 a.m., Dougie the keeper reported that the river was running at twelve inches, but he thought that it might go up a little during the day as there had been a small amount of rain earlier in the morning. Usually Mary and I share the rod, and on this occasion we intended the same. As it happened, though, there was still one remaining and we decided to take it as well.

Now before I go any further I must tell you that although we share the fishing, we do not in actual fact share the same fishing rod. She prefers to fish with her own rod, even though it is the same type as mine.

Rather than drive to the middle of the beat with the car we decided to leave it at the lodge and walk down to the bottom of the beat, the Battery Pool, a short walk of two to three hundred yards. We tackled up with 13½ft rods and a floating line, 10–12ft of 12lb nylon with a dropper about 6ft from the end of the fly line. Initially we selected size 10 for the dropper and size 8 for the point, both flies being trebles. Mary selected a magenta hairwing with a silver body of her own tying for the dropper and a Stinchar Stoat's Tail for the point; my choice of dropper fly was the same, and I selected a predominantly orange Willie Gunn for the tail fly. This was because I suspected that the water would be a little on the black side, and as it happened I was right. At times the Stinchar runs as black as a silage puddle, making it impossible to see the bottom where the water runs any more than a few inches deep. When it runs like this I favour a fly with a bit of colour in it.

Having tackled up it was not long before we arrived at the Battery. The head of this pool is fairly narrow and has a funnel-like neck, which has created a central channel in the top third section of the pool. The belly of the pool is slow and languid, but here it almost doubles in width. From head to tail trees line the far bank. In order to fish this pool correctly one must get into the water. To fish the top section of this pool from the high bank at this height of water I would not recommend, as every fish in the head of the pool would almost certainly be frightened. In order to get down the bank a steep wooden stairway is provided, which makes entering the water a little bit easier. I decided to go down the pool first. The first two or three back casts are restricted due to the close proximity of trees, but by employing a sort of makeshift roll cast, it is possible to get enough line out to work the rod. It is then a case of employing a single upstream mend after the cast is made to keep the fly hanging temptingly through the central gully. At the height of water we were fishing this would be where any running fish would be resting.

I fished my way down, cast and mend, to the end of the gravel shelf and at this point I could not go any further. I started winding in my line and had just started to secure my fly to the rod when Mary shouted 'Fish!' I turned around to find her rod bent and bucking under the weight of a salmon. What a surprise, I didn't even know she had started to fish and as I discovered later the fish had taken her fly on only the third or fourth cast. I scrambled up the bank and picked up both net and camera. The fish, a fresh-run silvered variety of 7lb, fought with spirit, making two energetic runs down and across the pool, with one final powerful run up into the neck, where it soon tired. As luck would have it I managed to get a few frames run off of her playing it before it was time to act as ghillie and net it out.

The fatal fly, the Stinchar Stoat's Tail, was well and truly embedded in the inside of the jaw and there was no way it was coming out other than by some unfortunate disaster. What a nice start to the day – a fish in the first fifteen minutes. Although we both fished down the pool twice more and saw other fish showing, we did not tempt another there.

We made our way upstream to the Greystanes Pool, a distance of some 400 yards. On arrival we discovered another angler already fishing it and while Mary stayed to fish, I moved upstream a little further. The bankings here are wooded, but every twenty or so yards a small opening allows relatively easy access to a series of small stone groins. From one of these I decided to have a few casts. It is one of those places where you cover the available water by lengthening line between casts. I had lengthened line about five times when I had a soft take. On lifting the rod I discovered not a salmon, but a small trout, hooked on the Willie Gunn. It was quickly unhooked and returned.

I fished the available water again but had no further offers. A good salmon did display itself in the stream above, however. Since it would be difficult to cover it properly from my side I wished the angler on the opposite bank luck and made my way up to the bottom of the Craig Run. This is a long,

fast stretch of water with a good-sized boulder-composed weir at the tail. I decided to give the tail just above the weir a try as I thought that perhaps a running fish might be resting in the deeper water immediately upstream. Before fishing it I changed my tail fly to a size 6 shrimp fly, which was in fact one I had tied the previous day. It consisted of golden pheasant breast fibres for a tail, a pearl tinsel body with a silver rib, a claret cock hackle half way-along, and a bright orange cock hackle tied in at the head.

This stretch of water is not the easiest to fish, with long grass and other assorted vegetation making access to the water's edge difficult. There is a thin path through this 'jungle' to one small clearing nicely placed to allow one to fish the tail. As before it is a case of lengthening line between casts to cover the water here, as step and cast is just not possible. I covered the water just above the lip of the weir with anticipation, but had no offers. Perhaps when fishing there I would have had more chance of a fish by using a sinking line to get the fly down just a little deeper. At the time I considered giving it a try, but due to laziness couldn't be bothered changing spools.

After fishing the tail I decided to go to the head of the run, wade along the side and fish my way back down to the tail, which may sound easy enough, but the going is anything but. At the head of the run there are a couple of trees. I cautiously entered the water a little upstream of them feeling the way with the toes of my waders as I went. Even though the water only came up to my thighs I could not see my knees beneath the surface and in addition a load of submerged rocks had to be navigated.

Once I got opposite the trees I started to put out some line by carefully flicking and rolling it out between the legion of overhanging branches. When I had about 15 yards out I started to mend the line to reduce the passage of the fly across the pool. On the other bank some grass cutting was being done by an elderly gentleman and a young lady both of whom acknowledged my presence with looks that questioned my sanity for fishing such a place.

Eventually, after four or five casts I was below the trees and had started to make my way back towards my own bank. There was still no welcome here as this vertical shore is thick with briers, nettles, bramble vines, long grass and other unwanted flora. I had edged myself up against this assortment of nasties when after perhaps three or four casts my fly was halted in its tracks about ten feet out from the opposite bank, right in front of the mowers.

I lifted my rod to feel the weight of a fish. and at this point the fish about turned causing a great disturbance. Not only had I hooked a fish, but I had an audience as well. 'What a hell of a place to hook a fish!' I exclaimed and started to kick down some of the long grass which was growing down to the water's edge, which was where, if luck was with me, I would have to land my fish. There was no way I could follow it. As I finished flattening the grass the fish about turned and started to head back upstream fast. Even winding as fast as possible I could not keep up with it and I knew I was starting to lose contact with it as the line started to wobble from side to side. When I did regain full contact it veered across towards me and started to sulk right under the rod top.

Try as I might I found it most difficult to move. By bringing the rod around and pulling from a more downstream position the fish lazily turned with the current. The power of the run that followed left me totally surprised. I had never before experienced such power in a fish. The fish stopped just as the rear taper of my line was going through the top ring and again about turned and headed back upstream, but this time I did manage to keep in touch.

As before, under the rod tip it went and started to sulk once again. I tried the same trick as before, but this did nothing to move it. I then reeled the tip down and applied more pressure than I have ever done to any fish before. It would not budge. All this time I was expecting the top of the rod to shoot skyward as the blood knot making my dropper failed. Suddenly, however, with no warning it made another sensational run down the centre of the pool, almost to the same spot as before. Here it came to the surface and thrashed about. I eased off the pressure slightly and it started back upstream towards the neck of the run. This time however it very obligingly stayed opposite me in midstream.

A few minutes later it showed its tail, a sure sign of tiring and within a further few seconds it was starting to show its silver flanks. On seeing this I palmed the rim of the reel and drew it closer to the bank. The fish kept coming and showed no signs of objecting. I was not expecting to get it as close to my bank as easily as this, considering its earlier exploits. When the fish was about two feet out from the side I swung the rod around so that its tip was pointing upstream. Next, holding the rod at arm's length above my head I pulled the fish closer. The fish, now amid the grass I had flattened earlier, wallowed languidly, the way they sometimes do when being lifted out in a net. This was my chance. As I bent down to tail it out its tail sank out of sight below the surface. This was where I would either have it or lose it. As I sank my hand under the surface I knew that if the fish had been having a breather it would object by thrashing its tail on feeling my hand. I found its wrist and started to lift, there was no resistance.

There came a round of applause from the opposite bank as the fish cleared the surface. I turned around putting myself between the fish and the water, while continuing to hold it steady by its wrist with my left hand. Next I laid the rod against some long grass and reached with my right hand for the priest that was in the pocket of my chest waders. Two swift chaps on the back of the head between the eyes and it was all over. A fresh-run silver cock fish of 9lb taken on the shrimp fly tied less than twenty-four hours previously. This fish and the challenge that the surrounding terrain imposed had tested me to the full and as such is one of my most memorable successes.

Of all the rivers I fish the Stinchar is by far my favourite. When the river is fining down after a good spate there is nowhere else I would wish to be wetting a line. Although the river is capable of providing double figure catches to a single rod in a day I chose the day recounted above because it was the day on which my wife took her first Stinchar salmon on fly and her very first sea-trout. I also chose it because of the satisfaction experienced by successfully landing such a hard-fighting fish from such a horrible place.

INDEX